An Approach to the
Design of Mediated Instruction

Prepared at the Great Plains National Instructional
Television Library and based on procedures developed
for Project ASERT at the Lincoln, Nebraska Public Schools

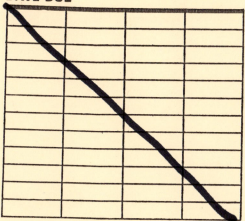
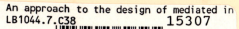
ons and Technology
C. 20036

Contents

Needs 49

Development 67

Goal 69

Display 177

Mediation 179

Diagnosis 211

Instructional Diagnosis 213

Dissemination   241

Glossary   255
Bibliography   269

Foreword

The critical conditions of American—and world—education today certainly seem to require a rational and massive exploitation of telecommunications technologies as the only likely means of coping efficiently with combined population, knowledge, and expectation "explosions." Yet, it is now generally realized by sophisticated instructional specialists that the learning ambiguities resulting from the misapplication of conventional classroom design procedures to the mass media are intolerable in light of the costs involved. If higher efficiency potentials of mass technology are to be achieved, new and more precise design methodologies must be brought to operational reality.

B. F. Skinner's historic development of the linear stimulus-response-reinforcement (S-R-X) procedures served as the foundation of all programed instruction. Until then, the idea that instructional experiences or materials could be empirically "validated" as to their learning effectiveness for selected groups of students lacked the specifics for implementation.

Under the Skinnerian design, instructional information was broken into very small units. Each unit was framed as a stimulus posed to cue a student to make a definite, correct response. The response was then psychologically reinforced by "rewarding" him with confirming knowledge of his results. During the preparation of these instructional programs, all S-R-X units of each linear sequence had to be tried out on carefully selected population samples, and then suitably modified to insure that response elicitation would be effective. The learning contingencies had to be, to a very high degree, exactly those intended. The resultant instruction was, in effect, *validated*.

Validation therefore depends on the application of certain rigorous contingency-management procedures to instruction tried out on appropriate population samples. (The original insistence on the "atomization" of information and linear sequencing is no longer a categorical demand on the programer who wishes to validate a particular learning experience or material. Both of these design elements underwent a functional transformation with the advent of Crowderian "branched" programing which has now eclipsed the less flexible Skinnerian forms.)

In the late 1960s, Nebraska's unique Elementary and Secondary Education Act (ESEA) Title III Project ASERT—conducted under the professional direction of C. Edward Cavert—attempted to devise a practical, everyday method for validating *televised* learning materials. The resultant methodological policies represented a considerable and significant professional achievement; and that, despite the unhappy fact that their practical effectuation within the project's tight time frame proved virtually impossible.

When it was decided to use Project ASERT to help develop a feasible system of validation techniques for ITV programing, Cavert undertook an extensive study of such apposite educational phenomena as Skinnerian and Crowderian programing, the short-interval, closed-looped behavioral model, criterion testing, etc. He sought the assistance of two top professionals as advisors from the University of Nebraska, Robert E. Stepp and Wesley C. Meierhenry. With their counsel, he began the painstaking development of a highly detailed procedural manual to articulate theory with sensible administrative practice in order to provide the project's Lincoln-based staff with a set of sound, comprehensive operational procedures.

The first manual has now been extensively revised and improved by Cavert during a three-year connection with the Great Plains National Instructional Television Library, a national organization deserving special credit for its major investment in this educational innovation.

The book you have before you is unique in its field. The book traces in fine detail the many faceted and interrelated steps requisite to the rational design, production, and operational management of a validated learning experience mediated by technology. Not only does it conform to current thinking in behavioral change models of the precise kind associated with such men as Robert F. Mager, but it makes an important effort to capitalize on the curricular taxonomies devised several years ago by Benjamin Bloom, David Krathwohl, and others.

Thus, the three domains of learning—the cognitive, affective, and psychomotor—have now been linked together into complex but logical design relationships which can guide the instructional designer in determining efficient lesson strategies, more by concrete principle than by capricious intuition.

I compliment my colleague, Dr. Cavert, and commend this book to all those who have faith in the new high science of education.

George L. Hall

Acknowledgments

The author is deeply indebted to many who contributed to this work. Specific persons must be singled out for their continued support and influence throughout the lengthy gestation period in which these concepts grew and developed constantly.

Thus, from a combination of efforts and influences came this approach to the design of mediated instruction: The initial faith in the project of Nebraska Commissioner of Education, Dr. Floyd A. Miller; the counsel of Project ASERT advisors, Drs. Wesley C. Meierhenry and Robert E. Stepp; the benefit of mistakes made by the original Project ASERT design and production staff; the courage of Lewis A. Rhodes for being first to advance concepts which few were ready for; the prodding and searching discussions with George L. Hall and his unshakable faith; the friendship of Dr. George Bair, Mr. James A. Fellows, Drs. Robert C. Gerletti and Robert E. Stepp, who were imposed upon to read many early versions of this manuscript; the commitment of Paul H. Schupbach to the potential for instructional television, through the Great Plains National Instructional Television Library; recognition of the manual's potential by the Association for Educational Communications and Technology; and, perhaps more than any other single factor, the understanding of a neglected family.

C. Edward Cavert

A Preface: WHY?

The educational community can no longer afford to speculate on whether or not to use instructional technology. It has come to the point in time where the only alternative is *how*. As the report of the Commission on Instructional Technology points out, "A society hurtling into the age of the computer and the satellite can no longer be held back by an educational system that is limping along at the blackboard-and-textbook stage of communication."

If television and other media of instructional technology are used *as a part* of the blackboard-and-textbook approach, the educational systems gains little. If instructional technology is used *instead of* something else that would otherwise have been done, the educational system profits and the individual learner benefits.

Much of instructional technology has, however, actively encouraged a process conducive to self-destruction. Perhaps no aspect or medium of instructional technology demonstrates this phenomenon more clearly than does instructional television.

Because teachers were not using television in their classrooms, millions of federal and foundation dollars were spent to improve television. As a result there is now a much better-looking product but one which is still not widely used in classrooms. This is a consequence of trying to improve television in isolation from the basic instructional process. What usually results are efforts to upgrade technical aspects and to increase production competencies as the means of improving quality.

The instructional roles of television and other instructional media are more important than technical quality. Where technology has succeeded, it has been used not as a resource *for* the system, but rather as a resource *of* the system. Where it failed, instructional technology had been applied incompetently, or inappropriately.

In discussing his systems approach to educational management, Donald R. Miller advances a concept that is beginning slowly to permeate thinking in instructional technology. According to Miller, "Our nation requires the development of an organic-adaptive system of education. Educational management must meet new demands, assume new roles, and offer new learning situations. To an extent never before true, schools represent the singular mechanism for developing the human capabilities that these changes demand."

And to an extent never before true, television, with other media of instructional technology, can serve a vital function to meet the demands for change in the development and organization of these human capabilities.

Leon M. Lessinger, the outspoken advocate of accountability, has often said that "Our schools themselves must assume a revised commitment—that every child shall learn. Such a commitment must include a willingness to change a system that does not work and find one that does; to seek causes of failure in the system and its personnel instead of focusing the failure solely on the students. In short, state departments of education must hold the school districts accountable for results in terms of pupil learning rather than solely in the use of resources."

So, too, must the school districts hold the resources they do use accountable for what happens to the individual learner. These resources include all of instructional technology.

The field of instructional technology has not been completely devoid of attempts to effect basic educational change. In 1965 the Nebraska educational community believed that Project ASERT could do more—more than just making available supplemental educational resources by television. The project served as a basis for a new approach to instructional design for television. In the project, attempts were made to at least move this resource out of the blackboard-and-textbook stage of instruction.

Freed from the restrictions imposed by local funding, ASERT was supported by Title III of the Elementary and Secondary Education Act (ESEA). Attempts were made to extend the environment for the individual learner by bringing resources of the state into his classroom through nonverbal communication techniques. Exclusive use was made of remote-location production to free instructional television experiences from the four walls of a studio. The whole instructional scheme in the project, however, evolved around a systematic approach to instructional design.

Encouraged by the Nebraska educational community to try something new, attempts were made in Project ASERT to demonstrate that innovation in instructional television was not adaptation but change. However, one of the most serious constraints in Project ASERT was the contractual obligation with the U.S. Office of Education to develop *television* programs. Therefore, television was used in many cases where a mimeograph machine might have mediated the instruction with more efficiency and perhaps with more effectiveness.

As recipients of a large federal grant for innovation in ITV, Nebraskans with their Project ASERT were confronted with accountability long before Leon Lessinger promoted the concept. The project had to struggle with measuring resultant learning at a time before concern over instructional effectiveness had become commonplace.

In Project ASERT it was realized that the instructional product had to be measured in terms of student learning gains. Thus, project efforts would have to shift from *producing television for instruction* to *designing instruction for television*.

Success was of a different sort. The project staff made almost all the operational errors that could be made. The architects of Project ASERT found they were then able to anticipate most problem areas in design, and armed with basic research in learning theory and systems analysis they fashioned an approach to instruction. This approach disciplined design efforts that focused on testable instruction or could result in specific ends amenable to testing.

With confidence in the universal application of these procedures to all of ITV, the Great Plains National Instructional Television Library continued to support this work after federal funding for Project ASERT was exhausted. Project ASERT's instructional design procedures underwent extensive revision at GPN. Developmental testing was conducted by working with these procedures in such diverse locations as Halifax in Nova Scotia, Shawnee Mission in Kansas, and Guadalajara in Mexico.

What resulted was an early version of these procedural guidelines for the design of media instruction. What remained then was to verify GPN's commitment to this work. This had to be done by extensive testing in the operational nitty-gritty of reality.

In late 1971, Great Plains National Instructional Television Library chose eight sites across the country to field-test this material. These sites were representative of most operational situations and administrative structures for mediated instruction. Participants were given a preliminary version of the procedural manual. They set out to demonstrate the operational feasibility of producing mediated instruction, amenable to testing, by following these specific guidelines in design.

These efforts led up to the 1972 Lincoln Leadership Conference in Instructural Design. Representatives from ITV stations and local school districts working with the GPN project met at a mid-February meeting at Nebraska's Educational Telecommunications Center in Lincoln to advise GPN on revisions to these procedures, based on extended actual use.

Out of the dialogue at this conference came a common realization that the concepts reflected in this approach to instructional design are essential to the future survival of technology in instruction.

Instructional Design

There is no aspect of human existence more complex than learning. And, there is no area of human concern more tenuous than causing learning to happen. Procedures to create conditions favorable for learning to occur cannot exist within the rigid limits of a structured formula, any more than they can exist in the complete freedom of human intuition. The "gut-level feeling" of the humanist's "Art of Instruction" and the disciplined structure of the behaviorist's "Science of Instruction" can be combined into a descriptive procedural scheme for instructional design.

When instruction is committed to a given medium, a detailed description of what *has* worked and *why* can become prescriptive guidelines to what *can* work and *how*. These procedures are not designed merely to be followed but to be used. When merely followed, they can become prescriptive shackles to the instructional technologist. When *used*, they become descriptive guidelines to what to expect—or not expect—from an effort to design instruction that works.

The Systematic Approach

Design procedures are not advanced as a theory of human behavior and development. They should serve as a self-disciplining device that helps focus design efforts to specific performance tasks. The prime purpose of these procedures is to prevent the total design effort from attempting to do too much and thereby weaken and diffuse instructional experiences.

These design procedures to not restrict creativity but discipline it toward a purposeful end.

The systematic approach, and its application in education, is defined by Hamreus as "An empirically derived framework that serves as a guide for systematically proceeding toward the solution of some defined problem in the educational system.

This approach provides not only the means for systematic planning, designing, organizing, and controlling the development of instruction, but it then builds upon that which has been found to work best and eliminates those parts that contribute least or negatively to the desired goals. A systematic approach is necessary because it is the most efficient means presently available for determining precise learning requirements and arriving at the most effective plan for eliciting the desired learning outcomes in an orderly fashion. It enables us to separate the 'need to know' from the 'nice know'" (Hamreus, 1968).

The final report of a National Association of Educational Broadcasters study urged the use of the systematic approach to instructional technology: "Systems analysis and design, to be manageable, requires means for providing for the systematic operation as well. The use of communications technology and the systems approach in education can no longer be viewed as separate processes or concerns. They need to be independent facets of the same approach to the management of a complex educational environment" (Rhodes, 1969).

The Operational Framework

The instructional technologist, for a while at least, must be an architect of a new mode of learning. He must be responsive to the individual but work within the restraints of an established system.

The systematic design of instruction requires a new breed able to cope with basic change. The term instructional technologist is more descriptive of a function than a person and is the focal point of the entire systematic approach. The technologist is required to implement or delegate responsibilities of design, development, display, diagnosis, dissemination, and management for the total instructional effort.

Confronted with new directions in instruction, people must cope with a whole new language. The jargon of instructional technology "turns people off." But jargon doesn't have to be interpreted as a "dirty word." Every professional field has its own jargon. There are those who admonish the instructional technologist for using terminology such as "the electronic display of stimuli for a cognitive learner response," because they fail to understand what the terms mean to their use of "modular scheduling in a team-teaching approach to an integrated curriculum." Or they fail to understand what it means to their use of "an SCA sideband FM transmission network" or their "2.5 gighertz fixed-service television carrier system."

The description of these design procedures is liberally sprinkled with the jargon of the instructional technologist. This was done not to "turn off" the reader. It was done because descriptive terms and phrases were needed to define complex concepts and functions.

Since much of the language used, and many of the ideas advanced, are not in the working vocabulary of many of those involved daily in the design and development of instruction or of some media, it is recommended that the following resources form the nucleus of a design library; and that those involved with implementing these procedures in an actual operational setting be familiar with them:

Athey, I. J., & Rubadeu, D. O. (Eds.) *Educational Implications of Piaget's theory.* Waltham, Mass.: Ginn-Blaisdell Co., 1970.

Bloom, B. S. (Ed.) *Taxonomy of Educational Objectives, Handbook I: Cognitive Domain.* New York: David McKay Co., Inc., 1956.

Gagné, R. M. *The Conditions of Learning.* New York: Holt, Rinehart, & Winston, Inc., 1965.

Gronlund, Norman E. *Preparing Criterion-Referenced Tests For Classroom Instruction,* New York, The Macmillan Company, 1973.

Hamreus, D. G. *The Systems Approach to Instructional Development.* Salem, Oregon: The Teaching Research Division of the Oregon State System of Higher Education, 1968.

Krathwohl, D. R., Bloom, B. S., & Masia, B. B. *Taxonomy of Educational Objectives, Handbook II: The Affective Domain.* New York: David McKay Co., Inc. 1964.

Mager, R. F. *Developing Attitudes Toward Learning.* Palo Alto, Calif.: Fearon Publishers, 1968.

Mager, R. F. *Preparing Instructional Objectives.* Palo Alto, Calif.: Fearon Publishers, 1962.

"A New Look at an Old Log," 16mm color, sound film. Produced for the National Association of Educational Broadcasters, Washington, D.C. 1969.

Pulaski, M. A. S. *Understanding Piaget: An Introduction to Children's Cognitive Development.* New York: Harper & Row, 1971.

Simpson, E. J. *Progress Report: Vocational and Technical Education Grant, Contract No. OE-5-85-104.* Department of Health, Education & Welfare, U.S. Office of Education, 1966.

Tickton, S. G. *To Improve Learning: An Evaluation of Instructional Technology, Vol. I & II.* New York: R. R. Bowker, Co., 1970.

Procedures for Design

The main justification for the existence of instruction is that it assists an individual to learning something. The main justification for electronically facilitated instruction is that it serves a logistic function to make learning more manageable and efficient. The main justification for a systematic approach to instructional design is that it disciplines efforts to those ends.

For the instructional technologists, the systematic approach structures a disciplined effort to produce something for which he can be held accountable. The mysticism of creative intuition must yield somewhat to getting a job done with relative assurance that it will not only look nice, but will also work. So, too, has the pure science of the systems approach had to yield somewhat to the constraints of time, talent, and available resources. The diagrammatic charts that plot out the functions and flow of responsibility characterizing pure systems approaches are helpful only to describe graphically the relationship of each individual function to the total effort in the modified systematic approach.

Task Analysis

Project ASERT personnel attempted to produce instructional results for which documented evidence could be provided to indicate success. The evolution of this systematic approach began when it was found that little of what was done in conventional planning of instructional television produced results that *could* be tested. Therefore, a new structure of planning and design had to be developed. The instruction, then, could be validated eventually when there was enough confidence in the tested results both to anticipate and to predict similar findings in almost any situation.

No formal task analysis was conducted in Project ASERT to determine how to reach that desired end in instructional television design. However, over the history of the project, the analysis did evolve through the constant reality of working toward validated instruction in an actual operational situation.

Although the zealous fanaticism favoring specific behavioral objectives was almost intimidating, it was soon realized that design could not begin with a statement of objectives. It had to be determined first *who* was going to make a response to *what* information or experiences. This decision had to be based on a studied analysis of *why* it was important that the learner respond in a particular way to that material. It was found quite early that systems approaches to instruction must be restructured for use in designing *mediated* instruction. When instruction is committed to some medium, there is often no possibility of direct contact with the learner. Allowances had to be made to accommodate other instructional intervention.

Before instruction could be validated, it had to be tested repeatedly to establish confidence that consistent results could be anticipated and predicted.

Before results could be tested, a learner had to make an anticipated response to the material mediated for him as a stimulus.

To determine what stimulus should be used to get that response, only that content essential to reach an objective would have to be identified and selected.

That meant, of course, that specific behavioral objectives had to be written into a planned approach and sequence appropriate to reaching both the learner and a valid and relevant goal.

It was found that a clearer goal would result if the intent was to provide for instruction found lacking in the experience of an individual—instruction that would fill learning deficiencies of a specific type of individual.

All of this culminated in the realization that the characteristics of a specific individual representative of the target population had to be identified before anything could be done in instructional design. Thus, a conceptual framework evolved in which the specific procedures for instructional design were implemented. This conceptual framework reflects the design functions identified in the eventual analysis:

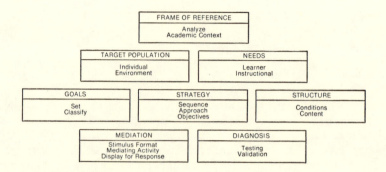

Procedural Analysis

The functional design model, based on the conceptual framework advanced in these procedures, has combined known educational theories into an operational structure for instruction. The resultant systematic approach disciplines efforts to produce instruction in which confidence in predictable results can be placed. These procedures will describe in detail the theory behind, and the requirements for using each of the following design functions:

Frame of Reference: A frame of reference must be established for entering the procedural scheme. This is done by analyzing the total academic content for design to know what elements must be acknowledged as constants and what elements will remain variables for design.

Target Population: Specific characteristics of an individual learner must be identified in relation to the academic, societal, and cultural environment in which he exists.

Needs: Learner needs are defined as deficiencies in the learned experiences of the individual. *Instructional needs* define what is lacking in the instruction required to fill learner needs.

Goal: The goal for instruction should be set and classified according to *how* the learner is expected to respond to *what* instruction.

Strategy: The instructional strategy is based on both the sequence of performance to reach the goal, and the approach to instruction to reach the learner. Both the sequence and the approach are reflected in specific objectives.

Structure: Content should be structured to include only what is essential to get the desired response.

Mediation: In preparing the actual experience for display to the target population, each element of instruction should be treated as a stimulus to the desired response.

Diagnosis: Testing and validation will provide the designer with information about how effective and consistent the instruction was in producing the desired results.

Very little in the systematic flow of these design responsibilities is new. However, this scheme organizes common sense and adds structure to the procedures already recognized as being essential to conscientious planning of instruction. It disciplines the designer to do only what is essential to reach a testable, and ultimately a tested and validated, instructional product.

These procedures for instructional design are dynamic and allow for adaption to constantly changing conditions and learner populations. Therefore, it is important that the design personnel be at least familiar with all procedures described. A comprehensive working knowledge of the theory behind these procedures and the systems analysis used to formulate them would be nice but is not really essential.

However, all design personnel who are affected by the resultant instructional effort should be comfortable enough with *why* certain procedures are advanced to be able to adapt them to the immediate situation in which they are working. It must also be realized that compromises with the procedures described will result in compromises in the instruction designed.

In brief, these are the procedures of instructional design that evolved within this conceptual framework:

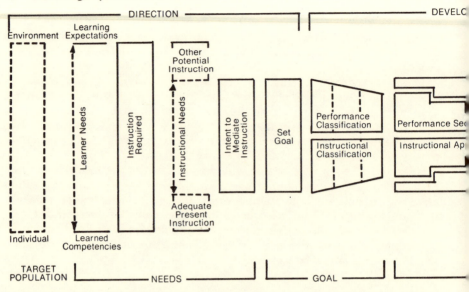

Design must begin by knowing what elements are already determined. From this FRAME OF REFERENCE, the other variable elements can be designed and these constant elements verified by using these procedures.

A TARGET POPULATION must be selected—an INDIVIDUAL from the total learner population. How the individual's ENVIRONMENT influences what he is expected to learn must also be known.

LEARNER NEEDS are evident when there is a difference between the LEARNING EXPECTATIONS and the way the individual is now able to respond from his base of LEARNED COMPETENCIES.

There is an INSTRUCTIONAL NEED if the PRESENT INSTRUCTION is not ADEQUATE, or if OTHER POTENTIAL convention or mediated INSTRUCTION cannot provide the INSTRUCTION REQUIRED to fill learner needs.

The GOAL SET for instruction should verify the INTENT TO MEDIATE INSTRUCTION for only what remains necessary to fill learner needs. The GOAL is CLASSIFIED according to the primary type of learner PERFORMANCE expected and according to the major kind of INSTRUCTION expected.

The STRATEGY of instruction is based on a step-by-step PERFORMANCE SEQUENCE that describes progressive levels of responses. Experiences mediated to lead toward the goal in this sequence must use an INSTRUCTIONAL APPROACH best suited to reach the learner in an academic environment. Specific OBJECTIVES are then written to describe responses that will evidence learning.

The objectives must reflect all performance levels in the sequence leading toward the goal of developing skills, increasing knowledge, or formulating values.

Objectives must also reflect whether the approach to reach the learner is direct or indirect. An indirect approach is unique to mediated instruction where changes can also be made to facilitate getting to the desired response through the existing academic structure.

Each objective is looked at individually to develop a STRUCTURE for the experience that is compatible with the approach and sequence. Implied in each objective

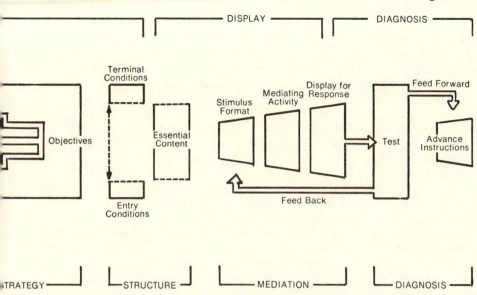

are the ENTRY CONDITIONS that tell where to begin instruction. Where to end instruction is described by what the TERMINAL CONDITIONS should be like when the objective is achieved. The ESSENTIAL CONTENT necessary to achieve that objective is then described by those CONDITIONS that will ENABLE the learner to make the response.

The essential content is reshaped as a STIMULUS in a FORMAT with other stimuli as an appropriate instructional experience. This composite experience is then translated by some MEDIATING ACTIVITY so that it can be DISPLAYED for the RESPONSE of the individual learner under controlled conditions.

The response is TESTED. By a DIAGNOSIS of the results, FEEDBACK is provided to reshape instruction if the response does not occur as expected. When the planned response is made, the diagnosis provides FEED FORWARD to ADVANCE INSTRUCTION to the next level.

When the tested instruction gives enough consistent results for the designer to have the confidence to guarantee it will do what was intended, when used under appropriate conditions for a specific target population, the instruction is VALIDATED.

CAUTION

The disciplined structure of these design procedures should be used only if the initial intent is instructional. The purpose in design cannot be other than directly effecting a change in the individual in his learning development. These procedures will not work efficiently—if at all—in other indirect attempts to influence learning.

One of the initial cautions that must be considered in instructional design is not to use these procedures to structure everything that is intended to be for the learner. Everything that happens in the classroom cannot be broken down into discrete behavioral responses to planned and identified stimuli. So, too, not every mediated stimulus can be expected to produce a direct, observable or measurable response in the individual learner.

Initial Considerations of Intent

There has been a general failure to define adequately the primary intent in the use of instructional technology. As a result, instructional technology has been held accountable for results which could not be validated as evidence of specific learning gains.

It has been said that if you don't know where you're going, any road will get you there. For example, in efforts to delineate clearly between Public Television, Community Television, Educational Television, and Instructional Television, it may have been forgotten that the basic intent to use any medium is pluralistic and not easily characterized by a single descriptive term. In efforts to agree on the name of the road, too often ITV has lost sight of why the road is there in the first place. This is common to other forms of instructional media as well.

At the risk of adding to the confusion of terms now struggling for acceptance inside and outside of instructional technology, there is a need for labels more descriptive of intent—terms that will describe why technology is used to reach a school audience.

The ultimate reason for instruction is to structure the way a learner is changed by his environment—learning. Any effort in the production of mediated instruction to reach an audience in schools has as its intent: to entertain, to enrich, to inform, or to instruct. Each intent tries to create the conditions in which learning can occur.

ENTERTAINMENT USES OF MEDIA   To a large extent, most forms of media are seen by the individual as vehicles for diversion or escape. People are entertained by television and other forms of media used in education. People are changed by entertainment and it can therefore be assumed that they do learn from entertainment. But in entertainment, much depends on what the audience itself brings to the experience. Whatever learning occurs is not predetermined by the entertainer or his writers.

It is ludicrous to ask that behavioral objectives and rigorous testing be designed for learning which occurs when the intent is to entertain a learner. However, that is not reason enough to say that the learner should not be provided with a vehicle for at least momentary escape from the sterile environment of his institution of learning. The only thing wrong with using instructional media to entertain is that so little is visible in the classrooms where it is needed.

ENRICHMENT USES OF MEDIA   When technology is used in a broad cultural fashion to enrich lives, the effect of a specific single effort cannot be isolated from the cumulative influences of other factors acting on the individual. Indeed, it is difficult not to group mass media with the family, the school, the church, and the community when speaking of environmental influences on the learning development of the individual.

Because of modern mass media, man is no longer isolated from the rest of humanity. The same advances that have freed man from his cultural isolation can also free him from his educational isolation. Man's isolation from what is happening around him is now a matter of personal choice rather than a technological restraint. Television has given man a "window to the world," and well beyond. It now takes less effort to observe man walking on the moon than it does to attend the local PTA.

While the McLuhanistic phenomenon of the "Global Village" may not be fully understood, the mass media have added a greater dimension to the educational influences on people. Even within the formal academic structure of a school, this use of communications technology can facilitate learning for an individual. It can expose him to a wider range of experiences that affect and enrich his life. But, this contribution to learning cannot be isolated from the individual's other experiences. This media alone cannot be held accountable for what learning is expected.

INFORMATIONAL USES OF MEDIA   In much the same manner, much of the use of television (and to no less extent, other instructional media) has been merely to inform. A plethora of monologs have paraded across the cathode ray tubes of classrooms and living rooms. Media, in its relationship to the individual's learning development can disseminate information which affects his behavior. In this context, television has as much a place in the classroom as it does in a living room with the dinner hour news. This informational use of media is designed to provide a variety of inputs without predicting the learner's eventual response. Specification and measurement of responses are out of place. There is no direct control over how the information will be used to get a response from the learner.

INSTRUCTIONAL USES OF MEDIA   When media is used to create conditions where the designer will predict the response the learner will make, the intent of the media is instructional. Ways to manage instructional situations must be designed in order to control the experiences or symbols to which the learner is exposed and to which he must respond. Here the specifics of behavioral objectives and the procedures for instructional design become operational.

FRAMEWORK FOR IMPLEMENTING AN INSTRUCTIONAL IN-TENT   Each of the preceding intents—entertainment, enrichment, information, instruction—is legitimate and worthwhile. In fact, adequate instructional media planning for schools should contain all in a studied balance. If instructional design is disciplined by a structure of procedural guidelines, the results can be predicted, tested, and validated.

The instructional technologist must now begin to work *with* the total educational structure to implement instructional efforts for a "systematic way of designing, carrying out, and evaluating the total process of learning and teaching in terms of specific objectives, based on research in human learning and communication, and employing a combination of human and non-human resources to bring about more effective instruction" (CIT, 1970). However, efforts to apply this definition to operational procedures must take into consideration the fact that any effort to design instruction is going to have to work, at least initially, in the formal learning institutions which exist today.

Since any instructional effort should effect learning in an individual, it is appropriate that the design of instruction for media be based on evidence from pertinent learning theory. For the instructional designer, the purpose of learning theory is not to reduce learning to a mathematical formula. Its chief usefulness is that it serves as a guide that will give the designer the best chance of knowing what learning to expect, or not to expect, from a given set of circumstances.

Following a set of rather complex procedures will not make the task of instructional design any easier, faster, or cheaper—just better.

The Management of Design

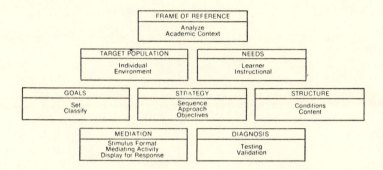

Specific aspects of the context in which instruction will be designed and the conditions under which the learner will be exposed to instruction will directly affect the use of these procedures for instructional design. A total management commitment to use these design procedures is required before any effort to mediate instruction can produce consistent results.

Frame of Reference

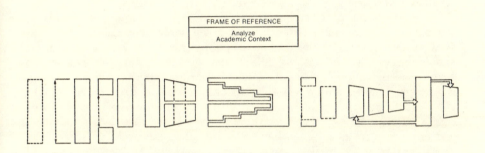

FRAME OF REFERENCE
Analyze
Academic Context

A frame of reference must be established from which to begin the procedural scheme. This frame of reference is established by analyzing the total academic situation to determine what elements must be acknowledged as constants and what elements will remain as variables for design.

Restraints on Instructional Design

It is unrealistic, even naive, to think that instruction can be designed in an open context, free from any imposed restraints.

Many restraints will not be apparent at the outset of the design effort. Thus, the procedures for instructional design may not always follow a prescribed sequence. Initially, then, the existing realities must be reconciled with procedural tasks in instructional design. Existing restraints—constant elements that should be variables in design—will establish a frame of reference from which each step in the procedures can be entered. Other restraints may become apparent after design begins.

Frame of Reference in Design

It is often difficult to reconcile change with the relative comfort of traditional ways of doing things. These procedures for design were formulated to use existing realities to establish a common frame of reference from which to begin.

For example, it may be asked that something be done by television to increase reading skills for sixth-grade students. These students may be predominantly from minority groups who live in a highly concentrated urban setting. It may be desired to increase their scores on a particular standardized test above that represented by national norms.

Here, the frame of reference from which to begin design is already restricted to certain characteristics of a given target population. From the content area given, learner and instructional needs may be assumed, but should be verified in design. The choice of the medium—television—has already been made. The basis on which learning results will be analyzed is known. The remaining variables in design are the steps to verify what goals are to be set for this mediated effort. It will then be possible to design a strategy by selecting specific objectives best suited to a sequence of learning performance, and then selecting the approach to instruction. Specific content essential to increased reading skills can then be structured for mediation and display to the target population by television. Consistent scores on the standardized test given will eventually lead to the confidence necessary for validation.

Without this specific frame of reference for entry into the procedures, the tasks of instructional design would be so all-embracing that using the design scheme would be without pragmatic or useful value. Once established within a frame of reference, the descriptive nature of these procedures can be used in designing units of mediated instruction which may be tested.

Frame of Reference Established by Design Management Policies

Since most efforts in instructional design are for formal systems of instruction, attempts must be made to reconcile any restraints imposed by instructional policies. While these restraints are usually present in terms of budget restrictions, time limitations and adequacy of staff, there may be others particular in each local situation.

The frame of reference from which design will begin may be established initially by budget limitations either in the amount of money available or in the ways in which the money be spent.

Efforts in the design of mediated instruction may be funded initially by sources outside the local school system. Such contracts impose special conditions on the money spent. These conditions are identifiable as restraints which form part of the frame of reference in which mediated instruction is designed.

The design of any mediated instruction will also be restrained by limitations imposed by the time available for production before use. In countless situations where there are sufficient funds, the limiting factor has been not enough time to do the job as it should be done. However, recognition of the time limitations in the design of mediated instruction will greatly reduce the frustrations of the instructional technologist when he is suddenly forced to compromise his design in order to display the mediated sequence on schedule.

There should also be adequately trained personnel to implement these procedures for instructional design. In many instructional television situations throughout the country, the design of instruction for mediation requires a type of training and experience ordinarily not provided or acquired by the staff.

This is no less true in other aspects of media, where title changes to conform to contemporary national thrusts have transformed the audiovisual coordinator into the school instructional materials supervisor, and then to the system's educational communications director and finally to the resident mediated instructional designer, without additional opportunities for professional growth and development.

Other restraints will be apparent at each step of these design procedures. The first task before beginning each design function is to seek out, recognize, and acknowledge the restraints imposed. From this frame of reference, design information can be provided more realistically.

Direction

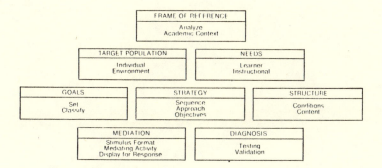

You can select a specific target population from the total population from the total learner population. Learner needs would be evident only when the individual does not have the learning competencies expected of him. Instructional needs are evident if the present instruction is not adequate to bring the learner to these expectations. When goals are set, they should satisfy the intent to fill only what instruction remains necessary to bring the learner up to learning expectations.

Target Population

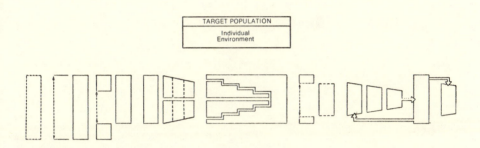

TARGET POPULATION
Individual
Environment

Specific characteristics of the individual learner must be identified and related to the academic, societal, and cultural environment in which he exists.

While learning is a highly individualized phenomenon, instruction most often occurs as a group activity. Attempts to individualize the procedures of instruction under current academic structures and media limitations may be much more difficult than will attempts to individualize the process for learning.

The starting point in these design procedures is not with a statement of objectives that specify what a teacher wishes to achieve. Rather, design begins with identification of a specific target population and the determination of its characteristics and needs. Instruction can then be designed for fulfillment of needs rather than for achievement of content.

Although demographic research data are generally available, the identification of the target population and the determination of its needs may be largely empirical in most practical situations. In many cases, the identification is based on a given restraint imposed by a teacher-planning committee decision that something has to be done for individuals with common characteristics.

It is not unusual, for example, to begin from the frame of reference of a committee-type identification of a target population as "a sixth-grade class with slow learners." However, the application of basic minimum identification procedures will allow instruction to be designed for a more specific segment of the total learner population.

For instructional design, much more must be known. It should also be asked: "What kind of learner?" "Does he live on an Indian reservation in Arizona, or in the inner-city ghetto?" "Does his society expect more of him than he is now capable of?" "What previous experiences does he bring to instruction?" "What instruction will be supported by his community outside school?" Answers to questions such as these in all areas of learner identification will make a difference in the way instruction is designed. It will especially make a difference in the way instruction is produced in some mediated form.

The target population, therefore, must not only be selected from the total population, but must also be analyzed to determine what influences the learner as he functions in an environment, as well as to determine the characteristics of the learner as he exists as an individual.

```
┌─────────┐
│Environment│   *The Individual*
│         │
│         │
│         │
│         │        Specific characteristics of an individual learner must be
│Individual│   identified to narrow the total population to a specific tar-
└─────────┘   get group.
```

FRAME OF REFERENCE FOR SELECTING
POPULATION FOR INSTRUCTION

This design function should begin from the frame of reference established by acknowledging any restraints imposed on identifying the specific characteristics of an individual learner in order to narrow the total population to a specific target group.

Often a predetermined group, classified by formal academic characteristics, will be a condition that must be considered in the frame of reference. For example, it is not uncommon to have to design instruction for all sixth-grade students, regardless of the diversity of learner characteristics within that classification.

Some characteristics of the individual learner may be omitted in design. For example, identifying learners by race or religion may smack of discrimination.

Judgments on the appropriateness of instruction to the learner's function outside school will be based on traditions as well as contemporary influences. This dualism may often prevent the identification of current community influences on the individual in the target population. For example, schools in large metropolitan areas often offer English language instruction inconsistent with the dominant language in the community. The common language of the community, whether a foreign language or nonstandard English, is often treated as a second language in school.

The relevance of instruction skills which the learner will use outside of school may often be assumed without examining community expectations as a part of design. Careless assumptions of this sort, for example, might eliminate vocational education programs in communities where the individual's economic survival might depend on employment in skilled or semiskilled jobs.

Characteristics of the Target Population

Many characteristics of the individual as a learner are similar to the characteristics of other learners. Therefore, in instructional design, it is possible—perhaps even desirable—to personalize the target population as a *single individual* who has characteristics in common with other learners. Generally, the combined numbers of people with these common characteristics are substantial enough to allow for the widespread dissemination of most kinds of mediated instruction.

There are differences, however, in how one deals with the target population in the singular and in the plural. These differences will have a noticeable effect on instructional design. One difference can be as simple and as basic to communication as the reactions of youngsters to a television teacher who greets them with, "Good morning, third-graders," and the personal friend on the screen who says, "Hi,pal!"

Many television directors condition television teachers to use the "you" approach (as in, "I want *you* to repeat after me"). There is a noticeable difference in communication, however, if the teacher using "you" is thinking of a singular "you" as an individual, or of the plural "you" as the whole sixth grade.

The following profile of a target population illustrates some of the detail necessary for complete discipline in instructional design:

Profile of a Target Population

The intent of instruction is to satisfy the requirements of increased community awareness and involvement.

The target population is identified as an individual in the sixth grade whose mental age is 9 years and who has a severe hearing loss. He has, however, displayed a positive attitude toward school, especially when his interest in nonverbal communication techniques is recognized.

He is surrounded by a cultural environment where the community would show understanding, not pity, with respect to his physical handicaps. The traditions of his culture reflect a "town meeting" attitude. Here, patterns of human thought are sequential, ordered and group-oriented.

The individual in the target population is influenced by a low-income socioeconomic group and has had limited resources available to him. He is also influenced by a societal community in which authority figures are associated with enforcement situations, resulting in an innate fear of authority rather than a respect for it. Because of his physical disability, his ecological relationship to his environment can be classified as "different" from whatever norm could be identified. The learner tends to over-preserve and protect elements of his physical environment that directly affect him.

The individual in the target population exists in an academic environment where the administrative structure provides special help for children with a hearing disability only through infrequent visits of a resource specialist. Efforts of this individual to overcompensate for his physical disability have made his socialization a concern rather than a normal functional problem. As a result, teacher autonomy in making immediate instructional decisions is dominant.

The individual is exposed to an instructional structure geared to a normal sixth-grade classroom in which the teacher has little or nothing with which to provide special learning opportunities for the kind of child in this target population.

Since the learner has not been exposed to a value system in which the functions of persons in authority can be respected rather than feared, these cultural and social needs are common to the academic expectations of increased knowledge in his immediate community.

Because of his physical limitations, instruction will have to be designed for communication with a large measure of nonverbal displays of experiences.

The elements contained in this profile will be more fully described in the sections following. While it appears this profile may be too highly detailed to do in a practical situation, all the information is necessary to provide input to the functions of later design elements. In fact, this profile may have to be honed to a sharper description of the target population for a specific instructional task.

For example, it would be apparent from this profile that test instruments should not rely on oral items or directions because of the individual's hearing loss. It will have to be known whether he can read well enough to take a written test, or whether some other kind of psychometric device will have to be designed to test his achievement of objectives.

[To put this concept of design into immediate operational terms, try formulating a target population profile of yourself—as you are now or as you were in school—as the elements of each of the sections of learner identification and classification are described.]

These following procedures to identify the target population are not necessarily sequential. Each element of the design procedures is not only cyclic, but highly interactive. The output of one function may often require a reassessment of a previously determined element of design. In this way, the application of these specific procedures for instructional design can allow a more detailed profile of a specific individual for whom a direct one-to-one interaction can be designed.

Social Characteristics of the Target Population

As an initial step, the target population can be selected from the total learner population by specific factors which characterize the individual in a social community.

ETHNIC CHARACTERISTICS   A specific target group can be identified from the total learner population by selecting only those individuals with a common ethnic background or those from the same ethnic group.

For example, the recent infusion of Black Studies in curricula in many schools has not adequately defined the target population for these courses of study. It would appear logical, at least on face value, that television programs dealing with black studies would be treated differently *for* the black community than they would *about* the black community for a predominantly white audience.

SOCIAL CHARACTERISTICS   A target population may also be selected from a specific portion of the community's social structure in order to narrow the total population to a specific target group.

Because of the nature of both federal and state funding for education, social stratification of the total population may often be necessary in order to select a specific target group for instructional design. Instruction supported by ESEA Title I funds, for example, cannot be used to benefit students other than those from a low income economic group.

GEOGRAPHIC CHARACTERISTICS   The total learner population can also be narrowed to a specific target group by selecting individuals from an identified geographic region. For example, an instructional experience about farming would be treated much differently for individuals from a rural area than it would for individuals from an urban setting. While this example may seem quite obvious, the principle behind this concept of identification is not so clear in actual practice. Countless producers of instructional television are at a loss to explain why programs designed for audiences in New York fail to get utilization in rural Kansas.

Imposed Characteristics of the Target Population

To narrow a learner population to a target group, the individual can be identified by age, grade, or ability-level classification characteristics that are imposed as a function of design. Identification by these factors will serve to narrow the total learner population logistically, but rarely functionally. It will provide a smaller group from which to identify more distinguishing characteristics of a single individual type for instructional design.

GRADE-LEVEL CHARACTERISTICS   The total population can be narrowed to a specific target group at an academic grade level. This will indicate the kinds of things that an individual is expected to do at that level.

The organizational structure of American public education assumes rather complete homogeneity of learning achievement in a highly compartmentalized system. An individual in the sixth grade is operationally assumed to function within the rigid tolerance levels established for the sixth grade in virtually all areas of learning. Deviation from these tolerance levels in any area is identified as a learning "problem," regardless of the direction of the deviation. Patterns of administrative behavior in the schools greatly facilitate, even demand, the design of instruction for children at a specific academic grade level.

While the target population *can* be characterized by a grade level, little is actually gained by this, for within each grade level there is a microcosm of the diversity of the total learner population.

Grade-level classifications lend themselves to administrative expediencies rather than to learning efficiency. Thus, grade-level characteristics are usually imposed on design so instruction will not deviate from the expected patterns of behavior or disrupt an established and traditional scope and sequence. It does, in fact, guard against extending a learner beyond his expected role at a specific grade in a traditional academic system.

AGE CHARACTERISTICS   The target population can also be identified at a specific chronological or mental age. Thus, it may be possible to design instruction across established grade-level patterns of organization.

Designing instruction for a person at a specific age may limit the learner population to a more homogeneous target group, but identification by chronological age offers little, if any, advantage over grade-level identification, since age is the foundation of grade-level compartmentalization.

Age-level characteristics are generally identified for a target population because of some arbitrary standards set by society about that to which the learner is expected to be exposed at that age. Society is abundant with arbitrary restrictions on the role of the individual based on his age. 17-

year-olds are not allowed to watch an "X-rated" film. Their 18-year-old brother can. Drivers' licenses, in most states, are limited to those who have reached the chronological age of 16, regardless of the kind of farm equipment the child may have been driving for the previous four or five years. Entry into the formal learning environment is governed by the year, month, and day the child was born.

However, the mental age of the individual has gained some respectability in the academic community through its widespread use and fairly reliable differentiation. If this identification is further honed to establish the mental age of the individual *in any given area of concern*, the design of instruction can be directed to a much more specific type of learner.

ABILITY-LEVEL CHARACTERISTICS   A specific target population can be identified by individuals at a specific ability level, determined either by standard testing programs or by the achievement of predetermined objectives within the area of instruction designed. An individual can display a wide range of readiness in any given area of concern. When this is combined with a knowledge of the top level of possible achievement, the specific ability level of the individual is known.

Identification by age or grade level may be relatively arbitrary and may guide design only to the extent it would be characteristic of the "norms" of the academic system. In combination, however, they may provide a profile of an individual specific enough for design. For example, a sixth-grade child with the mental age of nine would be classified as a "slow learner" in many school systems. Actually, however, the child may not be a slow learner but a "rapid forgetter," simply because instruction has not been geared to his abilities or interests. Ability grouping would enable the design effort to rely more on the physical, intellectual, and emotional maturity of the child regardless of his age or grade level.

The process of identifying the ability level of an individual is largely imperfect. Specific devices of measurement (and the interpretation of the results) are widely varied in the schools. Classifications such as "slow," "normal," or "gifted" are as broad and categorical as are age or grade-level characteristics.

So, too, ability classifications such as "disadvantaged" or "Title-I Qualified" are arbitrary standards set by federal funding provisions for specific groups. It is often assumed in these classifications that economic disadvantages bear exclusive and direct relationships to learning disadvantages, when in fact they do not. These classifications are familiar to the academic community and can be used for a coarse identification of a target population, if specific characteristics to describe the target group become a part of design later.

Natural Characteristics of the Target Population

The characteristics of the individual, as a person, can also be used to narrow the total learner population to a specific target group.

While the individual is characterized by many aspects, for the purpose of instructional design, at least the physical condition, the interests, and the emotional state of the individual can be identified. These should not be construed as the only elements of analysis and description that may be necessary. Other characteristics of the individual may be important to a specific design effort.

PHYSICAL CHARACTERISTICS   The target population can be described by identifying individuals who have recognized capabilities to respond because of certain physical characteristics.

Instruction may be limited for a target population of a specific sex. This might occur to determine needs in sex education or in certain vocational areas. A target population with some physical disability would manifest needs quite different from those in a "normal" group. Thus, for a learner identified as having a hearing loss, instruction would have to consider this disability. This learner would respond under different conditions than one without that condition. The physical condition of the target population will influence the treatment *for* the learner as well as the performance *of* the learner.

INTEREST CHARACTERISTICS   A specific target population can also be described as individuals who are known to want the same things because of their common interests. Instruction relevant to the individual can be developed in areas of immediate interest to the target population rather than in academic discipline areas alone. Attempts, therefore, to limit the learner population to a specific target group may identify common or specialized interests. Describing a learner as being interested in nonverbal communication will cause other design elements to be more disciplined.

Relating instruction to the interests of an individual is not a common phenomenon in American education. It has only been in recent years, for example, that the publishers have recognized that seven-year-old Dick might be less interested in Jane than he is in her father's car.

EMOTIONAL CHARACTERISTICS   A specific target group can be described by the emotional characteristics that indicate how the individual feels, or what his pattern of behavior may be.

It would be a great deal easier to design instruction if the emotional state of the target population could be *imposed* as a function of design. While this obviously is not possible, it is possible to discipline the design effort if certain emotional characteristics were known.

The target population will have a much different character if it is limited to those individuals with an unfavorable attitude toward school than if the population were identified by more positive attitudes. Although attitudes are neither stable nor clearly identifiable, even categorical generalizations, such as "drop-out prone" or "college preparatory," may discipline instructional design to some extent.

Intellectual Development of the Target Population

A general principle of instructional design should be to respect the sequence of learning development of the individual. Many psychologists and learning theorists maintain (as has Bruner in his idea of the "spiral curriculum") that it is possible to teach any subject to any child at any age. Yet, there is clear evidence to many other psychologists that the child's age at which instruction in any concept begins will strongly determine the way that this material should be treated.

In their introduction to the anthology of readings on the implications of Jean Piaget's theory of intellectual development to instruction, Irene J. Athey and Duane O. Rubadeau have synthesized these psychological principles from the Piaget theory:

First, Piaget tells us that thought is action internalized. Thinking is an organized activity which is seen in certain characteristic ways of interaction with the environment. It is this continuous activity that brings about the growth of intelligence in accordance with a predetermined biological pattern.

Second, the intellectual growth occurs in response to three variables: maturation of the nervous system, experiences with physical reality, and interaction with the social milieu. Learning takes place through adaptation of existing cognitive structures in which tension states caused by the imbalance between assimilation and accommodation are relieved. Thus, the need to explore and learn initiates with the organism and becomes self-perpetuating.

Third, the intellectual development is continuous, but results in qualitative differences. Aristotelian logic, which sets down the various operations that govern formally correct reasoning, according to Piaget, characterizes *adult* thought. This is fully operational thought, exploring the possible as opposed to the real. By contrast, according to Piaget's theory, the pre-operational thought of the child is tied to the world of physical objects, governed by perception rather than by reason. But, the extent of adult logical thinking depends on the richness of experience at each stage of intellectual development through which the child matures.

Finally, intellectual development occurs both horizontally and vertically, but not necessarily simultaneously. Horizontal development of cognitive concepts may occur related to one phenomenon (such as the conservation of mass), but may not be applied to other phenomena (such as the conservation of weight). The vertical development of cognitive concepts approaches a problem related to similar content with a completely different level of functioning at different stages of development to which the child has matured (Athey and Rubadeau, 1970).

In a very real sense, this is how the intellectual development theory of Jean Piaget relates directly to instructional design. It is not necessary to be a Piaget scholar, comprehending all of the intricacies of his vastly complex theory of human development, and engaging in the continuing intellectual intercourse about the application of the theory. What is important to instructional design is to understand that there is a sequence of intellectual as well as biological development in a child. Therefore, instruction should not be designed to expect intellectual activities of a child at levels to which he has not yet matured.

Frequently precise chronological ages are applied to each level of development and result in the misuse of Piaget's theory of intellectual development. As David P. Ausubel said, in the Piaget anthology, "The development stages imply nothing more than an identifiable sequential phase in an orderly progression of development that is qualitatively discriminable from adjacent phases and generally characteristic of most members of a broadly defined age range. As long as a given stage occupies the same sequential position in all individuals and cultures whenever it occurs, it is compatible with the existence of intraindividual, interindividual, and intercultural differences in age level and incidence and in subject matter" (Ausubel, 1970).

Thus, the age at which Piaget has observed that these stages of intellectual development occur are not fixed constants but will vary with each individual and the cultural environment in which he learns. Therefore, it is necessary to match the level of instruction to the level of intellectual development of the learner. For the purposes of identifying these characteristics of the target population, the levels of intellectual development advanced by Piaget are identified only to help keep instruction from being designed at levels for which the individual has not matured. These stages of intellectual development have been briefly and generally described by Marilynne Adler in another of the readings in the Piaget anthology:

SENSORY-MOTOR STAGE: Between the birth of the infant and the ages of one-and-one-half to two years, the child moves through six substages of sensory-motor intelligence. The scope of this development may be seen by comparing the earliest period, where the child has only a few reflexive schematas (e.g., looking, sucking, prehension), at his command; and the final period, where he is able to imitate an absent model, search for and find a hidden object, and show considerable evidence of internal mental activity. He realizes that objects which are no longer in the immediate here-and-now still continue to exist, but his appreciation of them is tied to concrete action.

PRE-OPERATIONAL STAGE: From two to four years, the child increases his capacity for stable internal images of external events and actions. Imitation, play, and language development are the primary achievements of this period. Thought, however, is "transductive;" the child reasons from particular to particular, and his symbolic activity is frequently very idiosyncratic. In the "intuitive" phase, he begins to show the beginnings of logical thought, but thinking is highly unstable

and is tied to perceptual arrangement. The issue of centration and de-
centration of thinking is relevant to this period and is most clearly
illustrated by reference to Piaget's studies of the concept of conservation. The investigator asks the child what will happen to a quantity of
liquid that is poured from a short, wide beaker to a tall, thin one, and
the child promptly responds by saying that the quantity will increase
("because it is now taller") or decrease("because it is thinner"), but
never that it will stay the same (i.e., that the increase in one dimension
is compensated for by a decrease in the other one). He is unable to de-
centrate his perception from the dimension upon which he is centrating
(concentrating); he cannot think without reference to visual images,
and when they mislead, his mental apparatus is not sufficiently developed to correct the distortion. Similarly, when two identical rows of
counters are placed before him, he can count them and realize their
equality. But if he is then asked to spread one row out so that it appears longer than the other, he says the longer one has more counters
in it, and seems undisturbed to discover that moving them back together again restores the equality. He cannot "conserve" numbers in
the face of irrelevant perceived changes. Another way of viewing this
stage is to say that the child sees things egocentrically; i.e., he is unable
to take the point of view of another, and Piaget, in fact, has an experiment where he shows that children at this stage cannot accurately
describe how a particular mountain would look if viewed from the
other side. Nonconservation occurs at this stage with respect to number, space, duration, length, quantity, classes, series, weight, volume,
etc.

CONCRETE OPERATIONS STAGE: Between the ages of seven to
eight and eleven or twelve, an important development of thinking
occurs. The child becomes capable for the first time of appreciating
the following four kinds of logical or mathematical operations, without
of course being able to state the principles formally:

(a) Combinativity or closure: Two classes or operations
can be combined to make a third: $(a + b = c)$.

(b) Associativity: Different operations lead to the same
result: $(a + b) + c = a + (b + c)$.

(c) Identity: The negation of an operation annuls it:
$a + (-a) = 0$.

(d) Reversibility: Each operation implies its converse:
$a \times b = b \times a$.

Reversibility, for example, in the case of the counters is achieved when
the child can think about the action of spreading them out and bringing them together again as a perfectly complementary opposite activity;
i.e., arrangement and rearrangement can lead back to the starting point.
Piaget likens thought at this stage to a film, which can be run forward,
backward, slower or faster, as desired. The child can thus realize that
number, quantity, etc., are capable of "conservation," that nothing
really changes when you reverse the action. However, this understanding is only effective in concrete situations with concrete materials at
hand. For example, the child can classify and order objects with respect
to some dimension, but he is unable to perform the same operations on
their verbal equivalents. His ability to synthesize dimensions such as
length and width in the beaker task, or even such concepts as classification and ordering into number, still does not permit him to reason
about ideas.

FORMAL OPERATIONS STAGE: The capacity for formal, perfectly logical, abstract thought appears fully at about age eleven or twelve. Reasoning about the "possible," about ideas and events which are in the past, the future, or the imagination, is now within the person's scope. Such conditional concepts as proportions, probabilities, permutation, combinations are available to the adolescent, as is the capacity to perform "logical experiments," to formulate hypotheses and test them, and to do all this without necessary reference to concrete materials or images. According to Piaget, thinking now manifests the qualities of pure mathematics or logic, and its capacity to appreciate such relations as identity, negation, reciprocity, and correlation. Thought is now mobile, flexible and free (Adler, 1970).

In sequencing of instruction in design, clusters of design elements about the learner, his expected performance, and the type of stimuli required to achieve the goal will become part of this procedural scheme. The stage of intellectual development of the individual is an important component of these Design Clusters. Piaget's stages of intellectual development have been described in five general classifications for use in these Design Clusters:

Stages of Intellectual Development for Instructional Design

SENSORY-MOTOR STAGE: If the individual can perceive, discriminate, and identify objects, usually without the use of verbal symbols, he is characterized as having matured to the Sensory-Motor Stage of intellectual development.

PRE-OPERATIONAL STAGE: If the learner can use symbols and representations and acts on perceptive imulses but is self-centered and displays static, irreversible thinking, he is characterized as having matured to the Pre-Operational Stage of intellectual development.

CONCRETE OPERATIONS STAGE: If the learner is conscious of dynamic variables, can measure or classify things in groups or series, he is characterized as having matured to the Concrete Operations Stage of intellectual development.

FORMAL OPERATIONS STAGE—LEVEL I: If the learner can analyze, hypothesize, synthesize, and displays abstract conceptual thinking, he is characterized as having matured to the first level (for the purposes of instructional design) of the Formal Operations Stage of intellectual development.

FORMAL OPERATIONS STAGE—LEVEL 2: If the learner can imagine, evaluate, and his reasoning is generalized, he is characterized as having matured to the second level (for the purposes of instructional design) of the Formal Operations Stage of intellectual development.

The work of Jean Piaget deserves much more studied attention than can be given here. Design will be greatly enhanced by an examination of all elements of Piaget's theory contained in "The Developmental Psychology of Jean Piaget," by Flavell.

Additional help in instructional design will be found in the anthology of readings contained in "Educational Implications of Piaget's Theory," edited by Irene J. Athey and Duane O. Rubadeau for the 1970 publication by Ginn and Company.

Harper & Row, publishers, in 1971 released the work by Mary Ann Spencer Pulaski called, "Understanding Piaget: An Introduction to Children's Cognitive Development." This volume gives less detail but is somewhat easier to read than the other two.

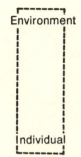

The Environment

The external influences on the individual make up his total environment. These influences must be identified in order to design instruction for use in the environment.

FRAME OF REFERENCE FOR ANALYZING THE ENVIRONMENT FOR INSTRUCTION

This design function should begin from the frame of reference established by acknowledging any restraints imposed on identifying how the environmental influences will affect what instruction is designed for the individual.

While environmental influences are always present, the frame of reference for design may be shaped by restrictions about which influences can be readily identified. More dominant, perhaps, will be restraints imposed by the formal academic environment. For example, administrative decisions allowing discretionary use of mediated instruction may block design efforts from relying heavily on a sequential structure.

The conditions for instruction within this context may not be flexible enough to allow for varied approaches to reach different learner populations. For example, if the course of study prescribes what instruction can be designed, deviations from the scope and sequence mandated in these guidelines will not be permitted.

The Educational Universe for Instructional Design

Ptolemy, the second century Greek astronomer, maintained from his observations that the earth was the center of the universe and that the sun, moon, planets, and stars all revolved around the earth. This Ptolemaic philosophy persisted up to the sixteenth century when the established beliefs were challenged by the Polish astronomer, Copernicus. He maintained that the earth was not the fixed center of the universe, but that the earth and other planets moved in orbits around the sun.

Today's evolution in the concepts held about the educational environment is not unlike this change in the concepts held about the total environment of our universe. Learning has always been an individual *process*. When the Egyptian high priests intervened to assure certain learning from the "writings of the dead," they created the *institution* called education. And, they added the teacher—and looked at learning from a new frame of reference.

The teacher is at the fixed center of the Ptolemaic educational universe. The environmental variables of time, space, knowledge resources, grouping arrangements, and professional personnel have become constants planned to facilitate the procedures for *teaching*.

The individual learner is at the center of a Copernican educational universe, where all elements are designed to facilitate the process of *learning*. Environmental variables thus remain flexible and responsive to the needs of the individual rather than to the institution in which instruction takes place.

Copernicus, with his new ideas, did not really change the elements of the universe. What he did was to view them in a different frame of reference. As a result, he influenced a change in a whole way of life and made possible new human accomplishments.

In effecting change in the educational universe, it may only be necessary to view existing elements and procedures from a new frame of reference. For instructional design, the entire educational universe should be responsive to the individual learner. Thus, the characteristics of the learner's environment must be known in order to design instruction that will be in harmony with the educational universe it seeks to serve.

Instruction must be relevant, not only to the individual, but also to the setting where learning will take place. The *educational* environment of the individual cannot be defined by a simple description of what happens within the walls of the formal institutions called schools. This environment includes all of the formal and informal structured interpersonal institutions of a society. The limits of the *academic* environment, however, can be more clearly described in terms of what influences the formal instructional institution has on the individual. An *instructional* environment can be defined as the mix of man, media, and machines that combine with ideas in any place where symbols and experiences are arranged for learning to take place.

Characteristics of the Instructional Environment

Before instruction can be designed, produced, tested, and used, a comprehensive survey should be conducted to establish influences in the environment that exists for instruction.

Even a detailed review of the current research conducted for instructional technology will yield very little information about those conditions thought to be necessary for effective design and use. There is little evidence that such research is even attempted to any great extent. There are nearly a thousand scientifically designed and statistically treated studies of instructional television and classroom teaching.

Most educational researchers see no further need to tax the capacities of the mimeograph machines and overhead projectors with reports of laboratory-pure comparative research punctuated by the characteristic "no significant difference." Research has "proven" that conventional techniques used by the teacher are as effective as the conventional techniques used by the teacher in the classroom. This research, however, may have obscured some issues basic to the discovery of realistic potentials of instructional technology for learning.

In spite of all this, however, the greatest concern of most researchers in instructional technology is that so little is done with so much of the research conducted. The whole emphasis of the report of the Commission on Instructional Technology is on urging educators to base instructional decisions on what is known about learning and communications. Thus, there is an urgency to shift the context in which educational research is placed. In the past it has indicated what the current conditions are, or what they have not been. The emphasis now is that research indicate what can be.

Concern with feedback to tell what *was* done should now become a concern with "feed forward" to tell what *has yet to be* done. These procedures for instructional design are based on experimental research in learning and communication but depend on applied research that examines the conditions that exist for efficient instruction.

Moreover, while additional experimental research in instructional technology may be superfluous, relatively little has been done in the field of applied research to provide any substantive market analysis data.

Until the 1967 and 1968 surveys of Nebraska schools for Project ASERT, the market analysis for instructional television did little more than count noses to indicate possible viewers and then to inventory the distribution of teacher's guides as a measure of actual use. These surveys for Project ASERT sought to provide a descriptive analysis of the instructional environment that existed for television's use in the Nebraska schools. These data were required in the project so that material could be designed, developed, produced, and tested and integrated into the total instructional process to which the learner was exposed.

The concept of instructional technology goes well beyond the operation of audiovisual devices. Data must be gathered and analyzed to assess the role that instructional technology has in the total academic structure. In translating Marshall McLuhan for schoolmen in a 1967 issue of *The Saturday Review*, John Culkin said:

> The whole process of formal schooling is now wrapped inside an environment of speeded-up technological change that is constantly influencing kids and learning and stuff. The jet speed of this technological revolution, especially in the area of communications, has left us with more reactions to it than reflections on it. Meanwhile, back at the school, the student whose psyche is being programed for tempo, information, and relevance by this electronic environment is still being processed in the classrooms operating on the postulates of another day (Culkin, 1967).

Culkin further says that when looking at the instructional environment to see if the boxes in which we contain the kids are adequate, we perhaps should look at the more basic concern of whether the boxes are necessary at all.

Despite visionaries like McLuhan, and spokesmen like Culkin, instructional technology for some time to come will be constrained to function in the existing academic system.

Nature of the Instructional Environment

For instructional design, it is important to know whether media are looked on as logistical devices to help teachers teach, or as a communication process to help the individual learn.

Lewis A. Rhodes, in the report on the activities of the NAEB's National Project for the Improvement of Televised Instruction, observed that the close association of the two processes in this pluralistic educational universe—teaching and learning—has resulted in failure to define adequately the differences between them when applying society's resources to facilitate the education of its people (Rhodes, 1969).

In the project's filmed report, *A New Look at an Old Log*, Rhodes points out that in our attempts to increase the efficiency and be effective at an acceptable cost for an inadequately defined educational process, elements of the educational universe which should be variables were regarded as constants. Rhodes identified these elements as:

SPACE   To be responsive to the learner, space should be a free element. Room should be provided for the individual learner to move, explore and discover. However, to facilitate teaching, space has become a rigid element. It is divided into self-contained classrooms with comfortable desks and uniform accessories, including the all-purpose teacher.

TIME   In a learner-oriented educational universe, time is allowed for the individual to learn. He can gain knowledge and relate it to an understanding of himself. However, to facilitate the procedures of teaching in the teacher-centered educational universe, the day has been sectioned off into specific class periods, repeated 180 times between September and June.

KNOWLEDGE RESOURCES   To facilitate learning, knowledge resources should provide opportunities for the individual to experience the real world, past and present, and to speculate about the future. However, these knowledge resources are often compartmented into academic discipline areas.

GROUPING ARRANGEMENTS   To be responsive to the needs of the individual, grouping arrangements should permit the learner to relate himself to other people. However, to be responsive to the logistical realities of the academic institution, students are typically placed into grades and classes with certain other students of the same chronological age.

PROFESSIONAL PERSONNEL   The professional is in similar groups. Where a learner-centered educational universe would provide people to understand and care about the child, a teaching-centered educational universe often provides the professional as the primary means of conveying information. Telling has become as important as caring in the process of education.

INTERRELATED NATURE OF THE INSTRUCTIONAL ENVIRONMENT   Rhodes concludes that what should be flexible elements in an educational universe are in reality often rigid constants and the learner is forced to be the variable (Rhodes, 1969).

Attempts to make one element of the educational universe responsive to the individual while the other elements remain constants are rarely completely successful. The interactive nature of the element of time, for example, cannot be altered in isolation. Modular scheduling will not work when teaching-centered grouping arrangements or when rigidly compartmented knowledge resources make the element of time, flexible in isolation, little more than shorter, rigid time blocks. Continuous progress education in an ungraded elementary school usually allows grouping arrangements to be responsive to the learner only until he is old enough to "graduate" to the more rigid and traditional junior high program.

So, too, instructional technology cannot be grafted on as an appendage to a system that is not designed to accommodate it. Attempts to use instructional media to make one element of the environment responsive to the learner must be done in harmony with the other interrelated elements. Fixed-schedule instructional television has rarely intruded successfully into the high school program. This is largely because bell schedules remain rigid. Other attempts to free the classroom teacher from the burden of lecturing have been thwarted by a lack of commitment to change more than one element in the academic system.

Instructional media will seldom be compatible in an academic environment where they are no more than appendages to the established environmental constants. Their value to any educational system is in the ability to manage these elements as variables that are responsive to the needs of the individual. Thus, a total mobilization of all elements may be required to effect the changes required to benefit from using instructional technology.

Change in the Instructional Environment

Responsive instruction seeks to modify the performance of the individual in some way to better equip him to exist in his environment. Within each environment there is a tolerance within which these changes can take place. In the academic environment, this tolerance for change has relatively well-defined boundaries. Efforts to change within the known tolerance boundaries will encounter less resistance than will efforts to change something outside this range.

However, instructional technology can facilitate the design for change in the cultural, societal, or academic environments as well as it can effect change in the performance of an individual. Therefore, it should be clearly distinguished whether the target population for instructional design is the individual, or the environment in which the individual exists—or both.

For example, if the community does not reward increased intellectual abilities in the individual, cognitive-oriented instruction would receive little reinforcement in the world outside the classroom. However, the inculcation of new cognitive standards into the community through mass media would eventually result in a change in how the individual is influenced. Then, planned intellectual growth in the individual could be designed more in phase with the newly created influences of the environment on the learner.

The educational system in its sociocultural community continuously experiences evolutionary growth and development with respect to internally as well as externally generated goals. However, efforts to change our cultural, societal or academic environments beyond traditional limits demand greatly diversified approaches. These efforts can be expected to encounter resistance from those who have vested interests in established patterns of behavior. Therefore, it is altogether likely that it will be a waste of time and resources to attempt anything radically new in instruction that is not part of a total educational commitment to change.

Change is not a free agent, nor will it come easily. David Engler pointed out in describing instructional technology and the curriculum,

> The basic media of instruction, such as textbooks, chalkboards and teachers, have sharply defined tolerance boundaries. Today, while teachers are better prepared, textbooks are better written and illustrated, and chalkboards have changed color, their functions and their relationships to the learner have not changed essentially in over a hundred years. Moreover, the process by which instruction is carried on has not changed in any fundamental respect for this period. It remains teacher-centered, group-oriented, and textbook-based (Engler, 1970).

For the purposes of instructional efficiency, it almost has to be assumed that the procedures by which instruction is carried out in the future must be more learner-centered, individual-oriented, and technology based.

For instructional technology, there is no obligation to change the universe in a 20-minute television program; only the obligation to effect change in a specified group of individuals to better equip them to live in their environment.

Thus, it is important to know what changes will be tolerated within the immediate instructional environment. Instruction designed to facilitate teaching will be quite different from designing mediated instruction to facilitate learning.

Influences on the Target Population

Specific influences on the individual should guide instruction to what is essential for the learner to meet the expectations of his environment outside as well as within the academic institution. The learner's relationship to the expectations of his environment will help define deficiencies to give direction to design.

A person must function as a part of a societal group that exists in a cultural community. The identification of various cultural and societal influences will establish the expectations against which known learner attributes can be compared.

The target population is defined as a *learner* who exists as an individual in a cultural environment. He functions as a part of a societal group. To enable the learner to function according to the demands of his society, he is more likely to be reached through the interactive dynamics of a group. To enable him to exist as an individual in a culture, the learner can be reached effectively as an individual. Instruction, therefore, must be designed for the learner as an individual as well as a part of a group. Thus, characteristics of the individual in the target population can be identified to see what is lacking to be able to get along in the community.

Instruction should reflect the influences of what the community expects the individual to be like as a result of instruction. If design efforts result in instruction that is "out of phase" with these community influences, the desired change in the individual is not likely to occur in any permanent form. Without establishing the influences of these cultural and societal expectations, there is no real standard against which to compare known learned competencies to determine needs.

The total design energies should not, however, be expended in conducting environmental analyses, leaving little energy for the pursuit of goals. Therefore, needs assessments should be made within the frame of reference established. It should also be limited to only those aspects that contribute to the attainment of a more precise description of the target population.

Cultural Influences

In discussing innovation in education as a new direction for American schools, Sterling McMurrin said that "Education is a major bearer of the culture of man. Its task is to transmit the basic values of the culture, cultivate the instruments for its criticism, and to communicate it to the next generation" (McMurrin, 1969). The cultural community of the individual establishes the moral, intellectual and aesthetic norms that are the determinants of the societal and academic environments in which the individual must function and receive instruction. Therefore, it is important to establish how that portion of the learner population selected as the target group is influenced by specific elements in the cultural environment.

McMurrin's descriptive observations of the relationship of education to a culture can be extrapolated into prescriptive procedures to give disciplined direction for instructional design. The cultural environment is organized around value systems, traditional beliefs and expressive symbols.

To be relevant to the culture in which the learner exists, it is necessary to identify and examine the influences on the learner of the value system in its mores—the belief system in its traditions—and the expressive symbols in its art forms.

INFLUENCES OF CULTURAL MORES   The mores of a people, in establishing a set of morally binding customs, are almost generic in their scope; but they are an overriding influence on the learner. The design of any instruction involving moral values would be treated differently to some extent for an individual influenced by one cultural environment than by another. The treatment would be different, not because the concept would vary to any great extent, but because outside the classroom the moral patterns related to the concept may differ.

Instruction that deviates beyond the established moral customs of a culture will generally not be supported by the influences exerted on the individual outside his formal learning environment. It is important to identify the expectations of an individual to conform to these moral customs. Then, subsequent efforts for behavioral change leading to the internalization of a value system, or change in the individual's pattern of behavior, can be developed from the base of how the learner conforms to the mores of the cultural environment.

INFLUENCES OF CULTURAL TRADITIONS   Each culture is advanced by the traditions of its people. In the process of handing down from generation to generation the patterns of human thought and behavior, the individual is constantly being influenced by cultural traditions. The identification of these influences is important to determine what intellectual abilities and skills are required to meet the expectations of the individual to examine the belief system of his cultural community.

INFLUENCES OF CULTURAL ART FORMS   The culture of a people is mirrored in its art forms and expressive symbols. Often the only tangible evidence of a culture exists in the heritage of its art. Hence, it becomes essential to identify those influences on the individual which are manifest in the legacy of these expressive symbols of a culture. These exist in the form of music, film, architecture, as well as in the art and language of a people. Only from a working knowledge of the expectations of a culture can creativity and expression needs be determined for the individual.

Societal Influences

The societal environment of the individual is by definition an interactive influence. A society establishes the rules of interpersonal relationships necessary to advance the intellectual and aesthetic norms of a culture. Of specific concern in instructional design is an analysis of the influences on the individual of the economic, political, and ecological elements that enable the individual to function as a part of a group. By identifying the degree to which the individual is influenced by these factors, the design of instruction can be more relevant to the individual as he is expected to function in society.

SOCIOECONOMIC INFLUENCES   The socioeconomic influences on the individual determine to a large degree the resources to which the learner can be exposed. In establishing the elements of instructional design, knowledge of the socioeconomic influences on the target population will determine those elements that are familiar to the learner as well as to identify those elements essential to survival in society to which the learner most likely has *not* been exposed. These socioeconomic influences are determined by the relationship of *things to people* in society.

For example, quite different needs would be identified for a target population influenced by an environment in which intercommunity mobility is economically possible than for a target group influenced by the restraint of even intracommunity mobility in a ghetto environment.

SOCIOPOLITICAL INFLUENCES   The sociopolitical aspects of an individual's environment describe the hierarchical power structure in which group interaction and interdependence must function. It is the relationship of *people to people* in society. The way in which an individual is influenced by this political structure in this environment will determine, in part, the nature and extent of his function in society. Thus, the individual in the target population is characterized by how he is expected to function in the hierarchical order of his social environment.

Instruction can be designed to support, as well as to question, respect for authority and the exercise of authority. The direction for instructional design is also determined, in part, by an analysis of the dynamics of the sociopolitical structure itself as well as by its influence on the learner.

SOCIOECOLOGICAL INFLUENCES   The socioecological influences on the individual are a function of the ability to contribute to the environment. While by definition, "ecology" is the total relationship of an individual to an environment, no single individual can create a society. It is always created and shared by groups. Therefore, societal ecology is the relationship of *people to things* in a community.

For instructional design, it is essential to analyze the characteristics of the individual beyond interpersonal relationships to include those elements that affect the ability to get along with an environment as well.

Cultural Lamination

Cultural lamination is a phenomenon that is typically, but not uniquely, American. It occurs when the societal environment requires that the academic environment impose other cultural values on those already held by an ethnic group.

The lamination of a culture is seen, for example, when society expects the educational system to impose the "White-Anglosaxon-Protestant" culture values dominant in a community on all cultural groups within that community. A western culture has been laminated on the cultural heritage of the American Indian or the Alaskan Eskimo, for instance, to enable him to function in and contribute to a community—and because the salable product of the expressive symbols of the culture of these people will be marketed in a western society.

This cultural lamination is detected in the gradual loss or distortion of cultural identity with the mores, traditions, or art forms to the dominant cultural market. More recently, this cultural lamination has taken an additional dimension. Attempts are now being made to laminate the original cultural values of a people to those that were previously imposed over their indigenous culture. For example, the "paleface" culture has been successfully imposed on that of many American Indians over the past century or so. Now, however, society's conscience is asking the academic system to restore the cultural values to the American Indian. It has been said, however, that the cultural values cannot be *restored* to a generation that never was influenced by them. They can be *re-established* and laminated on top of the existing cultural values that now influence the behavior of the current generation.

Cultural lamination must be recognized to establish relevant learner needs by an awareness of the nature and strength of the base culture on which the academic system may be expected by society to laminate or impose other cultural values.

While the depth of the sociological implications of cultural lamination is well beyond the scope of these design procedures to describe in detail, it is essential to be aware of this phenomenon in instructional design.

Influences of the Academic Environment

The structure of the whole academic process must allow for varied approaches to reach varied learner populations. Elements of the academic structure must also remain flexible if instructional technology is going to be an efficient educational methodology. Following procedures for the design of instruction will allow existing structures to take on new dimensions of effectiveness for the learner.

In attempting to explain instructional technology, Lewis A. Rhodes has said, "When we put the gasoline engine in the horse-drawn carriage, we had a horseless carriage, right? Wrong! We had the automobile that made a great many more things possible. The way of life created by automobile technology could not be possible if roads were designed, cities located, goods moved and vacations planned for horseless carriages" (Rhodes, 1971).

In its pure definition, "instructional technology" is more than the sum of combining instruction with technology.

Carroll V. Newsom described the phenomenon in this way:

> When the automobile was first developed, the motor was merely inserted into a buggy that was the traditional and accepted method of transportation. Now the new and powerful educational mechanisms that technology has provided are merely being inserted into the traditional educational buggy. We squeeze, we pinch, we pull, we tug, trying to make the new fit into the old. It seems to be so very hard for some educators to realize that new and important results in education are now possible if we will take proper advantage of what is available. Even content and organization of a program of study cannot be considered in isolation from the instructional resources that are now available and should be used (Newsom, 1971).

In an effort to take advantage of what is available for the design of instruction, these technologies and instructional conditions are not looked at in isolation but together as a part of the design procedure itself. To modify the behavior of an individual, instruction must be designed within the structure both of what now exists and what is possible.

Thus, it is important to assess the possibilities and deficiencies in the academic environment through the educational program, the instructional process, a specific course of study and ultimately through direct interaction with the learner.

COURSE OF STUDY INFLUENCES   For instructional design, a course of study can be defined as guidelines that exist for the scope and sequence of the content required for instruction. It then follows that to meet any expectations of the academic environment, the design procedures should be concerned with the influneces of whatever course of study is available for use by the teachers. Of principal concern is the influence of course of study guidelines for the curriculum that facilitates the classroom teaching structure to directly affect the individual learner.

In many content or discipline areas, especially in new areas of knowledge or in areas for specialized learner populations, there is relatively little available to guide the scope and sequence of the classroom teaching structure. The sudden awareness of a lack of Black Studies caught most of the educational community without an adequately structured course of study to provide relevant instruction in this aspect of the Afro-American culture. Similarly, the absence or inadequacy of the courses of study in science and math was underscored in the immediate post-Sputnik era. It may be found for design that no existing, or at least no adequate, course of study exists to map out the total articulated route for the learner's progress toward a goal.

Often, too, governmental agencies enact legislation that requires instruction in certain areas of local, state, or national concern. Unless the continuance of state aid is a factor, many schools are quite reluctant to adopt a course of study prescribed by the state educational agency in an attempt to satisfy legislative intent.

Generally, there is no one readily available to help interpret and use the guidelines. Even a well-designed course of study that has been demonstrated effective with learners often lies dormant in the warehouses of state education departments. This is not always because of the lack of confidence in these state-imposed structures. More often it is because of an inadequate system of making the existence and value of these guidelines known at the classroom level. Thus, instructional design may have to cope with a course of study that is imposed from some academic administrative body.

The almost universal determinant of the scope and sequence for a course of study is, of course, the textbook. But, similar guidelines appear in other mediated forms as well. Using the textbook to determine what should be taught and when, is not the kind of thing a good teacher likes to admit. Often, there is no real reason why educational eyebrows should be raised in righteous indignation at such uses of the textbook. Most are better organized than local guidelines for a subject. More expertise often went into their design than the teacher or school curriculum director alone could command. The instructional designer may be faced with basing instructional decisions in design around such a course of study that already exists.

INSTRUCTIONAL PROCESS INFLUENCES   The instructional process, in the context of design, is defined as what happens when a course of study is implemented in the school. Fundamental to instruction is the nature and extent of the material and methods that are needed according to the guidelines set forth in the course of study. Of principal concern to instructional design is whether the materials exist to implement the course of study and enable instruction to reach the goal.

Often the instructional process is set up with the assumption that teachers will be able to use materials they don't have or cannot get.

The story has been told about how American consultants to the government of Indonesia set up an elaborate course of study for chemistry for the schools of that archipelago. It was warmly accepted and dutifully praised by the Indonesians—then promptly put into a file and forgotten. The closest chemistry paraphenalia needed to implement the instructional process was some 5,000 miles away.

Also certain materials to implement an instructional process may indeed exist but cannot be used in a given classroom or school.

Other materials may be essential to implement an instructional process but by their nature, the classroom teacher does not want to use them. There is little doubt that experience is the best teacher, but few instructional processes require that the teacher take a first-grader and get him lost to teach him how to find his way home. In much the same way that the Link Trainer has translated the actual airplane from its original form to a highly faithful simulation, so too may the instructional designer be required to translate material from forms that are dangerous, offensive, or frightening in direct use.

EDUCATIONAL PROGRAM INFLUENCES　　The educational program is the structure in which the course of study can become instruction. In instructional design, the principal concern is the total dimension of the educational program, including the extent to which resources are or should be made available to equalize educational opportunity.

One of the ways the educational program will influence design of instruction is seen in the nature of the total environment for learning. This environment for learning is made up of people, places, and things that influence the individual as a learner. A pre-schooler may think milk comes from a store, not a cow, if his environment has been limited to a six-square-block community in the middle of the concrete wilderness in an urban setting. The Children's Television Workshop was made acutely aware that its "Sesame Street" was more fantasy than reality for the first generation of young viewers. In second-year production, the street was "dirtied up" to try to make it more like the real environment familiar to the target audience. Principally, it should be recognized that a learner exists in a rich environment the other 18 hours a day. The church, the family, the media, and the street are going to have an influence on what he learns and how. This is of prime concern in instructional design.

The influence of prior experiences of the learner must be considered in instructional design. It is too often assumed that the learner has experienced things that are really quite foreign to him. If the objective is to show a young child that a policeman is his friend, it will be important to know if the child has ever had experiences with policemen in other than arrest and enforcement situations.

It is often the case that the experiences of the learner are underestimated. With the mobility of today's population, many children have actually seen America before they ever looked at a map in a geography text, or learned the state capitals in school. To many, Nova Scotia is eight hours away from Nebraska, just on the other side of the Chicago and Montreal airports.

When the first "Sesame Street" generation descended on the schools, there was almost universal blindness in the kindergarten and first-grade programs to the fact that these children were bringing with them a whole new set of experiences and learning capabilities. It is easy to see why this aspect of the educational program is of concern in instructional design.

Motivation to learn within the educational program is much more difficult to define operationally, but the influence of motivation is important to analyze. Motivation can be looked at from the basis of the learner's *positive* approach tendencies toward a given instructional moment. It is much easier to reach a learner with something he wants than with something he doesn't really care about.

Motivation can be better described for instructional design from a specific point of view. Teacher-oriented motivation may be to make the student's perception of an instructional task the same as the teacher's perception of that task. From a learner-oriented view, motivation would be to make the teacher's perception of an instructional task the same as the student's perception of that task. The influence of motivation takes on a completely different perspective when looked at from each of these points of view.

The negative reinforcement aspect of instruction has been also used to describe motivation. Much of the over-thirty generation was motivated to learn by fear: fear of bad grades, fear of parental disapproval, fear of teacher wrath, fear of loss of social status, and so forth. Today motivation may be showing the learner that what he learns will be of some use to him.

The way the learner approaches instruction will be a concern in instructional design. Something must be designed to grab and hold the audience and to convince them that this instructional moment is the greatest thing since peanut butter.

Needs

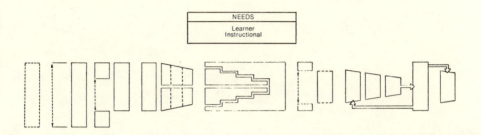

It is essential to know what is lacking in the individual's learning experiences in order to design the necessary instruction to fill that deficiency.

Needs are defined here as deficiences in the learning experiences of an individual. The identified characteristics of the target population form the base line from which to identify learner needs. Instructional needs define what is lacking in the instruction required to fill that lack in the learner's expected performance.

The ultimate responsibility in education is to the learner. Thus, needs must be established from the base of the learner.

Instruction is required only when there is an identifiable difference between the defined learned competencies of the individual and the level at which performance is expected.

Only when conventional or other mediated instruction has not been adequate to fill these learner needs is there an instructional need evident in the design of instruction.

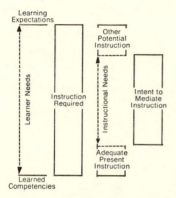

Learner Needs

Learner needs are defined as the difference between the expected performance and the way the individual is now able to respond to these expectations.

FRAME OF REFERENCE FOR DEFINING LEARNER NEEDS

This design function should begin from the frame of reference established by acknowledging any restraints imposed on defining learner needs in terms of learning deficiencies.

Learner needs may be determined by academic institutions rather than by the deficiencies in learner's experiences. For example, needs may be stated as the requirements for graduation rather than skills required of the learner after graduation.

It should be possible to determine what will modify the learner's behavior in such a way that identified needs, or deficiencies, can be reduced or eliminated.

The fact that needs may often be assumed rather than defined should be considered in the frame of reference from which this design function will begin. For example, all learners may be required to sit through sixteen weeks of French grammar before they can sit through sixteen weeks of conversational French even though some learners may already be fluent in the language.

Individual Needs

Since a person exists as an individual but functions as a part of a group, he has basic *human needs to exist* as well as *educational needs to function* in his environment. Attempts should be made to differentiate clearly between these two categories of need, even though there may be no sharp line of distinction between them. This differentiation is necessary in order to engage realistically in the design of instruction to fill needs that *can* be met.

The basic human needs to exist relate to the *personal growth* of the individual. The educational needs to function relate more directly to the *learning development* of the individual. Educational needs are the *responsibility* of the educational process, although attempts are often made (out of default) to meet basic human needs as a *function* of formal instruction.

The basic human needs of the human organism (derived from those advanced by Mazlow) are based on the recognition of existing or potential needs for personal growth that if not satisfied will lead to frustration and maladjustment to life. It is important to instructional design to recognize the basic human needs in order to differentiate them in analyzing the needs of the individual as a learner.

Basic Human Needs for Personal Growth

SURVIVAL: The avoidance and postponement of death in the want to live.

MATERIAL WEALTH: The avoidance of poverty in the want for economic security.

LOVE: The avoidance of solitude and lonesomeness in the want for social belonging and personal caring.

PERSONAL WORTH: The avoidance of shame and inferiority in the want for recognition and superiority.

HEALTH: The avoidance of illness, discomfort, and pain in the want for health, comfort, and a feeling of well being.

PLEASURE: The avoidance of monotony and boredom in the want for stimulation, activity, enjoyment, and satisfaction.

FREEDOM: The avoidance of regimentation, undue control, and imprisonment in the want for liberty and individuality.

SEX: The avoidance of sexual frustration in the want for sexual stimulation.

Satisfying these basic human needs requires human intervention. This is often neglected in formal academic situations because of the classroom teacher's concern for required academic expectations. If some approach to instruction is used to mediate the formal instruction of the classroom, the teacher can be "replaced" (that is, placed in a different functional role) to act as a warm human being, identifying the basic human needs and satisfying the personal wants of the individual. In other words, if instructional media are used to meet some of the basic educational needs, the classroom teacher's functional role can be changed from that of *confrontation* with the learner to an *interaction* with the learner to help meet basic human needs.

Efforts to satisfy basic human needs may well be beyond the responsibility and the scope of possibility in instructional design. For example, a television program to satisfy the want to avoid sexual frustration will undoubtedly frustrate other basic human needs of the designer. On the other hand, Fred Rogers has quite visibly satisfied the want for love, for at least half an hour a day, for many four-year-olds who find some avoidance of solitude and lonesomeness when they join him in "Misterogers Neighborhood" over the Public Television Network. So, too, has Bob Keeshan approached the basic human want of stimulation, activity, enjoyment, and satisfaction to meet a need to avoid monotony and boredom in his highly pleasurable and interactive role with children as "Captain Kangaroo."

The instructional technologist cannot be held accountable for the design of material that will satisfy human needs depending on personal human intervention. He *can* be held accountable for creating conditions in which this interaction can occur by attempting to satisfy educational needs that depend more on confrontation than on interaction.

In the overall conduct of instruction, there will always be elements of personal growth that must be recognized as being beyond the scope of mediated instruction. However, the specific goals for instruction should reflect the defined deficiencies in the learning development of the individual for treatment in design.

Learner Needs

Needs in education have almost universally been expressed as dogmatic statements of what the academic system expects of the individual. Statements of need such as, "the students need to be able to tell the difference between a numerator and a denominator," or "the student needs to develop an appreciation for the democratic way of life," are statements of administrative expectations rather than of learner deficiencies.

The needs of an individual are best defined as a void or deficiency between learned competencies and learning expectations. Through an analysis of the environment and of the individual, learner needs can be described by the degree to which the learned competencies characteristic in the individual can meet the cultural, societal and academic learning expectations. Wants are needs that are recognized by the individual.

Needs Defined by Cultural Influences

It is important to determine the needs of the individual to function as a part of a group in a cultural environment.

The cultural environment is organized around value systems, beliefs, and expressive symbols. The identification of the individual's needs in a cultural environment result from how well the individual conforms to the mores of a value system—how he criticizes the traditions of the cultural beliefs—and how well he can create art forms for the expressive symbols of a culture. Defining cultural needs that relate to the frame of reference established for design will result in instruction more appropriate to the individual and to his community.

NEED TO CONFORM   In the evolution of a set of morally binding customs of a culture, it is expected that the individual will conform to these mores within very rigid tolerances. The degree to which the individual now conforms to the cultural mores establishes the baseline from which the deficiencies between the characteristics of the learner and the expectations of his cultural environment can be determined. For example, a need in terms of a learning deficiency in conforming to cultural mores might be stated, "The individual has been denied exposure to conflicting moral stimuli and is thus not able to respond to situations where established cultural value systems are credibly challenged."

NEED TO EXAMINE   The traditions of a cultural belief system are based on the selective transmission of the patterns of human thought and behavior from one generation to the next. Hence, it is expected that the individual critically examine the accumulated knowledge in his cultural environment. The degree to which the individual can now examine the traditions of the cultural beliefs will determine what learning deficiencies can also be identified as cultural needs. An example of a need to examine might be stated, "The individual has not taken the opportunity to compare the traditional beliefs of his culture with those of another."

NEED TO CREATE   Since the tangible evidence of a culture exists in the heritage of its art, the cultural environment imposes expectations on the individual to create new and more expressive symbols. These expectations may be seen, not only in the more broadly conceived forms of art where the culture is mirrored directly in spoken or written words, but also in the expressive thought and communication expected of the individual within the culture. Any deficiencies between these expectations and the self-expression of the individual can also be identified as a cultural need.

Needs Defined by Societal Influences

The individual is influenced also by expectations of the economic, political, and ecological elements of his society. These societal needs are identified as the voids between the individual's ability to assimilate into a socio-economic environment—to cooperate in the expectations to function in a sociopolitical environment—and an ability to contribute to the perpetuation of an environment as expected by society. Defining societal needs will result in instruction more relevant to the individual and to his community.

NEED TO ASSIMILATE   In the relationship of things to people in society, there are elements basic to survival. How the individual has now learned to assimilate into a socioeconomic environment will determine the deficiencies which will be identified as part of a societal need. For example, the expectations of even limited intercommunity mobility, when assessed against an individual's economic ability to fit into such a social pattern, would determine the following kind of socioeconomic need: "The learner's economic status has denied him exposure to resources or situations outside his immediate environment."

NEED TO FUNCTION   In order to function in the relationship of people-to-people in society, the individual is expected to cooperate with the power structure in which group interaction and interdependence must function. Therefore, a societal need is expressed as the deficiency in the degree to which the individual's cooperation allows him to meet the expectations to function in society. Thus, a statement such as: "The individual does not relate to the functions of a policeman in other than arrest and enforcement situations," would be an example of a sociopolitical need stated in terms of a learning deficiency.

NEED TO CONTRIBUTE   The total aspects of the learner's behavior includes the relationship of people to things in an environment. For a measure of socioecological needs, for example, it may be expected that an individual preserve and protect those material elements of his environment essential to its continued existence. The extent to which an individual now has the learned competencies to contribute may determine socioecological needs.

Needs Defined by Academic Influence

In the academic environment, the individual is expected to achieve varied degrees of performance competencies in manipulative skills, to achieve levels of intellectual capabilities, and to adjust his pattern of behavior to accepted attitudes or values. The deficiencies between these expectations and the individual's actual manipulative ability, intellectual capability, and pattern of behavior determine the academic needs for instruction.

NEED TO PERFORM SKILLS   There are prescribed manipulative or motor skills that the individual is expected to learn within an academic system. The degree to which the manipulative ability of the individual allows the performance of these skills determines basic psychomotor needs. However, recognition of these needs must be made from the point of view of learning deficiencies. For example, a conventional statement of need would be: "The student needs to be able to type his own theme papers." This would have some impact on instructional design. However, a different approach will grow from stating the need in terms of a learning deficiency such as: "The learner does not have the amount of practice required to attempt habitual performance of typing skills."

NEED FOR INCREASED KNOWLEDGE   The acquisition of knowledge or the development of intellectual abilities and skills is perhaps more regimented than any other aspect of human life, within or outside of the academic environment. These cognitive expectations are usually precisely defined and form the core of the American educational system. Not only are these academic expectations for the individual's level of knowledge and intellectual abilities quite rigidly defined, but the methods to assess learning deficiencies by evidence of cognitive achievement are well developed and accepted by the academic community.

NEED TO DEVELOP ATTITUDES   Within the academic environment, affective expectations are generally limited to observable patterns of behavior in the learner's interest, attitude, appreciation, and value systems. It is not uncommon to see affective needs stated as deficiencies in the *ability* of the learner rather than in terms of deficiencies in his *disposition toward* formulating some sort of characteristic pattern of behavior. The difference between the expectations for affective learning, and the degree to which the individual's pattern of behavior now indicates he is disposed to meet these expectations, determines academic affective needs.

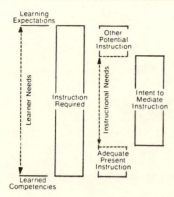

Required Instruction

Instruction will be required to satisfy learner wants that are defined as the recognition of the existence of needs by the learner.

Instruction Required to Fill Needs

Required instruction is determined by what is necessary to reduce or eliminate the deficiencies that are recognized as such by the learner. In the rigorous application of these procedures to instructional design, learning deficiencies identified as needs are quite often greater in scope than can be met by any series of mediated experiences. Hence, the process of defining instruction involves selecting only those needs which are recognized by the individual as learning wants.

It is highly desirable to reduce or eliminate *all* learning deficiencies. But, because of the brief and often transient encounters with the individual through mediated instruction, it becomes essential that some judgments be made on what needs should be met. For relevancy as well as efficiency in instructional design, the learner should be aware of any learning deficiency. Learning wants, therefore, are defined as recognition within the individual of an evident need.

A great deal of caution is urged at this point in working with "learning wants." "Learning wants" are not to be defined nor thought of as what the learner himself *desires*, but simply as what he recognizes as an existing need. The term is used to make comparisons possible with the "basic human wants" used by most learning psychologists.

For example, a learner influenced by a way of life where regimentation and rather rigid control over everyone's behavior is accepted as a part of a societal structure, may not realize that a basic human need for freedom exists. Until this need is recognized by the individual, he will not have the drive or urge to seek conditions in which he can avoid regimentation and undue control in his want for liberty and individuality, even in another and different societal context.

In the same manner, unless learning deficiencies are recognized by the individual as "learning wants," instruction may be quite foreign, perhaps even alien to the individual. A learner who has driven a car for years, for example, may reveal a deficiency in his knowledge and application of basic rules of safety. Unless he realizes such a need exists, no amount of instruction is going to reach him—he knows it all now (he thinks).

The test, perhaps, is the greatest single element in defining "learning wants" in more conventional instruction by making the learner aware of his learning deficiencies. The student, even after a cursory analysis of his corrected examination, will be more inclined to receive additional instruction on items of which he did not demonstrate a mastery than on those that were judged as being correct.

In actual practice in the design of instruction, "learning wants" should *not* be thought of as the affective response of the learner in a desire for or interest in approaching some instructional moment. It is simply an awareness of a learning deficiency in a well-defined area.

Requirements to Meet Learner Needs

Learner needs have been defined by the expectations of the cultural, societal, and academic environmental expectations of the individual. Since each need has been defined as a learning deficiency, if the learner recognizes this deficiency and sees benefit to himself—or to his society—in filling this need, a "learning want" has been defined. Specific instruction required to reduce or eliminate these learner needs and to satisfy these "learning wants" can then be determined.

INSTRUCTION REQUIRED TO MEET CULTURAL NEEDS   If the learner is expected actively to indicate a preference for the established value system, for example, there is a deficiency in his learned competencies if he has never been exposed to conflicting values. If he is asked to recognize the worth of a value system which may challenge that accepted by his cultural environment, he has no learned base from which to do so. If the individual has recognized this deficiency as a need, and is convinced that it would benefit him to have his performance modified to fill this need, then some instruction is required to satisfy a "learning want." Thus, instruction is required so that this learning deficiency may be reduced or eliminated by introducing a conflicting set of values to the learner in a planned instructional experience.

INSTRUCTION REQUIRED TO MEET SOCIETAL NEEDS   To meet a societal need where, for example, the individual has not been exposed to the functions of policemen in other than arrest and enforcement situations, instruction would require that the individual be exposed to other functions of policemen. If the individual has recognized this learning deficiency as a need, and is convinced that it would benefit him to be exposed to some instruction that would modify his behavior to fill this need, then some instruction is required to satisfy a "learning want." Instruction could then be designed, for example, to allow the individual to distinguish other police functions from the more familiar functions of arrest and enforcement.

INSTRUCTION REQUIRED TO MEET ACADEMIC NEEDS   Requiring that all high school sophomores take a course in Latin, for example, may fill an expectation in the academic requirements for graduation imposed by system or state authorities. However, if actual cognitive learning gains are recognized by the learner as relevant, then required instruction assumes a much different posture. Defining the instruction required to fill evident learning needs would necessitate more specific identification of those elements that relate more directly to the recognized needs of the individual and will result in an instructional effort more relevant to the individual.

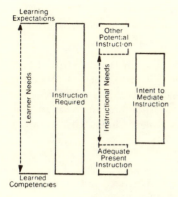

Instructional Needs

Instructional needs are described as the difference between what instruction is presently adequate to enable the learner to reach his learning performance expectations, and what instruction is required.

FRAME OF REFERENCE FOR DESCRIBING INSTRUCTIONAL NEEDS

This design function should begin from the frame of reference established by acknowledging any restraints imposed on describing, as instructional needs, any deficiencies in the instruction required to fill learner needs.

Instructional needs may be based on institutional requirements. For example, even though instruction has been identified as being required to fill an immediate learner need, it may not be appropriate if it will extend the learner beyond what is expected of him at a certain academic grade level. Working from this frame of reference might prevent kindergarten instruction in basic reading skills for the "Sesame Street" generation of children.

The required instruction may have to fit within some academic discipline area, even though its identification in design would indicate more effective treatment in isolation from traditional patterns. Instruction in American foreign policy, for example, would assume a much different character if it were confined to a war-by-war structure of history than if it could be treated as a study in human behavior.

Instructional Needs

The purpose for the design of mediated instruction must be to provide instruction which is not now available or adequate. Attempts to design instruction for mediation beyond these limits may result in a redundancy of experiences in the classroom. Or, it may result in a superfluous expenditure of effort in attempting changes that make no real difference to the learner or to the community in which he must live and function. Through mediation, it may not be possible to provide all the instruction that remains necessary to fill learner needs. Mediated instruction may have to be integrated with other potential conventional or mediated instruction to be planned for at a later time.

NEED TO MEDIATE INSTRUCTION   To the extent that design restraints will permit, only what is required to fill learner needs should be reflected in the instructional needs for the design of mediated instruction. This determination is made by assessing the adequacy of present instruction against the potential of other conventional or mediated instruction to determine deficiencies that can be filled.

ADEQUATE PRESENT INSTRUCTION   Through an analysis of the conditions that now exist in the academic environment, it can be determined what instruction now is adequate to fill some or all of the identified learner needs. It is not unrealistic to discover, at this point in design, that the present instruction in conventional or other mediated forms is quite adequate to fill these learner needs. Thus, any attempt to design additional instruction for mediation would impose a redundancy on the instructional conditions for the individual. It may also be possible, however, for present instruction to be adequate only to partially fill learner needs within the academic environment.

For example, instruction could be quite adequate in the present academic structure to provide for the required instruction in the Process Approach to Science if teachers could use the guidelines they now have. Thus, the eventual instructional need identified for mediation may be to facilitate the use of these existing guidelines. Some mediated instruction could reinforce them by showing how they should be used in a more conventional classroom structure.

Perhaps also, adequate instruction could exist if there were enough instructional materials for the teacher to use to implement the course of study. Thus the nature of the instructional needs would assume a much different character than if there were no materials at all in the conventional program to which the learner is exposed.

It is also possible that adequate instruction now exists, but lacks the fullness possible for complete effectiveness. Efforts to complement the existing educational program may be all that are needed to be done through mediated instruction.

It is also possible, however, that no adequate instruction now exists in a conventional or other mediated form, and none seems likely to exist unless initiated or carried on in some mediated form. Instructional needs could then be determined by examing the extent to which mediated instruction provides what is required and how it must be integrated with other potential conventional or mediated instruction.

OTHER POTENTIAL INSTRUCTION   While the instruction now presently adequate to provide what is required to fill learner needs forms the baseline for determining the needs for mediated instruction, the potential of what can be done in a mediated form sets reasonable expectations against which instructional needs can be described. There may be levels of learning or types of instruction impossible to mediate. This instruction must rely on conventional means to extend the required instruction completely to fill learner needs. Or, present efforts to mediate instruction may be more efficiently designed to lead to other planned mediated instruction.

For example, in developing both the manipulative and cognitive skills as a pilot, some "hangar flying"—or ground school—about the basic principles of flight is desired before the learner steps into a cockpit to attempt to pilot a plane. It would be quite appropriate, in this instance, to determine that mediated ground school instruction could be designed to lead to future potential, conventional, flight instruction.

Or, it may be obvious at this stage of design that it is possible to design instruction for mediation in Second-Grade Science that could lead either to conventional instruction in Third-Grade Science or to other mediated instruction at that level.

NEEDS FOR MEDIATED INSTRUCTION   Instructional needs for design can be described if it is possible to commit what instruction remains between the present adequate instruction and any other potential instruction to some form of mediation. This instructional need must, however, also be based on learner needs common to achieving cultural, societal, and academic expectations.

For example, the individual may be influenced by a societal community structure where fluency in a second language is not expected. Instruction toward cognitive learning in a language may fill expressed needs in the requirements toward graduation, but there are relatively few common elements to justify treatment by mediated instruction. This is not to say that languages should not be a part of the total instructional experience for the individual. But, because they are not expected by the community, their priority for mediated instruction should be relatively low.

On the other hand, instruction required to fill a need to extend the learner's ability to examine the traditions of a cultural belief system may well be common to instruction required to reduce or eliminate deficiencies in the individual's knowledge of the patterns of human thought and behavior required by the academic institution. If the purpose for designing mediated instruction is to reduce learning deficiencies, satisfy learning wants, and fill instructional needs, relevant goals can be more effectively developed for a mediated instructional setting.

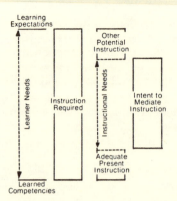

Intent

At this point in design, it is necessary to verify that the intent is primarily instructional in nature and that the purpose is to design mediated experiences to fill needs.

FRAME OF REFERENCE FOR VERIFYING INTENT TO MEDIATE INSTRUCTION

The frame of reference from which this design function can begin is established by the restraint inherent in the procedures themselves—that the intent must be instructional in nature. Look for and acknowledge other restraints which may affect what is done at this point in design.

Needs could indicate an intent other than instruction for designing mediated experiences. If the finished product could be described by what "it tells about . . .," rather than by what "it expects the learner to . . .," the intent would most likely be informational rather than instructional. If the intent would be satisfied with "a good program" instead of with "sound instruction," the use of media for enrichment would be appropriate. The use of these procedures with a frame of reference other than the intent for instruction will weaken the basic scheme.

Primary Intent

In order to use the design procedures with maximum efficiency and effectiveness, the primary intent must be instructional. These procedures guide and discipline efforts in using technology to directly effect a measurable change in what the learner does, knows, or feels. It is only under these conditions that instruction can be held accountable for any learning that takes place.

The instructional intent reconciles mediated experiences with what now exists and what is possible in an academic context. Thus, the intent reflects the purpose to mediate instruction for learner needs and recognized wants.

Intent to Fill Instructional Deficiencies

Once it has been established that the primary intent is instructional, efforts in design must be to mediate only those experiences that conventional classroom interaction with the learner or other mediated efforts in instruction will permit.

INTENT TO DESIGN INITIAL INSTRUCTION   The instructional needs may indicate that mediated experiences should begin the instruction for the learner. If this possibility is indicated, then the intent in design should be to mediate instruction that is prerequisite to later mediated or conventional classroom learning experiences.

INTENT TO DESIGN ADDITIONAL INSTRUCTION   The instructional needs may also indicate that mediated experiences should continue previous instruction toward later instruction. When these conditions exist, the intent in design should be to mediate instruction that builds on previous learned experiences and leads to future learning experiences either in a mediated form or in conventional classroom interaction with the learner.

INTENT TO DESIGN COMPLETE INSTRUCTION   The instructional needs may indicate that mediated experiences should provide complete instruction that does not depend on other mediated or conventional classroom interaction with the learner. Then the intent in design should be to mediate instruction that is a self-contained learning experience.

Intent to Reach the Target Population

With the widely varied educational, instructional, teaching, and learning resources in local schools, instructional media can greatly facilitate efforts to equalize learning opportunities for the individual as well as to equalize instructional opportunities for the teacher. The instructional intent can equalize learning conditions by trying to reach the learner directly. The intent may be to equalize the conditions for conventional instruction by efforts to control or manage the situation in which learning can take place.

INTENT TO REACH THE LEARNER DIRECTLY   To satisfy an instructional need where there is not an adequate program in the field of study, the instructional intent can be to reach the learner directly with mediated experiences.

INTENT TO MANAGE THE STRUCTURE FOR INSTRUCTION

To satisfy an instructional need where there is not an adequate course of study to guide the classroom teaching structure for the learner's response, the instructional intent may be to reach the learner through what the classroom teacher does in conventional instruction by upgrading teacher skills.

INTENT TO MANAGE THE MATERIAL FOR INSTRUCTION   To satisfy an instructional need where there is inadequate material to fully implement the instructional process in an established course of study that guides conventional classroom teaching, the instructional intent can be to reach the learner more indirectly by providing material for the teacher to use in the instructional process.

INTENT TO MANAGE THE CONDITIONS FOR INSTRUCTION

To satisfy an instructional need where it is desired to add a fuller dimension to the total educational program in which an established (and well supplemented) instructional process exists for the course of study that guides classroom teaching to get a learner response, the instructional intent can be to reach the learner by managing the conditions that exist in the total academic context of the learner. For example, additional mediated resources may be provided to complement the existing educational program.

Verification of Intent

Media may be used in an academic context for purposes other than instruction. Although not mutually exclusive, any effort using media to reach a school audience would have as its primary intent to entertain, to enrich, to inform, as well as to instruct. Each of these intents is legitimate and worth while. In fact, a balanced service to the schools should contain all four in a studied balance. However, only with an instructional intent do the specifics and discipline of the procedures for instructional design become operational.

One of the initial cautions in the use of these design procedures was to insure that they be used only to design material with an *instructional* intent. (See pages 10 - 12.) On the basis of an analysis of both learner and instructional needs, it is necessary to verify at this point in design that the intent is instructional.

INTENT TO ENTERTAIN   The disciplined structure of these procedures for design will not be operationally feasible if the primary purpose to use technology is for diversion or escape, either within or outside of the formal academic environment of the individual.

INTENT TO ENRICH   The disciplined structure of these procedures for design will also not be operationally feasible if the primary purpose to use technology is to add cumulatively to other influences of the family, the church, the school, and the community to create the total cultural environment for the individual.

INTENT TO INFORM   The disciplined structure of these procedures for design will also not be operationally feasible if the primary purpose to use technology is to present a body of knowledge which becomes a part of the individual's repertoire of information that is used by others in learning situations out of the direct control of design.

INTENT TO INSTRUCT   It is only when the intent is to directly effect a change in the individual's learning performance or in the environmental conditions that will directly affect performance that the disciplined structure of these procedures for design becomes fully operational.

Development

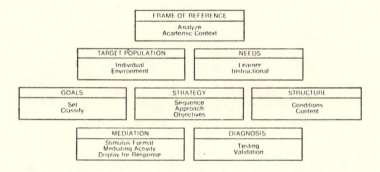

Based on the direction established, these procedures now provide guidelines for the development of units of instruction. Goals must be set and classified according to the kind of performance described by learner needs and by the kind of experiences described by instructional needs. From these classifications, a sequence of instruction can be established in a step-by-step arrangement that describes progressive levels of responses leading toward the goal.

Experiences mediated for this performance sequence must use an approach best suited to reach the individual in an academic context. Specific objectives are then written. Objectives must describe responses that show evidence of learning in the sequence leading toward the goal. They must also reflect the instructional nature of the approach selected to reach the learner.

Goals

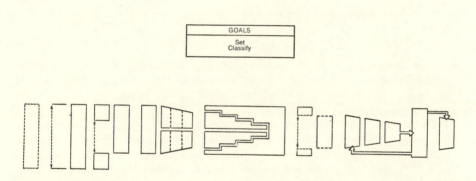

```
        GOALS
         Set
       Classify
```

The goal for instructional design should be set and classified according to how the learner is expected to respond to what instructional experience.

Setting a specific goal for instructional design requires translating the instructional intent into operational terms that describe how to modify the performance of an individual or alter the way he is influenced by his environment. In turn, the instructional intent reflects what is required to reduce or eliminate any deficiencies identified as learner and instructional needs.

Even if the design effort is to be directed to effect change in the environment, for learning in an indirect way, the ultimate responsibility in education is to the individual. Needs from which the goal is derived must be learner-based. Experiences designed to satisfy instructional needs will therefore be consistent with the intent of instruction. Classifying goals will give direction to a performance sequence and will help establish what approach to instruction will best be used to reach the individual in his academic context.

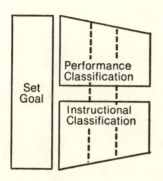

Set Goal

The goal of design states the intent of having instruction fill the needs defined in terms of learner and instructional deficiencies.

FRAME OF REFERENCE FOR SETTING GOALS

This design function should begin from the frame of reference established by acknowledging any restraints imposed on setting a specific goal for instruction that will describe precisely *how* the learner will be expected to respond to *what* instruction.

The intent of instruction may run against traditional goals; this prevents determining in design what the community expects as a result of instruction. Thus, it is possible that the educational goals established in the school will no longer be supported by the community outside the school. If so, this design function must begin from that frame of reference.

On the other hand, translating community intent into specific goals of instruction may not reflect what is expected of the individual in the school itself. For example, well-documented community desires for sex education may not influence goals in an academic institution that is prohibited by some state administrative agency from staffing and implementing a course of study in this area.

The assumed relevancy of goals may be an element of the frame of reference from which design will begin. Thus, it may not be possible to find out, as a function of design, what the individual himself expects to be like after instruction. Often, for example, a learner is exposed to content areas because "it's good for him," regardless of whether attempts have been successful in convincing the learner of that fact.

Set Goal

The basic reason for instruction is to fill recognized needs. To establish what has to be done in instruction, direction is given by setting specific goals. These goals state how, by satisfying the instructional intent, learner wants or instructional deficiencies will be reduced or eliminated.

However, learner-oriented goals are based on needs that grow out of the knowledge of the capacity for learning. Goals that can be realistically met in instructional design must be set from a full understanding of what *can* be done for the learner and still be integrated into an existing academic structure.

Verify Goal for Instruction

The goal should reflect other elements determined previously in design—the influences of what the community and the school expect the individual to be like as a result of instruction. Instruction designed to reach the goal should be appropriate to the cultural influences on the individual if it is going to be supported by the community outside of school. Instruction designed to reach the goal should also be of use to the individual as relevant to his interactive role in society. It is important, too, that instruction leading toward the goal be accepted in the academic context to insure integration into the educational structure of the formal learning environment.

SET GOAL TO BE APPROPRIATE TO CULTURAL INFLUENCES
Goals should indicate instruction appropriate to cultural influences to be supported by the community outside the school. Instruction designed to effect moral change, for example, will have little lasting effect on the learner's ability to function in a cultural environment where the community's value system exerts no influence on the individual in support of the change. When instruction is not in phase with the cultural influences in the community, what happens to the learner the other 18 hours a day, when there is no direct influence by school, can negate any instructional effort. Instruction should be completely supported by the things around the student outside school. Where this is not advisable, efforts may first have to be directed to change the cultural influences to support the planned mediated instruction.

SET GOAL TO BE RELEVENT TO SOCIETAL INFLUENCES Goals should indicate instruction that is relevant to the individual's role in society in order for it to be used by the individual in the learning environment outside school. Instruction, for example, that would expect rote memorization of the capitals and natural resources of South American countries would be of little use to the learner outside of school (unless an extensive South American tour is planned). On the other hand, too often the existence of an industrial training program in the business community witnesses the fact that instruction in the formal academic institution has not been relevant to what some learners must use in their societal environment outside school.

SET GOAL TO BE ACCEPTED WITHIN THE ACADEMIC INFLU-ENCES Goals should indicate instruction compatible with the academic influences to be accepted by the educational program of the formal learning environment. For example, if some state or local legislative agency prohibits or will not support instruction in a given field of study, no amount of design efforts will enable the mediated instruction to be accepted by and integrated with the conventional academic program for the student. Or, if preschool programs that lead toward specific cognitive gains are not accepted by the academic structure in a community, learners are going to be exposed to redundant instruction in the kindergarten or first grade. In many communities across the country where the Children's Television Workshop's ideals and philosophy were ignored or not accepted by the schools, the first "Sesame Street" generation faced such a condition.

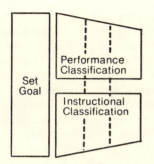

Performance
Classification of Goal

Goals should indicate a specific sequence of instruction to modify the learner performance in order to fill learner needs.

FRAME OF REFERENCE FOR CLASSIFYING GOALS FOR PERFORMANCE SEQUENCE

This design function should begin from the frame of reference established by acknowledging any restraints imposed on the type of learner performance by which the goal can be classified.

The level at which the goal will be classified for the performance sequence may be predetermined. This would establish a part of the frame of reference from which this design function could begin. The dominant learner needs may relate to developing manipulative abilities and skills. Design, however, may be restrained to increase the learner's knowledge about the performance act because of an aversion to the training function in the philosophy of the academic setting.

Performance Classification of Goal

The sequence of instruction will have a more disciplined structure if the goal is classified according to the major area of learning performance expected. To provide a conceptual framework for the performance sequence, a hierarchical structure of learning development is used. That is, any given field of learning can be said (at least for the purposes of instructional design) to be dependent on a sequence of competencies, building on the simple to achieve the more complex, from the familiar to the unfamiliar, or from lower levels of competency to higher.

This formal, structured dimension of learning was recognized at least as early as 1948 when David R. Krathwohl reported on a meeting of a group of psychologists who then began a project to develop a "Taxonomy of Educational Objectives." Krathwohl admitted this group was aware that all too frequently, educational goals were stated as meaningless platitudes and cliches. Some people viewed them as an opportunity to use a type of prose found frequently in the superlatives used by advertising men and the builders of political platforms. It was felt by Krathwohl and the others, however, that if goals were to give direction to the learning process, and were to be used to determine the nature of the evidence desired in appraising the effects of a learning experience, the terminology must be not only clear and meaningful, but standardized (Krathwohl in Bloom, 1956).

In the design of the "Taxonomy of Educational Objectives," these psychologists sought something beyond a simple classification scheme. They envisioned the possibility of revealing a hierarchical order among learning outcomes. Thus, in 1948, this group, meeting at a convention in Boston, speculated that the order and principles of arrangement might be of value in developing a theory of learning, or at the very least, the establishment of a hierarchical order of human learning outcomes that could be used to structure instruction for the individual.

In looking at the work that was started by Bloom, Krathwohl, and the others, Robert Sylwester observed that:

> Most educational conferences die quickly and quietly after the last resolution of appreciation has been passed. This one didn't. The problem was too important. During succeeding years, several dozen people continued to meet and work on the task they considered most pressing—that of developing a universal system for classifying educational objectives. Their efforts led them to develop a classification scheme that was sequential and cumulative— so arranged that each category in the system included some form of all categories that existed beneath it (Sylwester, 1971).

What developed from these speculations were taxonomies of educational objectives for the intellectual as well as the attitudinal development of the learner. Later, through the work of Elizabeth Jane Simpson, came a similar scheme for the area of development in manipulative or motor skills. Thus, to discipline instructional design, it is important to classify the goal at a specific level in a given structure of learning development.

The instructional model used in these procedures develops a learning hierarchy into a sequential structure to design instruction rather than to see these hierarchies only to classify instruction already designed. Classifying a goal in a specific domain of learning—affective, cognitive, or psychomotor—cannot follow any prescriptive rules. There are often components of all three areas of learning in any given instructional task. Generally, the goal is classified according to where the *primary* concern is placed in the intent of instruction.

A graphic representation of the model used will be found on page 79. In this illustration it can be seen that the nature of learner *needs* determines the learning domain in which the primary design effort will be concentrated. The general category of learning within the hierarchy of the domain is where the instructional *goal* has been classified. There is a specific level at a step within the category where specific performance is described. The *objective* then is an indication of the response that will be accepted as evidence that the level of the goal has been reached, or that progress is being made at levels leading to the goal.

PSYCHOMOTOR DOMAIN HIERARCHY OF LEARNING

For the ability to perform manipulative or motor skills

PERCEPTION
3 TRANSLATION
2 CUE SELECTION
1 SENSORY STIMULATION

SET
6 EMOTIONAL SET
5 PHYSICAL SET
4 MENTAL SET

GUIDED RESPONSE
8 TRIAL AND ERROR
7 IMITATION

MECHANISM
9 MECHANISM

COMPLEX RESPONSE
11 AUTOMATIC PERFORMANCE
10 RESOLUTION OF UNCERTAINTY

CREATION
13 ORIGINATING
12 ADAPTING

PERCEPTION	SET	GUIDED RESPONSE	MECHANISM	COMPLEX RESPONSE	CREATION
	Becomes aware of the performance of an act	Prepares or adjusts for the performance of an act	Mechanism	Performance becomes habitual	Masters performance of complex act
					Performs Habitually
			Initiates Performance	Initiates Performance	Initiates Performance
			Preparation to perform	Preparation to perform	Preparation to perform
		Awareness of performance	Awareness of performance	Awareness of performance	Awareness of performance
READINESS		ATTEMPTED	HABITUAL	MASTERY	CREATION

Psychomotor Classification of Goals

While most educators dislike reference to the training function instruction, the fact remains that an individual is expected to have a wide repertoire of manipulative skills.

Performance Levels for Psychomotor Instruction

Some classifications of goals relate to an individual's ability to perform some manipulative task. To reach goals within this area, for example, it may be expected that the individual learn how to hold a golf club or master the finely coordinated skills involved in flying an airplane. Any goal in which it is expected the individual will develop physical skills is classified somewhere in the structure of psychomotor learning.

When instruction requires the development of manipulative or motor skills to fill learner needs, design efforts are concentrated at levels within the psychomotor domain. "The Taxonomy of Educational Objectives" developed by Elizabeth Jane Simpson[1] for the psychomotor domain forms the structural model for the performance sequence.

Performance Levels
For Psychomotor Instruction

PERCEPTION STEP: The learner becomes physically aware of objects, qualities, or relations through his senses.

Level 1—Sensory Stimulation: The learner receives stimulation of one or more of his sense organs.

Level 2—Cue Selection: The learner decides what stimulus affects the motor act.

Level 3—Translation: The learner relates the stimulus to the motor act.

SET STEP: The learner prepares to perform a motor act.

Level 4—Mental Set: The learner is mentally prepared to perform a certain motor act.

Level 5—Physical Set: The learner is physically ready to perform a certain motor act.

Level 6—Emotional Set: The learner is emotionally favorable to having the motor act take place.

GUIDED RESPONSE STEP: The learner actually performs a motor act by following instructions.

---

[1]Adapted from: Simpson, Elizabeth Jane, *Progress Report: Vocational and Technical Education Grant, Contract No. PE 5-85-104*, Department of Health, Education and Welfare, USOE, 1966.

Level 7—Imitation: The learner actually performs a motor act while watching another person doing it.

Level 8—Trial and Error: The learner tries various ways of performing the motor act until he is successful.

MECHANISM STEP: The learner performs the motor act out of habit.

Level 9—Mechanism: The learner achieves confidence and a degree of skill in the performance of a motor act.

COMPLEX OVERT RESPONSE STEP: The learner performs a complex motor act that involves coordination.

Level 10—Resolution of Uncertainty: The learner performs an act without consciously thinking about the sequence of movements.

Level 11—Automatic Performance: The learner performs a finely coordinated motor skill with a great deal of ease and muscle control.

CREATION STEP: The learner adapts or creates a motor act to meet the requirements of a new situation and his personal characteristics.

Level 12—Adaptation: The learner adapts an action to meet specific requirements of a situation.

Level 13—Origination: The learner creates new patterns of action to solve a specific problem.

Psychomotor Classification of Goals

For the purpose of sequencing goals for design, the 13 levels of psychomotor performance have been synthesized into five categories. Each of these becomes a component part of a cluster of elements that will be used to design instruction to reach the desired goal.

The instructional goal can be classified at specific levels of skills performance within the category of the psychomotor domain. To classify goals, it must be determined at what category of readiness, attempted or habitual performance, or the mastery or creation of an act, performance is expected. Then, a specific sequence can be determined by identifying the performance level of manipulative or motor skills on a step in the category selected.

READINESS PERFORMANCE CATEGORY OF PSYCHOMOTOR GOALS   If the learner is expected to become physically aware of something through the senses, or if the learner is expected to prepare to perform some motor act, then instruction leading toward the goal would be designed for the *Perception* or *Set* steps in the psychomotor domain.

ATTEMPTED PERFORMANCE CATEGORY OF PSYCHOMOTOR GOALS   If the learner is expected to actually perform a motor act by following instructions, then instruction leading toward the goal would be designed for the *Guided Response* step in the psychomotor domain.

HABITUAL PERFORMANCE CATEGORY OF PSYCHOMOTOR GOALS   If the learner is expected to perform a motor act out of habit, then the instruction leading toward the goal should be designed for the *Mechanism* step in the psychomotor domain.

MASTERS PERFORMANCE CATEGORY OF PSYCHOMOTOR GOALS   If the learner is expected to perform a complex motor act that involves coordination, then the instruction leading toward the goal would be designed for the *Complex Overt Response* step in the psychomotor domain.

CREATES PERFORMANCE CATEGORY OF PSYCHOMOTOR GOALS   If the learner is expected to devise a new way of performing the motor act to meet the requirements of a new situation or of his own personal characteristics, then the instruction leading toward the goal would be designed for the *Creation* step in the psychomotor domain.

Cognitive Classification of Goals

The individual is constantly being classified by some academic agency on the basis of his relationship to the accumulated knowledge of man. The intellectual capability of the individual will be seen to be central to the design of instruction for most purposes.

Performance Levels for Cognitive Instruction

Learning can be concerned with the individual's knowledge about something or with developing the skill to use the knowledge he has. For example, the learner may be expected simply to memorize facts and to parrot them back to someone. Quite different from this "recall and regurgitation" type of knowing is the learner's skill to use the knowledge in a practical situation, or to make some intellectual decisions about the things he has learned. If the learner is expected to know something, or is espected to use that information in an intellectual way, the performance is classified as cognitive learning.

If instruction is required for the recall or recognition of knowledge, or the development of intellectual abilities and skills, design efforts are concentrated at levels in the cognitive domain. Instruction is then based around the model structured in the *Taxonomy of Educational Objectives*, edited by Benjamin S. Bloom (and almost universally known throughout the educational community as "Bloom's Taxonomy").

COGNITIVE DOMAIN
HIERARCHY OF LEARNING

For the recall or recognition of knowledge and the development of intellectual abilities and skills

						EVALUATION
						21 EXTERNAL CRITERIA
						20 INTERNAL EVIDENCE
					SYNTHESIS	Develops new material from component parts
					19 ABSTRACTIONS	Analyzes Material
					18 DESIGN	
				ANALYSIS	17 COMMUNICATION	Uses Abstractions
				16 ORGANIZATION	Breaks down material into its component parts	
			APPLICATION	15 RELATIONSHIPS	Uses Abstractions	Understands Material
			13 APPLICATION	14 ELEMENTS	Understands Material	Recognizes Patterns
		COMPREHENSION		Uses abstractions in concrete situations	Recognizes Patterns	Aware of Procedures
	UNIVERSALS	12 EXTRAPOLATION	Understands material being communicated	Understands Material	Aware of Procedures	Recalls Specifics
	11 INTERPRETATION	Recognizes patterns structures and settings	Recognizes Patterns	Aware of Procedures	Recalls Specifics	
PROCEDURES	10 TRANSLATION		Aware of Procedures	Recalls Specifics		
9 THEORIES	Aware of methods and processes	Aware of Procedures	Recalls Specifics			
8 PRINCIPLES		Recalls Specifics				
SPECIFICS	Recalls Specifics					
7 METHODOLOGY	Recalls specific bits of information					
6 CRITERIA						
5 CLASSIFICATIONS						
4 TRENDS						
3 CONVENTIONS						
2 FACTS						
1 TERMINOLOGY						

RECALL — UNDERSTANDING — APPLICATION — OPERATIONS — EVALUATION

COGNITIVE DOMAIN HIERARCHY OF LEARNING

Need of individual determines the domain from which we draw our planning activities

The individual does not have pre-requisites to be able to respond to objectives describing behavior at levels higher than that indicated by the goal.

General category of achievement expected by the individual determines the goal.

Level at which the individual is expected to perform determines the top level of sequence. The performance sequence is determined by the levels remaining between the entry level and the goal.

Level at which the learner can now demonstrate performance and competency defines the entry level.

FOLLOW-UP
After the individual has evidenced he has reached the goal, he is then ready to function at the next level of the hierarchy.

OBJECTIVE
Indication of the response that will evidence goal has been reached.

PRE-REQUISITES
The individual must be able to function at all levels lower than that indicated by the goal.

EVALUATION
EXTERNAL CRITERIA
INTERNAL EVIDENCE

SYNTHESIS
ABSTRACTIONS
DESIGN
COMMUNICATION

APPLICAT(ION)

COMPREHENSION
EXTRAPOLATES
INTERPRETS
TRANSLATES

PROCEDURES
THEORIES
PRINCIPLES
METHODOLOGY
CRITERIA
CLASSIFICATIONS
TRENDS
CONVENTIONS

SPECIFICS
FACTS
TERMINOLOGY

	CATEGORY I	CATEGORY II	CATEGORY III	CATEGORY IV	CATEGORY V
EVALUATION					Develops new material from component parts
APPLICATION				Uses abstractions in concrete situations	
COMPREHENSION			Recalls patterns structure and settings	Recalls Patterns	Recalls Patterns
PROCEDURES	Recalls methods and processes	Recalls Procedures		calls cedures	Recalls Procedures
SPECIFICS	Recalls specific bits of information	Recalls Specifics	Recalls Specifics	Recalls Specifics	Recalls Specifics

Performance Levels
For Cognitive Instruction[1]

KNOWLEDGE OF SPECIFICS STEP: The learner recalls specific bits of information.

> *Level 1—Recall of Terminology:* The learner recalls what specific verbal and nonverbal symbols represent.
>
> *Level 2—Recall of Specific Facts:* The learner recalls dates, events, persons, places, etc.

KNOWLEDGE OF PROCEDURES STEP: The learner is aware of ways to deal with specifics.

> *Level 3—Awareness of Conventions:* The learner is aware of different rules of treating and presenting information.
>
> *Level 4—Awareness of Trends and Sequences:* The learner is aware of the sequence of related information with respect to time.
>
> *Level 5—Awareness of Classifications and Categories:* The learner is aware of the ways information is arranged for a given purpose.
>
> *Level 6—Awareness of Criteria:* The learner is aware of the criteria by which information is tested and judged.
>
> *Level 7—Awareness of Methodology:* The learner is aware of the way information is treated in studying particular problems.

KNOWLEDGE OF UNIVERSALS STEP: The learner recognizes the major schemes and patterns by which information is organized.

> *Level 8—Recognition of Principles and Generalizations:* The learner recognizes when general principles summarize information, ideas or material.
>
> *Level 9—Recognition of Theories and Structures:* The learner recognizes when two or more general principles fit together to describe complex information, ideas or material.

COMPREHENSION STEP: The learner knows what is being communicated and can make limited use of the information.

> *Level 10—Translation:* The learner copies information from one form of expression to another.
>
> *Level 11—Interpretation:* The learner explains or summarizes information by stating it in a different way.
>
> *Level 12—Extrapolation:* The learner extends the given information to determine implications, consequences, corollaries, effects, etc., that are in accordance with the original conditions.

APPLICATION STEP: The learner uses the information beyond the context in which it was originally given.

> *Level 13—Application:* The learner uses abstractions in particular and concrete situations.

ANALYSIS STEP: The learner breaks down information so that the order of ideas is made clear and the relations between the ideas are explicit.

> *Level 14—Analysis of Elements:* The learner discriminates between the bits of information included in the idea.
>
> *Level 15—Analysis of Relationships:* The learner describes the connections and interactions between the bits of information in the idea, or between other ideas.

---

[1]Adapted from:Bloom, Benjamin S. (ed.), *Taxonomy of Educational Objectives, Handbook I: Cognitive Domain*, New York: David McKay Co., Inc. 1956.

Level 16—Analysis of Organizational Principles: **The learner studies the arrangement and structure of information that holds the ideas together.**

SYNTHESIS STEP: The learner puts together ideas to form a whole.

Level 17—Production of a Unique Communication: **The learner develops new material in which he conveys the ideas, feelings and experiences of others.**

Level 18—Production of a Plan or Proposed Set of Operations: **The learner develops a plan of work or proposes a plan of operations.**

Level 19—Derivation of a Set of Abstract Relations: **The learner derives new material by using abstractions to classify or explain ideas.**

EVALUATION STEP: The learner judges the value of information for a given purpose.

Level 20—Judgment in Terms of Internal Evidence: **The learner evaluates the accuracy of information from such evidence as logical accuracy, consistency, and other internal evidence.**

Level 21—Judgment in Terms of External Criteria: **The learner evaluates information with reference to other selected and remembered criteria.**

Cognitive Classification of Goals

The goal for instruction can be classified at a specific level of intellectual performance within the hierarchy of the cognitive domain. For the purpose of sequencing goals for design, the 21 levels of cognitive performance have been synthesized into five categories. Each of these becomes a component part of a cluster of elements that will be used to design instruction to reach the desired goal.

It can be determined what category of recall or understanding of information, the use of knowledge, or the operation with, or evaluation of material at which performance is expected. The specific sequence of instruction can then be determined by the level of the recognition of knowledge or the development of intellectual abilities or skills on steps within the category selected.

RECALL CAREGORY OF COGNITIVE GOALS   If the learner is expected to recall specific bits of information, to be aware of methods or procedures of dealing with specifics, or to recognize information about patterns, settings, or structures, then instruction leading toward the goal would be designed for the *Knowledge of Specifics* step, the *Knowledge of Procedures* step, or the *Knowledge of Universals* step in the cognitive domain.

UNDERSTANDING CATEGORY OF COGNITIVE GOALS   If the learner is expected to know what is being communicated and is expected to make limited use of the information, then instruction leading toward the goal would be designed for the *Comprehension* step in the cognitive domain.

APPLICATION CATEGORY OF COGNITIVE GOALS   If the learner is expected to use ideas beyond the context in which they were originally given, then instruction leading toward the goal would be designed for the *Application* step in the cognitive domain.

OPERATIONS CATEGORY OF COGNITIVE GOALS   If the learner is expected to break down ideas so the order of information is made clear and the relationship between other ideas is explicit; or if he is expected to put together ideas to formulate new information, then instruction leading toward the goal would be designed for either the *Analysis* step or the *Synthesis* step in the cognitive domain.

EVALUATION CATEGORY OF COGNITIVE GOALS   If the learner is expected to make judgments about the value of material for a given purpose, then the instruction leading toward the goal would be designed for the *Evaluation* step in the cognitive domain.

Affective Classification of Goals

Of all the academic classifications and influences on the individual, those dealing with his attitudes and values are the most elusive. Identification of these characteristics in a learner is realistically limited to looking for the visible, outward things a learner does because of these internalized attributes.

Performance Levels for Affective Instruction

Instruction may be concerned with developing within the individual an interest, attitude or appreciation of something. Or, within this type of learning, it may be expected that the learner form some sort of value system that will govern the way he acts in his day-to-day activities. Affective learning is different from cognitive learning in the sense that the learner is expected to have adopted some pattern of behavior about what he is doing, or about what is known. For instance, memorizing the lines of a poem is different from an appreciation of poetry. So, too, is the recall of multiplication tables different from an interest in mathematics. Affective learned attributes are the individual's ability to deal with concepts, values, or value systems.

If, to meet learner needs, instruction is required for the development of interest, appreciation, attitudes, values, or personal adjustment, the design efforts should be focused on those levels in the hierarchy of the affective domain. David R. Krathwohl's *Taxonomy of Educational Objectives* for the affective domain thus becomes the basic structure to give the direction to instructional design.

AFFECTIVE DOMAIN HIERARCHY OF LEARNING

For the development of interest, appreciation, attitudes, values and adequate personal adjustment

RECEIVING	RESPONDING	VALUING	ORGANIZATION	INTERNALIZATION
3 CONTROLLED ATTENTION 2 WILLINGNESS 1 AWARENESS	6 SATISFACTION 5 WILLINGNESS 4 ACQUIESCENCE	9 COMMITMENT TO VALUE 8 PREFERENCE FOR VALUE 7 ACCEPTANCE OF VALUE	11 ORGANIZATION 10 CONCEPTUALIZATION	13 CHARACTERIZATION 12 GENERALIZED SET
				Evaluates a value system
			Appreciates the worth of the concept as a value	Appreciates the worth of the concept as a value
		Shows interest in the concept	Interested in the concept	Interested in the concept
	Becomes Aware of a concept	Aware of a concept	Aware of a concept	Aware of a concept
AWARENESS	INTEREST	APPRECIATION	VALUES	ADJUSTMENT

Performance Levels
For Affective Instruction[1]

RECEIVING STEP: The learner knows that a concept exists and is willing to pay attention to it.

Level 1—Awareness: The learner is merely conscious of something—he takes into account a situation, phenomenon, object or state of affairs.

Level 2—Willingness to Receive: The learner is willing to tolerate a given concept, not to avoid it.

Level 3—Controlled or Selected Attention: The learner pays attention to only those concepts that are relevant to him or his situation.

RESPONDING STEP: The learner is actually actively paying attention to the concept—or at least he is doing something with or about it besides merely being aware of it.

Level 4—Acquiescence in Responding: The learner complies with a concept without fully accepting the necessity for doing so.

Level 5—Willingness to Respond: The learner is sufficiently committed to the concept that he accepts it willingly.

Level 6—Satisfaction in Response: The learner accepts the concept with a feeling of satisfaction generally of pleasure, zest, or enjoyment.

VALUING STEP: The individual recognizes that related concepts have worth as a value.

Level 7—Acceptance of a Value: The learner ascribes worth to a concept or to related concepts.

Level 8—Preference for a Value: The learner is sufficiently committed to the worth of concepts as a value to pursue it, to seek it out, to want it.

Level 9—Commitment: The learner has a high degree of certainty about the worth of concepts as a value.

ORGANIZATION STEP: The learner can organize values when he encounters situations for which more than one value is relevant in order to build his own value system.

Level 10—Conceptualization of a Value: The learner sees how the value relates to those he already holds or to a new one he is coming to hold.

Level 11—Organization of a Value System: The learner brings together a complex of values into an ordered relationship with each other.

INTERNALIZATION STEP: Values already have a place in the learner's value hierarchy and are organized into some kind of internally consistent system. These values have controlled the behavior of the learner long enough that he has adapted to behaving in this way.

Level 12—Generalized Set: The learner has internal consistency in his system of values at any given moment.

Level 13—Characterization: A value system has become completely internalized into the learner's way of life.

[1]Adpated from: Krathwohl, David R., Bloom, Benjamin S., and Masia, Bertram B., *Taxonomy of Educational Objectives, Handbook II: Affective Domain*, New York: David McKay, Co. Inc., 1964.

Affective Classification of Goals

The goal for instruction can be classified at a specific level of attitudinal performance in the hierarchy of the affective domain. For the purpose of sequencing goals for design, the 13 levels of affective performance have been synthesized into five categories. Each of these becomes a component part of a cluster of elements that will be used to design instruction to reach the desired goal.

It must be determined what category of awareness, interest, appreciation, value, or adjustment to a value system at which performance is expected. The sequence of instruction can then be determined by identifying the specific level of attitudinal performance on a step in the category selected.

AWARENESS CATEGORY OF AFFECTIVE GOALS   If the learner is expected to know that a concept exists and is willing to pay attention to it, then the instruction leading toward the goal would be designed for the *Receiving* step in the affective domain.

INTEREST CATEGORY OF AFFECTIVE GOALS   If the learner is expected to pay attention actively to a concept—or at least do something with or about it besides merely being aware of it, then the instruction leading toward the goal would be designed for the *Responding* step in the affective domain.

APPRECIATION CATEGORY OF AFFECTIVE GOALS   If the learner is expected to recognize that a concept has worth as a value, then the instruction leading toward the goal would be designed for the *Valuing* step in the affective domain.

VALUES CATEGORY OF AFFECTIVE GOALS   If the leaner is expected to organize values when he encounters situations for which more than one value is relevant in order to build his own value system, then the instruction leading toward the goal would be designed for the *Organization* step in the affective domain.

ADJUSTMENT CATEGORY OF AFFECTIVE GOALS   If the learner is expected to have a hierarchy of values that form an internally consistent system to control his behavior, then the instruction leading toward the goal would be designed for the *Internalization* step in the affective domain.

The operational definitions of the terms associated with the affective domain in popular use may contribute to increased confusion in classifying goals for attitudinal performance. Krathwohl noted in the *Taxonomy of*

Educational Objectives for the affective domain that:

> The terms such as interest, attitude, appreciation and value have a wide range of meanings. When we examined the range of meanings for any one term (in formulating the affective taxonomy) and compared this range to the taxonomy structure, we found that each term generally took on meanings over a section of the continuum (Krathwohl, 1964).

The range illustrated by Krathwohl is shown on the graphic representation of the affective domain levels on page 84. The descriptive definitions given in the taxonomy have been used in these design procedures to identify the range as well as the primary focus of design in classifying goals. Krathwohl described how these ranges were arrived at in this way:

> Interpretation of the term *interest* ranged all the way from the student's being aware that a phenomenon exists to the behavior of avidly seeking the phenomenon. Apparently *interest* typically describes behavior that would be classified at the lower levels of the taxonomy. Rarely would it be interpreted as describing behavior we would describe at the level of "Commitment" or higher.
>
> Interpretation of the term, *appreciation*, in popular use, shows that it may refer to such simple behavior as the person's being willing to attend to certain aspects of a phenomenon, to his feeling a response to some stimulus, or to his showing a preference for certain behavior or stimuli. Thus, *appreciation* would not be interpreted typically as including the behaviors at the lowest levels of the taxonomy nor at the highest.
>
> Similarly when we examined the range of interpretations given to the terms *attitude* and *value* in popular use, it was found they ranged from situations where the student was expected to display a particular behavior, especially with a certain amount of enthusiasm, warmth, or even disgust, if appropriate, to situations in which he might go out of his way to display the value or to communicate to others about it. Thus *attitudes* and *values* extend from the levels of "Willingness to Respond" to "Conceptualization of a Value."
>
> The term *adjustment* appears to take on a range of meanings, from a simple display of appropriate behavior in social interaction to the interrelation of one aspect of self to another—one's outlook on life. Thus, the range of meanings for *adjustment* extends from the level of "Willingness to Respond" through "Characterization." It has the widest potential range of meanings of any of the terms, extending nearly across the entire range of taxonomic categories (Krathwohl, 1964).

Since there is a great deal of overlapping, and since no one term describes performance that spans the entire hierarchy, these terms can be used in instructional design to define the parameters of design responsibility and performance expectations. If, for example, the intent of instruction indicates the development of attitudes or values toward some concept or idea, instruction should begin from the level of "Willingness to Respond" on the Responding step and not extend beyond the "Conceptualization" level on the Organization step. Or, in other words, if the goal is classified at lower levels than "Willingness to Respond," what is really meant in the intent of instruction is developing appreciation or interest, not attitudes. Similarly, a goal classified at the "Characterization" level would guide design to meet an intent related to the personal adjustment of the learner, not to his appreciation of something.

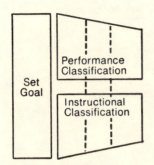

Instructional
Classsification of Goal

The approach to instruction will have a more disciplined structural core if the goal is also classified according to the type of experiences expected to fill learner needs.

FRAME OF REFERENCE FOR CLASSIFYING GOALS BY INSTRUCTIONAL APPROACH

This design function should begin from the frame of reference established by acknowledging any restraints imposed on the kind of instruction by which the goal can be classified.

The approach to instruction may also be based on a predetermined classification. It might be more appropriate to classify the goal according to the major kind of experiences required to fill the primary instructional needs. For example, it may be determined that instruction might be more efficiently designed for mediation as a self-contained unit. The approach, however, may have to be decided from the frame of reference established by the restraint that design must be made a part of an existing teaching structure.

Instructional Classification of Goal

Once classified according to the performance required to fill learner needs, the goal should also be classified by the type of experiences required to satisy the instructional needs. This classification of the goal will help decide on the approach to instruction that will be used to reach the learner. Where performance classifications were based on the dominant kind of learner need, so, too, the instructional classification is based on the dominant void in experiences required to fill these learner needs in an academic context.

Instructional Classification Categories

In classifying goals, instructional needs may be satisfied by experiences that will be prerequisite to later instruction. Or, efforts to satisfy instructional needs may require experiences in a continuing sequence of instruction. The instructional needs may also relate more directly to experiences provided as self-contained units of instruction.

INITIAL EXPOSURE CLASSIFICATION OF GOALS   If the intent is to mediate instruction that is prerequisite to later mediated or conventional classroom learning experiences, then the goal is classified in the initial exposure category and the instructional task will be to supply input for later instruction.

In any instructional process, there is always a starting or entry point for a sequence of experiences that consecutively build on previous learning. In such a planned, sequential structure, instructional experiences are blocks upon which are later built other instruction. It may be apparent that experiences essential to satisfy instructional needs may require a base that is prerequisite to later instruction. Therefore, mediated instruction may include essential elements to which the learner has previously had no exposure or with which he is relatively unfamiliar.

The instructional task, then, would be based on a rather thorough analysis of what adequate instruction actually exists now and a comparison of this to required instructional experiences in order to satisfy learner needs. If the identified instruction is not present, learning in the area may never even get started.

For example, in order to fill a recognized need to read in a learner who has never been exposed to the written symbols of speech sounds, instruction may first depend on giving the child exposure to the letters in the alphabet. Then the learner can be expected to associate these symbols with actual sounds. If these experiences are not adequate in the existing instruction, a need for experiences prerequisite to later instruction (mediated or conventional) is evident. It would then be necessary for the mediated instruction to be modified in such a way that it is possible to provide a body of experiences to which the learner will have initial exposure.

ADDITIONAL EXPOSURE CLASSIFICATION OF GOALS   If the intent is to mediate instruction that builds on previous learned experiences and leads to future learning experiences, then the goal is classified in the additional exposure category and the instructional task directed to expand present instruction that will supply input for later instruction.

The learner may already have had exposure to instruction, but requires additional experiences to progress through a given content area or field of study. Thus to satisfy the instructional need, experiences may be dependent on previous exposure and are themselves prerequisite to later experiences in a planned sequential structure.

An instructional need may be evident if these experiences are not now adequate for the learner. The goal of additional exposure occurs when experiences are required in addition to those already given to the learner before learning can proceed any further. These instructional goals may be very broad in scope. This would be the case where the learner would be expected to be exposed to trigonometry after he has been exposed to instruction in geometry and before he could respond to instruction in calculus. Or, the instructional need may be more limited. The learner could be expected to be exposed to the structure of information he understands before he can analyze the information presented.

Thus, to satisfy the instructional need, it may be necessary to modify the instructional process in such a way that the learner will have additional exposure in an area already familiar.

COMPLETE EXPOSURE CLASSIFICATION OF GOALS   If the intent is to mediate instruction as a self-contained learning experience, then the goal is classified in the complete exposure category. The instructional task is concentrated on providing complete, self-contained instruction which may or may not be based on previous instruction.

In any planned sequence of instruction, there may also be microunits that relate to but are not integral in the total structure. Thus, the instructional need may be satisfied by experiences that are complete and autonomous within themselves. For example, it may be expected that students of architecture have complete mastery of the slide rule. While the use of the slide rule may be essential to desired responses in the broader field of study, instruction in its use may not be a part of the planned course of study.

An instructional need may be evident for a rather narrow portion of the target population which has not been exposed to direct instruction in the use of the slide rule. This classification of instructional need may be somewhat tangential to the main thrust of instruction. If nothing now exists in the academic setting for experiences in the instruction required to fill learner needs, the instructional task will be to provide all the experiences as complete units of instruction.

Strategy

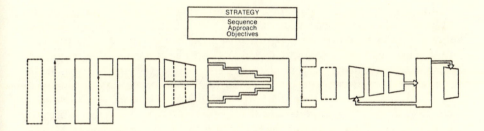

The instructional strategy is based on the performance sequence and the instructional approach and is reflected in specific objectives.

Instruction must be given direction in design if it is to function in an articulated learning sequence. A sequence of instruction should be developed from relevant learning theories. The hierarchical structure of learning used in these design procedures is not advanced as a panecea of learning theory. It is used because it has been developed from a studied and demonstrated effective way to discipline design of mediated instruction.

It is also important to concentrate design in a specific approach to instruction. The selection and sequencing of content symbols to which the individual must attend for the anticipated performance are based on what approach will be used to best reach the learner. In these design procedures, the approach to instruction defines rather narrow limits within which creative freedom of the designer is allowed.

An observable response is not necessary for learning to occur—although a response is essential if it is desired to know if learning has occurred. Therefore, objectives that specify an observable or measurable response must be written for evidence that the level of the goal has been reached. When it has, further display of instruction may be redundant, even confusing and boring to the learner.

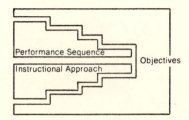

Performance Sequence

The sequence of instruction is determined by the requirements identified in the performance classification of the goal.

FRAME OF REFERENCE FOR THE SEQUENCE OF INSTRUCTION

This design function may have to begin from the frame of reference established by acknowledged restraints or constraints in using this disciplined structure. While the performance sequence is limited to rather arbitrary levels within certain clusters of design elements, strict adherence to these design elements may need to be relaxed if the structure itself stands in the way of efficient design procedures. For example, the goal may be classified at the level where it is expected the learner apply knowledge he has gained in a real and practical situation. Design could be arbitrarily limited to lower levels of intellectual competency if contingencies of time, talent, or money would prohibit developing all the instruction necessary to bring the learner to the desired level.

Sequence of Instruction

Instruction can be sequenced for the requirements of a specific cluster of elements about the learner and his expected performance.

The intellectual development of the individual provides an essential input to instructional design. Jean Piaget's scheme has been used to identify specific levels of intellectual development for design. Piaget is quoted by Charles Silberman in his book, *Crisis in the Classroom*, as saying:

> The essential conclusion about intellectual development is that learning cannot explain development but that the stage of development can in part explain learning. Development follows its own laws, as all of contemporary biology leads us to believe, and although each stage in the development is accompanied by all sorts of new learning based on experience, this learning is always relative to the development period during which it takes place, and to the intellectual structures, whether completely or partially formed, which the subject has at his disposal during this period (Piaget in Silberman, 1970).

Thus, regardless of *when* it happens, if it is assumed that a child does go through set periods of intellectual development, identification of these stages for instructional design will guide efforts to produce only that for which the child has demonstrated maturity to learn.

There is no decisive evidence that learning occurs in the orderly, sequential manner indicated in the hierarchies used for these design procedures. There are also no hard data to evidence that it does not. The taxonomies from which this hierarchical structure was derived were based on observations of patterns of teaching, not on patterns of learning. Yet, it has been demonstrated that a sequential pattern of instruction based on this structured approach does result in learning to achieve confidence not realized in other structures. A sporadic "shotgun" sequence in design has almost universally characterized mediated instruction in the past. Instruction has often been designed at performance levels beyond those where the learner can respond, or at levels for which he has already demonstrated performance some time in the past. In short, the learner was either confounded with instruction he was not ready for, or bored with material he already knew. As a result, instruction planned with abandon is much more difficult to use than that provided for in a more structured sequence.

In the instructional model used in these design procedures, it is assumed that the individual has the prerequisite learning to enable him to function at all levels of the hierarchical structure lower than that indicated by the goal (or by his known entry level). (See charts, pages 75, 80, 84.) It is therefore also assumed that the individual does not have the prerequisites to respond to instruction for responses at levels in the hierarchy higher than that indicated by the goal. After the individual has evidenced that he has reached the level of the goal, he *then* has the prerequisites to function at the next higher level to extend the instructional experience.

In the hierarchical structure of the domains of learning, it must be assumed that performance at *all* levels prior to that identified by the goal are prerequisite to the performance characteristics described at the goal level. For this, and other reasons, caution is advised in setting the level of the goal too high for learner (as well as for design) competencies. The design of some instruction for mediation has not always been honest or realistic about the goals it can hope to achieve.

In *Schools and the Challenge of Innovation*, Sterling M. McMurrin speaks of innovation and the purposes of education. It is his contention that school education is essentially an intellectual enterprise and the *cognitive* function of instruction lies at its center. The cognitive task is not only achievement of knowledge. The cognitive domain also includes skills in the inductive, deductive, and intuitive processes. It includes the ability to use techniques of analysis and generalization. It involves both sensory knowledge and abstract thought. And, for the lower schools, it involves especially the cultivation of the skills of literacy—the capacity for reading, writing, oral expression, and computation—that makes the acquisition and use of knowledge possible (McMurrin, 1969).

Often relegated to the separatism of vocational education are those *psychomotor* functions of instruction that relate to the manipulative or motor performance skills of the learner. The learner's ability, not only to perform tasks but to adapt and create patterns of performance, are not elements that occur as a function of physical maturity alone. They are also essential concerns of instruction.

In McMurrin's view, the *affective* functions of instruction, about which we now know far too little, relate to much that is precious in the experiences of the child. These functions are concerend with the child's pattern of behavior in life. McMurrin also feels that the inner life of feeling and appreciation and the countless values associated with that life deserve far more attention than they commonly receive. The arts, for instance, are often regarded as fringe concerns in a school, not as something comparable in worth to the sciences (McMurrin, 1969).

Often, however, affective goals are set for expected *emotional* change in the individual. For the purpose of instructional design in these procedures, affective learning does not include those behavior characteristics where the learner experiences a physiological change along with a strong feeling in response to a stimuli. Thus, behavior characteristics such as love, hate, fear, happiness, etc. (that involve some bodily reactions as well as mental responses), are more appropriately classified in a yet undefined "emotional domain." No pretense is made here that these learned characteristics can be caused exclusively by instruction. They are recognized as being the result of the total influences acting on the individual as a learning environment. Affective behavior, as defined in the *Taxonomy of Educational Objectives* edited by David R. Krathwohl and as used in these design procedures, is limited to performance characteristics associated with interest, appreciation, attitude, values, and personal adjustment to a value system.

At the risk of oversimplification, the distinction between cognitive behavior and affective behavior used in these procedures for the design of instruction is this: Cognitive learning can be thought of as how information or ideas relate to the individual; affective learning can be thought of as how the individual relates to information and ideas.

Instruction designed for electronic distribution, such as television, is more suited to cognitive functions because of the rather rigid tolerance for change associated with affective functions, or the actual performance requirements of psychomotor functions. Thus, cognitive goals will be more easily, and perhaps more appropriately, reached by mediated instruction. Efforts for psychomotor or affective instruction would be better limited to the cognitive-like lower levels in these domains (that are well within the tolerances of the academic context as well as of the medium itself). This does not mean that psychomotor or affective goals should not be included in design. Perhaps they should be related to cognitive learning wherever possible.

For example, higher levels of psychomotor learning require actual movement experiences by the learner. Lower-level psychomotor performance relates more directly to the cognition functions that can be treated by electronic media. For instance, you can show an individual on television how to swing a golf club and demonstrate the various aspects of the movement patterns involved. But at some point in the learning hierarchy, the individual is going to have to swing that club himself.

Higher levels of affective learning required delayed performance in an environment usually different from the one in which a person is exposed to instruction. Robert F. Mager advises caution in the affective area and warns that "The murky waters of affective goals and objectives are populated more by good intentions than by knowledge or experience" (Mager, 1968). It is expecting too much from a 20-minute television program (or even a series of 20-minute television programs) to provide the exclusive stimuli to change the attitudes or values that have been established over a lifetime. Affective values do require, however, cognitive-like prerequisites. And, mediated instruction can be used to formulate the cognitive base for a general disposition of an individual to respond to higher affective instructional goals.

Even the higher levels of cognitive functions would be difficult to treat in some forms of instructional media. Here, the display of symbols becomes secondary to the internalized reasoning capabilities of the learner.

Generally, as one moves upward in the hierarchies for each domain of learning, the nature of the stimuli change from external presentation to an internalized selection of past experiences.

In short, there is some finite point in any hierarchical learning structure where it is necessary to admit that instruction can no longer be mediated for display to the individual. At this point there has to be the recognition of the internalized attributes of the person himself as the medium for instruction.

Sequence Strategy

A sequence of instruction should follow a hierarchical pattern to avoid skipping essential steps in determining performance capabilities.

The descriptions of the hierarchical order of human growth and of individual learning cannot be used in isolation in the design effort. They must be combined into a working strategy to give discipline to instructional design. The strategy for the sequence of instruction combines the hierarchical elements of intellectual development and learning performance (for the selection of stimuli later in design) into a sequential, interacting order of *Design Clusters*.

In design, caution is advised against using the hierarchy of Design Clusters to describe the sequence of human behavior and learning development. The interactive structure restricts both performance expectations and stimulus design requirements to rigid tolerances—much more so than exist in actual human learning. However, in exposure to mediated instruction, the learner must be expected to attend to a display of stimuli to achieve a specific result with a predetermined and often very limited period of time. The designer cannot afford the luxury of exploring learner capabilities within the instructional experience itself. Instead, he must be assured that the design of stimuli will be appropriate to cue a desired response at known levels of learner capability and readiness.

The designer also cannot afford the possibility of designing stimuli for learner performance at one level and expecting an actual response at another. This results either in a superfluous expenditure of effort, or in inadequate treatment of stimuli that may not be appropriate to the level of performance desired. For example, if all that is expected of the learner is the recall of specific information, it might be an inefficient use of time and resources to design stimuli for Problem Solving instructional conditions even though the desired performance may be achieved. In the same manner, it is highly doubtful that learner performance in the mastery of a skill would be successful if the symbols were designed as stimuli for Verbal Association instructional conditions. The actual design of stimuli for each of the Design Clusters will be treated more in detail in these Design Procedures when the structure of specific elements for mediation are described (see pages 180 to 182).

These Design Clusters are to be used only as a disciplined structure for instructional design. By selecting a specific Design Cluster and restricting all efforts to the requirements described in that cluster only, the total design will then achieve a more targeted effort.

Design Cluster Characteristics

When combined into an interactive structure, the levels of intellectual development and learning performance form five basic Instructional Design Clusters for the selection of stimulus and the development of an instructional strategy:

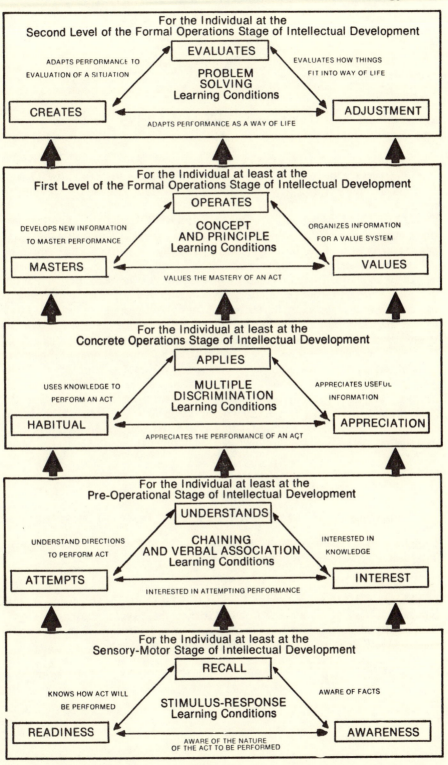

LEARNER LIMITATIONS IN THE DESIGN CLUSTERS

It is necessary to restrict performance expectations to only those Design Clusters at which the learner's intellectual development will allow him to respond.

INTELLECTUAL MATURITY OF THE INDIVIDUAL   The intellectual development of the individual refers to the level at which the individual's maturity will allow him to respond correctly to instruction to which he will be exposed. Piaget's scheme has been grossly simplified for use in the design of mediated instruction to determine the top level of intellectual development in the target population. Its use will also guard against developing instruction—especially in the early childhood years—beyond the intellectual maturation of the individual. For example, if the learner has demonstrated that he is conscious of dynamic variables, that he can measure or classify things in groups or series, but that he has not yet shown the ability to analyze, hypothesize, synthesize, or display abstract, conceptual thinking, he is classified at the Concrete Operations stage of intellectual development. Therefore, the design of instruction would be better limited to the first, second, or third Design Clusters and not at (or to design stimuli for) Design Cluster Four or Design Cluster Five (see pages 33 to 34 for the description of the levels of Intellectual Development).

Performance Characteristics in the Design Clusters

Instructional design should be limited to the characteristics of performance described for the level at which the goal has been classified.

LEVEL OF PRIMARY GOAL CLASSIFICATION   The primary goal has been classified at a specific level within the psychomotor, the cognitive, or the affective domain of learning. The category in which the goal is classified will determine what Design Cluster will be used.

For example, if performance is expected at the Extrapolation level on the Comprehension step of the cognitive domain (and the learner has demonstrated the appropriate level of intellectual development and cognitive readiness), all further design efforts should be limited to the cognitive category of *Understanding* in Design Cluster Two.

However, there may be some justifiable speculation as to just where the primary goal classification should be set. Often it may be necessary to set the goal at a level slightly higher within a category than that at which learned experiences will be applied. For example, if the performance characteristics involved in formulating these design procedures were the result of instruction, the goal would have been classified at the level of "Production of a Plan or Proposed Set of Operations" on the Synthesis step of the cognitive domain (see page 81). However, actually to formulate this plan or proposed operational procedure, performance at the next higher level ("Derivation of a Set of Abstract Relations") is required to classify or explain the abstractions involved and to get the pertinent relations needed to formulate this set of basic propositions. Thus, it could be speculated that actual *learning* at one level of the domain could often result in visible *performance* at a slightly lower level within the same classification.

SECONDARY GOAL PERFORMANCE CHARACTERISTICS   A secondary goal can be considered by the horizontal relationships between the levels of the three domains in the same or in prerequisite Design Clusters.

It must be acknowledged that learning is not exclusively restricted to performance in the domain at which the primary goal has been classified. Indeed, it may even be desirable to recognize the possibility of learner performance in other domains within the same or lower Design Clusters. If the goal has been classified in the affective domain, it is possible to identify affective dispositions to levels of psychomotor or cognitive learning within the same or at lower Design Clusters. A cognitive capacity for levels of affective and psychomotor learning within a Design Cluster can also be recognized. It is also possible that performance at a psychomotor level within a Design Cluster will provide the learner with the ability for certain interrelated cognitive and affective learning at the same or at lower levels.

For example, within Instructional Design Cluster Three, there is this horizontal relationship of performance between each of the three domains:

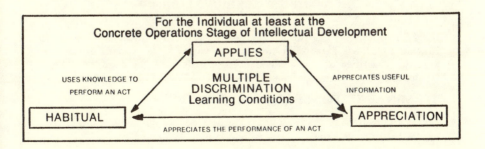

There is an affective disposition to cognitive functions in that the learner appreciates information that is useful to him. There is the cognitive capacity for the psychomotor level for it could be expected that the learner will use the knowledge he has in the actual habitual performance of an act. And, there is the possibile psychomotor ability for affective learning if, through the habitual performance of an act, the learner develops an appreciation of it.

Sequence of Learner Performance Characteristics

The level of the goal assumes that prerequisite levels of performance have a direct relationship to the expected response level.

VERTICAL PREREQUISITES   Prerequisite performance characteristics within the same domain of learning will determine the level from which instruction will be sequenced. To establish the entry level in any domain of learning, it is first essential to identify the performance characteristics of each successive level in the domain up to the level at which it is desired that the learner respond. For example, if the goal has been classified at the Extrapolation level in the Understanding category of the cognitive domain, the vertical prerequisites would be those characteristics of performance at *each* lower level. However, it is not always necessary to compile long lists of these prerequisites for each increment within the same instructional experience. While it is not advisable to skip levels within a hierarchy, it may not always be necessary to spell out all prerequisite levels in complete detail. Once identified completely, a statement of the level immediately prerequisite to the goal assumes capability to respond at all lower levels.

In the following examples, each of the prerequisite levels for a goal is identified by the performance characteristics at each level described in the appropriate domain of learning:

Example of Vertical Prerequisites
In the Cognitive Domain

INSTRUCTIONAL GOAL: To increase the learner's understanding of the functions of those persons in authority to whom he is exposed in his community. (Classified at the Understanding Catetory of the cognitive domain for design efforts in Design Cluster Two.)

TERMINAL RESPONSE CHARACTERISTICS

UNDERSTANDING CATEGORY: The learner should know the total pattern of behavior that characterizes a policeman in a community.

Level 12—Extrapolation: The learner will seek out and identify a number of non-enforcement functions of policemen other than those to which he has been exposed to show evidence that he knows policemen function in a community in ways other than arresting drunks, giving parking tickets, or shotting looters.

VERTICAL PREREQUISITES OF PERFORMANCE

Level 11—Interpretation: The learner should know about the non-enforcement functions of the policemen to which he has been exposed by relating these functions to other, more familiar community situations.

Level 10—Translation: The learner should state in his own words, what any non-enforcement functions of a policeman are when he is exposed to them.

KNOWLEDGE OF UNIVERSALS STEP: The learner should know about other behavior that is characteristic of the functions of a policeman, without necessarily relating them directly to non-enforcement functions.

Level 9—Recognition of Theories and Structures: The learner should recognize the complex role of the policeman as a combination of the familiar functions of enforcement and other functions with which he may not be familiar.

Level 8—Recognition of Principles and Generalizations: The learner should recognize the general role that persons in authority have in the community.

KNOWLEDGE OF PROCEDURES STEP: The learner must have at least a passive awareness of the ways of organizing, studying, and criticizing the functions of policemen in a community.

Level 7—Awareness of Methodology: The learner should know how to observe situations in which the non-enforcement functions of policemen are seen, and should know when to look for these non-enforcement functions.

Level 6—Awareness of Criteria: The learner should know how to discriminate between the functions of the policemen to enforce laws and to be a source of assistance.

Level 5—Awareness of Classifications and Categories: The learner should know how to classify functions that policemen have in a community.

Level 4—Awareness of Trends and Sequences: The learner should know how to identify all functions of a policeman before he can completely identify and characterize the policeman's function in a community.

Level 3—Awareness of Conventions: The learner should know how to recognize the non-enforcement functions of a policeman in a specific situation.

KNOWLEDGE OF SPECIFICS STEP: The learner is expected to recall specific bits of information about the policeman and about the situations where policemen may be expected to function.

Level 2—Knowledge of Specific Facts: The learner is expected to recognize a uniformed policeman either on foot, in a patrol car, or on a motorcycle.

Level 1—Knowledge of Terminology: The learner is expected to have a working vocabulary of the arrest and enforcement functions as well as to recognize terms associated with some non-enforcement functions of law officers in general and of policemen in particular.

This example of the vertical prerequisites to a cognitive goal was taken from the work done for Nebraska schools during the early days of Project ASERT. Perhaps not all levels of performance would satisfy the rigorous test against a narrow interpretation of the levels in the cognitive taxonomy, but this effort to define prerequisites precisely not only helped to clarify what should be done in instruction, but also helped to identify characteristics expected in the performance of the target population. (For a detailed description of the taxonomy of educational objecties from which these performance prerequisites were formulated, see pages 78 to 83.) This same goal developed for Project ASERT also had an affective component. The sequence analysis conducted to get the prerequisite performance identified for the affective secondary goal was derived from the Affective Taxonomy of Educational Objectives (pages 80 to 87) and is outlined below:

Example of Horizontal Prerequisites
In the Affective Domain to a Primary Cognitive Goal

INSTRUCTIONAL GOAL: To stimulate in the learner an interest in the understanding of those elements necessary to formulate a new value system toward those persons in authority to whom he is exposed in his community. (Classified in the Interest Category of the affective domain for development efforts in Design Cluster Two.)

TERMINAL RESPONSE CHARACTERISTICS

INTEREST CATEGORY: The learner will be expected to attend actively to information about the patterns of behavior that characterize a policeman in a community but which are not now a part of the value system he holds to ward policemen.

> *Level 6—Satisfaction in Responding:* The learner will be expected to enjoy knowing about the things a policeman does in the community other than arresting people and enforcing laws.

VERTICAL PREREQUISITES OF PERFORMANCE

> *Level 5—Willingness to Respond:* The learner is expected to receive willingly stimuli that will sensitize him to the existence of another value system related to persons in authority.

> *Level 4—Acquiescence in Responding:* The learner should comply with the expectations to discover the non-enforcement functions of the policemen.

> *Level 3—Controlled or Selected Attention:* The learner should be able to relate to a policeman in non-enforcement situations despite competing stimuli of his prior experience with law enforcement.

> *Level 2—Willingness to Receive:* The learner should pay attention to situations in which non-enforcement functions of policeman are presented.

> *Level 1—Awareness:* **The learner should be aware of the fact that a policeman, in a given situation, is doing something besides arresting someone or enforcing a law.**

Operational Strategy in the Use of Design Clusters

At first glance (indeed, perhaps even after detailed study) the quite rigid structure for learning and instruction dictated by the Design Clusters would appear to "dehumanize" the learning process. While there is nothing inherent in the use of the Design Clusters that will "dehumanize" learning, it is possible to fall suspect to the same arguments advanced that the behavior-oriented approach has dehumanized the entire instructional process. There is an increasing number of scholars (such as William A. Deterline and others) who believe that a structured approach, wisely applied without over-zealous fanaticism, may well be a direction for "rehumanizing" education by offering the learner the opportunity for learning and "re-placing" the teacher in the proper human role as the manager of learning. Thus, the whole traditional emphasis of the stimulus-response theory of learning, which is the core of these Design Clusters, needs to shift in emphasis from a concentration on the stimulus to a real concern for the response (Deterline, 1970).

There is, perhaps, no stronger dehumanizing force in education today than the lockstep traditional educational mode. These Design Clusters are not advanced as a lockstep procedure, but as a dynamic structure, yielding not only to the learing demands of the individual but to the structural demands of the emerging theories about how people learn. Yet, they must discipline a design structure to resist relapses into more comfortable and conventional ways of doing things.

Instructional Design Cluster One

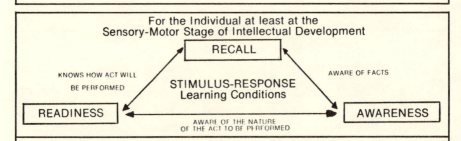

Intellectual Development Limitations
For the individual at least at the
Sensory-Motor Stage of Intellectual Development

Primary Goal Performance Characteristics
READINESS category of psychomotor goals:
  The learner gets ready to perform an act.
RECALL category of cognitive goals:
  The learner recognizes and recalls information.
AWARENESS category of affective goals:
  The learner is willing to receive and pay attention to something.

Secondary Goal Performance Relationships
Affective Disposition to the Primary Psychomotor Goal:
  The learner can be expected to be receptive to the nature of the act to be performed.
Cognitive Capacity for the Primary Psychomotor Goal:
  The learner can be expected to recall specific bits of information about how the act will be performed.
Psychomotor Ability for the Primary Cognitive Goal:
  The learner can be expected to have whatever physical readiness is required to recognize or recall bits of information.
Affective Disposition to the Primary Cognitive Goal:
  The learner can be expected to be receptive to the facts or specific bits of information that he will recognize or recall.
Psychomotor Ability for the Primary Affective Goal:
  The learner can be expected to have the physical readiness to want to attend to something related to his interest or appreciation of a concept.
Cognitive Capacity for the Primary Affective Goal:
  The learner can be expected to know specific bits of information about the concepts he will be aware of and pay attention to.

Sequence Strategy for the Psychomotor Goal

Before Instruction:

It is assumed that there are no prerequisite levels of performance for goals set in Design Cluster One.

For Instruction:

The psychomotor goal is classified at a level in the PERCEP-
TION or SET STEP:

Level 1—SENSORY STIMULATION

The learner can be expected to receive stimulation of one or
more of his sense organs, to become aware of the motor act.

Level 2—CUE SELECTION

The learner can be expected to decide what stimulus affects
the motor act.

Level 3—TRANSLATION

The learner can be expected to relate the stimulus to the
motor act.

Level 4—MENTAL SET

The learner can be expected to be mentally prepared to perform a certain motor act.

Level 5—PHYSICAL SET

The learner can be expected to be physically ready to perform a certain motor act.

Level 6—EMOTIONAL SET

The learner can be expected to be emotionally favorable to
performing the motor act.

To Extend Instruction:

The learner has the prequisities to extend instruction for performance described in Design Cluster Two:

GUIDED RESPONSE STEP: The learner can now be expected to actually perform a motor act by following instructions.

Sequence Strategy for the Cognitive Goal

Before Instruction:

It is assumed that there are no prerequisite levels of performance for goals set in Design Cluster One.

For Instruction:

The cognitive goal is classified at a level in the KNOWLEDGE
OF SPECIFICS, PROCEDURES or UNIVERSALS STEP:

Level 1—RECALL OF TERMINOLOGY

The learner can be expected to recall what specific verbal
and non-verbal symbols represent.

Level 2—RECALL OF SPECIFIC FACTS

The learner can be expected to recall dates, events, persons,
places, and so forth.

Level 3—AWARENESS OF CONVENTIONS

The learner can be expected to be aware of different ways
of treating and presenting information.

Level 4—AWARENESS OF TRENDS AND SEQUENCES
The learner can be expected to be aware of the sequence of related information with respect to time.
Level 5—AWARENESS OF CLASSIFICATIONS AND CAT-EGORIES
The learner can be expected to be aware of the ways information is arranged for a given purpose.
Level 6—AWARENESS OF CRITERIA
The learner can be expected to be aware of the criteria by which information is tested and judged.
Level 7—AWARENESS OF METHODOLOGY
The learner can be expected to be aware of the ways information is treated in studying particular problems.
Level 8—RECOGNITION OF PRINCIPLES AND GENER-ALIZATIONS
The learner can be expected to recognize when general principles summarize information, ideas or material.
Level 9—RECOGNITION OF THEORIES AND STRUC-TURES
The learner can be expected to recognize when two or more general principles fit together to describe more complex information, ideas or material.
To Extend Instruction:
The learner has the prerequisites to extend instruction for performance described in Design Cluster Two:
COMPREHENSION STEP: The learner can now be expected to know what is being communicated and make limited use of the information or ideas.

Sequence Strategy for the Affective Goal

Before Instruction:
It is assumed that there are no prerequisite levels of performance for goals set in Design Cluster One.
For Instruction:
The affective goal is classified at one of these levels in the RECEIVING STEP:
Level 1—AWARENESS
The learner can be expected to be merely conscious of something and to take into account a situation, phenomenon, object or state of affairs.
Level 2—WILLINGNESS TO RECEIVE
The learner can be expected to be willing to tolerate a given concept, not to avoid it.
Level 3—CONTROLLED OR SELECTED ATTENTION
The learner can be expected to pay attention to only those concepts that are relevant to him or his situation.
To Extend Instruction:
The learner has the prerequisites to extend instruction for performance described in Design Cluster Two:
RESPONDING STEP: The learner can now be expected to

actively pay attention to a concept—or at least do something with or about it besides merely being aware of it.

Stimulus Design Requirements

Prerequisite Instructional Conditions:

Signal Learning may be prerequisite to Stimulus-Response Learning. The learner may be expected to make a conditioned response before he is expected to make a precise response to a discriminated stimulus.

Conditions for Instruction:

Stimulus-Response Learning: The stimuli must be designed so the learner can make a simple response to a single stimulus.

Extended Instructional Conditions:

Stimulus-Response Learning is prerequisite to *Chaining and Verbal Association Learning*. The learner is now ready to acquire two or more stimulus-response connections.

DESIGN LIMITATIONS BY LEVEL OF INTELLECTUAL DEVELOPMENT

The individual must have matured at least to the *Sensory-Motor* Stage of intellectual development if he is to respond to the experiences or symbols as stimuli in Design Cluster One. At this level of development, the learner must at least perceive, discriminate and identify objects—usually without the use of verbal symbols.

Performance Conditions for Design Cluster One

PSYCHOMOTOR PERFORMANCE CHARACTERISTICS In Design Cluster One, performance characteristics for manipulative or motor skills are described at levels for the *Readiness* classification of psychomotor goals. At this category, the learner is expected to become physically aware of something related to a motor act, through his senses.

For example, the characteristics of sensory-stimulation in the Readiness step of psychomotor learning may anticipate that the learner be sensitized to the auditory cues in playing a musical instrument as a member of a group. He might also be expected to recognize the operating difficulties with machinery through the sound of the machine in operation. Or, he might be expected to demonstrate an ability to follow a recipe in preparing food. For mental, physical, and emotional set performance of psychomotor learning, he may be expected not only to know what to do to swing a golf club, but to assume the proper grip and bodily stance and to display an actual desire to perform the act.

COGNITIVE PERFORMANCE CHARACTERISTICS   In Design Cluster One, performance characteristics for the recall or recognition of knowledge are described at levels for the *Recall* classification of cognitive goals. At this catetory, the learner is expected to recall specific bits of information, to be aware of methods or procedures dealing with specifics; or to recognize information about patterns, settings or structures.

For example, the learner might be expected to recall specific facts by defining technical terms—giving their attributes, properties, or relationships. He might also be expected to recall the major facets of a particular culture. Where awareness of the procedures to deal with specifics is expected, the learner might recall the scientific procedures for evaluating the occurrence of a chemical phenomenon (without actually being expected to make the evaluation itself). He may also be expected to recall how certain elements combine into the theory of evolution to demonstrate his awareness of universals or abstractions.

AFFECTIVE PERFORMANCE CHARACTERISTICS   In Design Cluster One, performance characteristics for the development of interest or appreciation are described at levels for the *Awareness* classification of affective goals. At this category, the learner is expected to know that a concept or idea exists and be willing to pay attention to it.

For example, the learner may be expected to be aware of the aesthetic factors in dress, furnishings, architecture, city design or art. He might also be expected to be willing to receive information about the cultural patterns exhibited by individuals from other religious, social, political or economic groups. For performance at the controlled or selected attention level, the learner might be expected to be alert to human values and judgments on life as they are recorded in literature.

Instructional Strategy for Performance Goals

Once performance characteristics have been identified at a level in Design Cluster One, it is possible to design the arrangement of response conditions for the sequence of instruction.

VERTICAL PERFORMANCE PREREQUISITES   Since the categories of Design Cluster One represent the theoretical base of performance, there are, of course, no defined prerequisite categories of learner performance. However, within the category selected for the instructional goal, actual learner performance may require that the individual respond at lower levels in these steps as a prerequisite to the goal level.

For example, before the learner can respond to instruction at the Cue Selection Level in the psychomotor category of Readiness, he will be expected to be sensitized both to the normal and abnormal sounds of a particular machine in operation. Then he can be expected to recognize any operating difficulties with that machinery through its sound in operation. Performance characteristics for the cognitive Recall category of Design

Cluster One would require that the learner know the specific facts about chemical phenomena and be familiar with the terminology used in the scientific procedures before he could be expected to be aware of how these scientific procedures are used for evaluating the occurrence of a chemical phenomenon.

In the affective Awareness category of Design Cluster One, if the learner is expected to be willing to receive or attend to a stimulus, not to avoid it, it is essential that he first take that stimulus into consideration or at least be aware that it does exist. For example, before he can be expected to be willing to receive or to tolerate information about the cultural patterns of other groups, he must first be aware of the nature and existence of the information that describes these cultural patterns.

HORIZONTAL PERFORMANCE RELATIONSHIPS   A secondary goal can be considered by the horizontal relationships between the levels of the three domains in Design Cluster One.

The horizontal relationships between learning domains in Design Cluster One are quite basic. And, since the performance described in each domain is very similar, the specific delineation of the relationships between domains may be a very grey area in design. It is at the other Design Clusters that this horizontal relationship becomes increasingly important.

However, performance at levels within the psychomotor Readiness category of Design Cluster One may have a relationship to a cognitive capacity to respond. It could be expected, for example, that the learner know the terms used and the specific facts given about the act he is getting ready to perform.

In a like manner, there may also be an affective disposition to respond at this psychomotor level. Awareness (leading eventually to an interest) of what the act involves may be necessary in order to prepare to perform the act. However, at this level it is doubtful if it is necessary to develop an interest or an appreciation of the act if all that is expected is that the learner prepare himself physically, mentally and emotionally to perform it.

Performance at levels within the cognitive Recall category of Design Cluster One may require—or permit—a psychomotor readiness to respond. Demonstrated psychomotor skills of readiness may be required before the learner could be expected to repeat facts and terminology given to him in instruction toward a cognitive goal.

Performance within the cognitive Recall category may also have a horizontal relationship to an affective Awareness in order to respond. It is quite obvious that the learner must be aware of something—in the sense of more than an impingement on the senses of stimuli—before he can commit this information to memory for recall.

Performance at levels within the affective Awareness category may also have a relationship to a cognitive capacity to respond. It may be desired, for example, to be assured that the learner can recall specific bits of information before this information can be used to make him aware of something in which he will eventually (but not at this level of performance) ascribe some appreciation and worth.

It is also possible to expect a psychomotor readiness to respond to this affective Awareness level. The emotional and mental set descriptions of performance at this psychomotor level are interrelated directly with the descriptions of performance at the affective level of Awareness.

EXTENDED PERFORMANCE EXPECTATIONS   Performance in any learning domain within the categories that are a part of Design Cluster One will provide prerequisite levels to extend performance expectations of the learner to those categories in Design Cluster Two.

Demonstrated skill performance in the Readiness category of psychomotor learning will provide the learner with the prerequisites for the Attempted Performance category of Design Cluster Two. For example, after the learner has demonstrated that he knows what to do to swing a golf club, he has assumed the proper grip and stance, and really wants to swing the club, he has acquired the prerequisites to expect that he will now attempt to swing the club himself under the guidance and instructions of a golf pro.

Demonstrated intellectual performance in the Recall category of cognitive learning will provide the learner with the prerequisites for performance in the Understanding category of Design Cluster Two. For example, once the learner recalls what he has been told about the formulation of the theory of evolution, he might be ready to restate, or translate, this information into his own terms without necessarily seeing its fullest implications or relating it to other information.

Demonstrated attitudinal performance in the Awareness category of affective learning will provide the learner with the prerequisites for performance in the Interest category of Design Cluster Two. For example, after it has been demonstrated that the learner is alert to human values and judgments on life as they are recorded in literature, it can then be expected that he will respond to instruction in some way, such as reading the literature for these values and judgments even though he may not as yet fully accept the necessity for doing so.

The examples used to illustrate performance characteristics for Design Cluster One were taken largely from those given in the Condensed Version of the *Taxonomy of Educational Objectives* for each domain of learning to enable the use of these taxonomies to be related to the concept of Design Clusters. It is recommended that more detailed study be made of the performance concept in the Taxonomies of Simpson, Bloom and Krathwohl.

Instructional Design Cluster Two

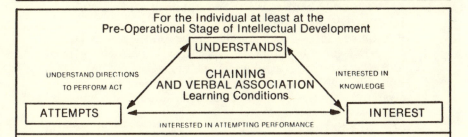

For the Individual at least at the
Pre-Operational Stage of Intellectual Development

UNDERSTANDS

UNDERSTAND DIRECTIONS
TO PERFORM ACT

CHAINING
AND VERBAL ASSOCIATION
Learning Conditions

INTERESTED IN
KNOWLEDGE

ATTEMPTS

INTEREST

INTERESTED IN ATTEMPTING PERFORMANCE

Intellectual Development Limitations
For the Individual at Least at the
Pre-Operational Stage of Intellectual Development

Primary Goal Performance Characteristics
ATTEMPTED PERFORMANCE category of psychomotor goals:
  The learner performs an act by following instructions.
UNDERSTANDING category of cognitive goals:
  The learner knows what is being communicated and makes limited use of the information.
INTEREST category of affective goals:
  The learner actively pays attention to a concept or idea—or at least does something with or about it besides merely being aware of it.

Secondary Goal Performance Relationships
Affective Disposition to the Primary Psychomotor Goal:
  The learner can be expected to be interested in the guidance of an instructor in the performance of an act.
Cognitive Capacity for the Primary Psychomotor Goal:
  The learner can be expected to make limited use of information in following the directions of an instructor to perform an act.
Psychomotor Ability for the Primary Cognitive Goal:
  The learner can be expected to attempt to perform some manipulative act in order to understand the information.
Affective Disposition to the Primary Cognitive Goal:
  The learner can be expected to be interested in the material or information he will understand.
Psychomotor Ability for the Primary Affective Goal:
  The learner can be expected to attempt to perform some manipulative act to be interested in something.
Cognitive Capacity for the Primary Affective Goal:
  The learner can be expected to make limited use of informa-

tion to know what is being communicated in order to want to pay attention actively to a concept.

Sequence Strategy for the Psychomotor Goal

Before Instruction:

Prerequisite to psychomotor performance at levels in Design Cluster Two, the learner is expected to have demonstrated learned competencies at all levels in Design Cluster One:

PERCEPTION STEP: The learner should now be physically aware of objects, qualities, or relations through his senses as they relate to a motor act.

SET STEP: The learner should now be prepared to perform a motor act.

For Instruction:

The psychomotor goal is classified at one of these levels in the GUIDED RESPONSE STEP:

Level 7—IMITATION

The learner can be expected to actually perform a motor act while watching another person doing it.

Level 8—TRIAL AND ERROR

The learner can be expected to try various ways of performing the motor act until he is successful.

To Extend Instruction:

The learner has the prerequisites to extend instruction for performance described in Design Cluster Three:

MECHANISM STEP: The learner can now be expected to perform a motor act out of habit.

Sequence Strategy for the Cognitive Goal

Before Instruction:

Prerequisite to cognitive performance at levels in Design Cluster Two, the learner is expected to have demonstrated learned competencies at all levels in Design Cluster One:

KNOWLEDGE OF SPECIFICS STEP: The learner should now recall specific bits of information.

KNOWLEDGE OF PROCEDURES STEP: The learner should now be aware of the ways specifics are dealt with.

KNOWLEDGE OF UNIVERSALS STEP: The learner should now recognize the major schemes and patterns by which information is organized.

For Instruction:

The cognitive goal is classified at one of these levels in the COMPREHENSION STEP:

Level 10—TRANSLATION

The learner can be expected to copy information from one form of expression to another.

Level 11—INTERPRETATION

The learner can be expected to explain or summarize information by stating it in a different way.

Level 12—EXTRAPOLATION:
The learner can be expected to extend the given information to determine implications, consequences, corollaries, effects, etc., of ideas which are in accordance with the original conditions.

To Extend Instruction:
The learner has the prerequisites to extend instruction for performance described in Design Cluster Three:
APPLICATION STEP: The learner can now be expected to use ideas beyond the context in which they were originally given.

Sequence Strategy for the Affective Goal

Before Instruction:
Prerequisite to affective performance at levels in Design Cluster Two, the learner is expected to have demonstrated learned competencies at all levels in Design Cluster One:
RECEIVING STEP: The learner should now know that a concept exists and should now be willing to pay attention to it.

For Instruction:
The affective goal is classified at one of these levels in the RESPONDING STEP:
Level 4—ACQUIESCENCE IN RESPONDING
The learner can be expected to comply with a concept without fully accepting the necessity for doing so.
Level 5—WILLINGNESS TO RESPOND
The learner can be expected to be sufficiently committed to the concept that he accepts it willingly.
Level 6—SATISFACTION IN RESPONSE
The learner can be expected to accept the concept with a feeling of satisfaction, generally of pleasure, zest or nejoyment.

To Extend Instruction:
The learner has the prerequisites to extend instruction for performance described in Design Cluster Three:
VALUING STEP: The learner can now be expected to recognize that related concepts have worth as a value.

Stimulus Design Requirements

Prerequisite Instructional Condition:
Stimulus-Response Learning is prerequisite to Motor and Verbal Association Learning. The learner must make individual stimulus-response links before he can be expected to connect the links into a verbal or non-verbal chain.

Conditions for Instruction:
Motor and Verbal Association Learning: The stimuli are designed so the learner can acquire two or more stimulus-response connections.

Extended Instructional Conditions:
Motor and Verbal Association Learning is prerequisite to *Multiple Discrimination Learning.* The learner is now ready to make a number of differently identifying responses to stimuli that may or may not resemble each other in physical appearance.

DESIGN LIMITATIONS BY LEVEL OF INTELLECTUAL DEVELOPMENT

The individual must have matured to at least the *Pre-Operational* stage of intellectual development if he is to respond to the experiences or symbols designed as stimuli in Design Cluster Two. At this level of development, the learner must now also use symbols and representations and must also act on perceptive impulses. He is characterized by static, irreversible thinking and is usually self-centered. For instruction in Design Cluster Two, the learner may be at a higher level of intellectual development, but it is highly unlikely that he would respond as desired if his intellectual development were at a level lower than the Pre-Operational Stage.

Performance Conditions for Design Cluster Two

PSYCHOMOTOR PERFORMANCE CHARACTERISTICS   In Design Cluster Two, performance characteristics for manipulative or motor skills are described at levels for the *Attempted Performance* classification of psychomotor goals. At this category, the learner is expected actually to perform a motor act by following instructions.

For example, the learner might actually attempt to operate some piece of machinery under the guidance of a foreman, or by using an instruction manual. Or, through trial and error, he might be expected to find the proper combination of colors needed to get a specific hue by actually mixing paint until the desired color is achieved.

COGNITIVE PERFORMANCE CHARACTERISTICS   In Design Cluster Two, performance characteristics for the development of intellectual abilities and skills are described at levels for the *Understanding* classification of cognitive goals. (At this Design Cluster, performance characteristics are beyond the levels of the recall or recognition of knowledge in the cognitive domain.) At this category, the learner is expected to know what is being communicated and is expected to make limited use of the information.

For example, intellectual performance for this hierarchy in Design Cluster Two would expect the learner to develop skill in translating verbal material into symbolic statements. It might also expect that the learner interpret the thought of a piece of literature as a whole at any desired level of generality. The learner might also be expected to extrapolate the conclusions of some literary work in terms of the immediate inference made from explicit statements.

AFFECTIVE PERFORMANCE CHARACTERISTICS　　In Design Cluster Two, performance characteristics for the development of interest, appreciation, attitudes, values or adjustment are described at levels for the *Interest* classification of affective goals. At this category, the learner is expected to pay attention actively to a concept or idea—or at least do something with or about it besides merely being aware of it.

For example, the learner might be expected to acquiesce to playground regulations. The learner may also willingly acquaint himself with significant current issues in international political, social and economic affairs through voluntary reading and discussion. The learner might also be expected to find pleasure in reading for recreation.

Instructional Strategy for Performance Goals

Once the performance characteristics hae been identified at a level in Design Cluster Two, it is possible to design the arrangement of response conditions for the sequence of instruction.

VERTICAL PERFORMANCE PREREQUISITES　　Learner performance for each category of Design Cluster Two requires and assumes learner performance capability at all levels in that same hierarchy of Design Cluster One. In addition, learner performance at higher levels of Design Cluster Two would require performance at a lower level in that category.

Prerequisite to performance for the psychomotor category of Attempted Performance of Design Cluster Two, it must be assumed that the learner can respond at all levels of Readiness in Design Cluster One. For example, before the learner can actually try to operate a piece of machinery under the guidance of a foreman, he must be aware of the various aspects of the nature of the machine and must have made the necessary physical, mental and emotional adjustments required to operate the machine. Performance under the guidance of the foreman, then, would provide the prerequisites within Design Cluster Two for attempted operation of the machine himself through trial and error.

For cognitive learning, it must be assumed (or known) that the learner can recall specific bits of information, methods and procedures as well as be aware of patterns, structures and settings (characteristic of performance described in Design Cluster One), before he can be expected to respond at the Understanding category of Design Cluster Two. For example, before the learner can be expected to develop a skill in translating mathematical verbal material into symbolic statements, the learner must recall the symbolic statements used and recognize the structure of the symbolic representation of the mathematical verbal material. However, once he translates this verbal material into symbolic mathematical statements, he is then ready to perform at the next level within Design Cluster Two that would involve some interpretation or explanation of the mathematical symbols that have been translated from the verbal statements.

Before the learner can acquiesce to respond to something at the expected level for the performance characteristics of the affective Interest category of Design Cluster Two, he must be aware of its existence and must be willing to pay attention to the specific stimulus. For example, before the learner can be expected to obey playground regulations, he must first be aware of and pay attention to these regulations. Once he has displayed this attitudinal performance, he could then be expected to show a willingness to obey the playground regulations in response to instruction designed at the next level in Design Cluster Two.

HORIZONTAL PERFORMANCE RELATIONSHIPS   A secondary goal can be considered by the horizontal relationships between the levels of the three domains within Design Cluster Two or in prerequisite Design Clusters. While related performance in other domains may occur, it is highly unlikely that instruction would be necessary or efficiently designed for a horizontal relationship to levels higher than those described in Design Cluster Two.

In Design Cluster Two, performance at levels within the psychomotor Attempted Performance category may have a relationship to a cognitive capacity to respond. At this level, it could be expected that the learner know what is being communicated to him and make limited use of that information before he could attempt the performance of some motor act. For example, in almost any motor act there are instructions that must be followed. Unless it can be assured that the learner has the cognitive capacity to know what the instructions are and to use them—even in a limited way—he could not adequately respond to instruction designed at the Attempted Performance psychomotor category.

In a similar manner, performance at this psychomotor level may also require, or permit, an affective disposition to respond. It would be reasonable to expect, for example, that the learner actively pay attention to the performance of an act—and at least be aware of why it is being performed—before he can be expected to attempt its performance by following instruction.

Performance at levels within the cognitive Understanding category may permit a psychomotor ability to respond. At this level it could be expected that the learner attempt the performance of some motor act before he could know what is being communicated and make limited use of the information. For example, verbal descriptions of how to shift gears in an automobilw may be easier to respond to for the learner who has actually attempted to shift gears in an automobile or simulator.

Similarly, performance at this cognitive level may also indicate an effective disposition to respond. Performance expectations for this horizontal relationship between domains may require the learner to be interested in knowledge or information that is useful to him. If it is expected the learner make even limited use of the directions for baking a cake, it is reasonable to assume that he will be willing to pay attention to these directions, demonstrating his interest in them.

Performance at levels within the affective Interest category of Design Cluster Two may require, or permit, a cognitive capacity to respond. At this level, all that could be expected would be that the learner have an understanding—that he know what is being communicated and make limited use of the information—before he could develop an interest in the topic of that communication. For example, to enable the learner to respond by paying active attention to the idea of social ecology may first require that the learner have a limited understanding of what the concept means and the ability to use the concept within a limited scope to demonstrate learned competencies.

Performance at this affective level may also have a horizontal relationship to a psychomotor ability to respond. If the learner cannot perform a motor act by following directions, it is highly unlikely that he will develop an interest in the act or actively seek out doing that act.

EXTENDED PERFORMANCE EXPECTATIONS   Performance in any learning domain within the categories of Design Cluster Two will provide prerequisite levels to extend performance expectations of the learner to those categories that are a part of Design Cluster Three.

Demonstrated skill performance at the Attempted Performance category of psychomotor learning in Design Cluster Two will provide the learner with the prerequisites for the Habitual Performance category of Design Cluster Three. For example, after the learner has demonstrated that he can, through trial and error, mix paints to achieve a specific hue, he could then be expected to achieve some confidence and a degree of skill in mixing paint and the act would become habitual.

Demonstrated intellectual performance at the cognitive Understanding cetegory of Design Cluster Two will provide the learner with the prerequisites for performance in the Application category of Design Cluster Three. For example, if it has been demonstrated that the learner has gained enough cognitive confidence to deal with the conclusions of some literary work in terms of the immediate inferences made from the explicit statements within that work, it might be expected that he is now ready to apply these inferences to other literary works or to abstract principles from what he reads.

Demonstrated attitudinal performance at the Interest category of affective learning will provide the learner with the necessary prerequisites for performance expectations in the Appreciation category of Design Cluster Three. For example, if it has been demonstrated that the learner finds pleasure in reading for recreation, it might be expected that he is then ready to indicate whether he feels what he has read has some worth.

The examples used to illustrate performance characteristics for Design Cluster Two were taken largely from those given in the Condensed Version of the *Taxonomy of Educational Objectives* for each domain of learning to enable the use of these taxonomies to be related to the concept of Design Clusters. It is recommended that more detailed study be made of the performance concepts in the Taxonomies of Simpson, Bloom and Krathwohl.

Instructional Design Cluster Three

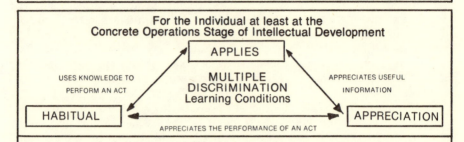

Intellectual Development Limitations
For the individual at least at the
Concrete Operations state of intellectual development

Primary Goal Performance Characteristics
HABITUAL PERFORMANCE category of psychomotor goals:
   The learner performs a motor act out of habit.
APPLICATION category of cognitive goals:
   The learner uses information beyond the context in which it
   was originally given.
APPRECIATION category of affective goals:
   The learner recognizes that a concept has worth as a value.

Secondary Goal Performance Relationships
Affective Disposition to the Primary Psychomotor Goal:
   The learner can be expected to recognize the worth of the
   performance of a motor skill.
Cognitive Capacity for the Primary Psychomotor Goal:
   The learner can be expected to make use of knowledge in the
   performance of a motor skill.
Psychomotor Ability for the Primary Cognitive Goal:
   The learner can be expected to habitually perform an act in
   making use of some form of knowledge.
Affective Disposition to the Primary Cognitive Goal:
   The learner can be expected to recognize the worth of useful
   information.
Psychomotor Ability for the Primary Affective Goal:
   The learner can be expected to habitually perform an act in
   commiting himself to a value.
Cognitive Capacity for the Primary Affective Goal:
   The learner can be expected to use his knowledge to appreci-
   ate something or to recognize the worth of something.

Sequence Strategy for the Psychomotor Goal

Before Instruction:

Prerequisite to psychomotor performance at levels in Design Cluster Three, the learner is expected to have demonstrated learned competencies at all levels up to those in Design Cluster Two:

PERCEPTION STEP: The learner should now be physically aware of objects, qualities, and relations through his senses as they relate to the motor act.

SET STEP: The learner should now be prepared to perform the motor act.

GUIDED RESPONSE STEP: The learner should now have tried various ways of performing the motor act until he has been successful.

For Instruction:

The psychomotor goal is classified at the level in the MECHANISM STEP:

Level 9—MECHANISM

The learner can be expected to achieve enough confidence and a degree of skill to perform the motor act out of habit.

To Extend Instruction:

The learner has the prerequisites to extend instruction for performance described in Design Cluster Four:

COMPLEX OVERT RESPONSE STEP: The learner can now be expected to combine simple actions into a complex motor act that involves sequence and coordination.

Sequence Strategy for the Cognitive Goal

Before Instruction:

Prerequisite to cognitive performance at levels in Design Cluster Three, the learner is expected to have demonstrated learned competencies at all levels up to those in Design Cluster Two:

KNOWLEDGE OF SPECIFICS STEP: The learner should now recall specific bits of information.

KNOWLEDGE OF PROCEDURES STEP: The learner should now be aware of the ways specifics are dealt with.

KNOWLEDGE OF UNIVERSALS STEP: The learner should now recognize the major schemes and patterns by which information is organized.

COMPREHENSION STEP: The learner should now know what is being communicated and make limited use of the information or ideas.

For Instruction:

The cognitive goal is classified at the level in the APPLICATION STEP:

Level 13—APPLICATION

The learner can be expected to use abstractions in particular and concrete situations.

To Extend Instruction:

The learner has the prerequisites to extend instruction for performance described in Design Cluster Four:
ANALYSIS AND SYNTHESIS STEPS: The learner can now be expected to break down information so the order of information is made clear and the relationship between other ideas is explicit; or he is able now to put ideas together to formulate new material.

Sequence Strategy for the Affective Goal

Before Instruction:

Prerequisite to affective performance at levels in Design Cluster Three, the learner is expected to have demonstrated learned competencies at all levels up to those in Design Cluster Two:
RECEIVING STEP: The learner should now know that a concept exists and should now be willing to pay attention to it.
RESPONDING STEP: The learner should now actively pay attention to the concept—or at least have done something with or about it besides merely being aware of it.

For Instruction:

The affective goal is classified at one of these levels in the VALUES STEP:

Level 7—ACCEPTANCE OF A VALUE

The learner can be expected to ascribe worth to a concept or to related concepts.

Level 8—PREFERENCE FOR A VALUE:

The learner can be expected to be sufficiently committed to the worth of concepts as a value to pursue it, seek it out, want it.

Level 9—COMMITMENT:

The learner can be expected to have a high degree of certainty about the worth of concepts as a value.

To Extend Instruction:

The learner has the prerequisites to extend instruction for performance described in Design Cluster Four:
ORGANIZATION STEP: The learner can now be expected to organize values when he encounters situations for which more than one value is relevant in order to build his own value system.

Stimulus Design Requirements

Prerequisite Instructional Conditions:

Motor and Verbal Association Learning is prerequisite to Multiple Discrimination Learning. The learner must have previously acquired, in isolation, each of the chains that make up the set to be learned.

Conditions for Instruction:

Multiple Discrimination Learning: The stimuli are designed so the learner can discriminate among the common traits stimulus-response connections, regardless of their physical appearance, in order to recognize a class of stimuli.

Extended Instructional Conditions:

Multiple Discrimination Learning is prerequisite to Concept and Principle Learning. The learner is now ready to make a common response to a class of stimuli that may differ widely from each other in physical appearance and to combine two or more concepts into a chain to form a principle.

DESIGN LIMITATIONS BY LEVEL OF INTELLECTUAL DEVELOPMENT

The individual must have matured to at least the *Concrete Operations* stage of intellectual development if he is to respond to the experiences or symbols arranged as stimuli in Design Cluster Three. At this level of development, the learner is now also conscious of dynamic variables and can measure or classify things in groups or series. For instruction in Design Cluster Three, the learner may be at a higher level of intellectual development, but it is highly unlikely that he would be able to respond as desired if his intellectual development were at a level lower than the Concrete Operations stage.

Performance Conditions for Design Cluster Three

PSYCHOMOTOR PERFORMANCE CHARACTERISTICS   In Design Cluster Three, the characteristics of performance for manipulative or motor skills can be described at the level of the *Habitual Performance* classification of psychomotor goals. At this category, the learner can be expected to perform some motor act out of habit.

For example, performance characteristics of this classification would expect that the learner achieve some confidence and a degree of skill in the performance of an act. This would be seen out on the golf course where the learner habitually swings his club with some degree of skill but still must get some sort of mental picture of the task beforehand.

COGNITIVE PERFORMANCE CHARACTERISTICS   In Design Cluster Three, performance characteristics for the development of intellectual abilities and skills are described for the *Application* classification of cognitive goals. At this category, the learner is expected to use information beyond the context in which it was originally given.

For example, the learner might be expected to use the phenomena discussed in one paper in the application of scientific terms or concepts in other papers. Or, he might be expected to predict the probable effect of change in a factor on a biological situation previously at equilibrium.

AFFECTIVE PERFORMANCE CHARACTERISTICS   In Design Cluster Three, performance characteristics for the development of interest, appreciation, attitudes, values or adjustment are described at levels for the *Appreciation* classification of affective goals. At this category, the learner is expected to recognize that a concept or an idea has worth as a value.

For example, the learner's recognition that something has worth might be seen in his desire to develop the ability to speak and write effectively. His preference for a value might be demonstrated in his deliberate examination of a variety of viewpoints on controversial issues with a view to forming opinions about them. The learner might also be expected to make a commitment to a value by his certainty about, and faith in, the power of reason and the methods of experimentation and discussion.

Instructional Strategy for Performance Goals

Once the performance characteristics habe been identified at a level in Design Cluster Three, it is possible to design the arrangement of response conditions for the sequence of instruction.

VERTICAL PERFORMANCE PREREQUISITES   Learner performance in each category of Design Cluster Three requires and assumes learner performance competency at all levels within that same hierarchy of Design Cluster One and of Design Cluster Two. In addition, learner performance within the affective hierarchy in Design Cluster Three would require achievement at a lower level in that category. Since there is only one level in the psychomotor and cognitive hierarchies in Design Cluster Three, there would be, of course, no prerequisite levels in those domains other than the performance described at levels of previous Design Clusters.

Before the learner can respond to instruction for a psychomotor goal at the Habitual Performance category of Design Cluster Three, it must be assumed that he can respond at all levels of Readiness of Design Cluster One and at all levels of Attempted Performance of Design Cluster Two. For example, before the learner can swing a golf club habitually, he must have progressed through the learning hierarchy to the point where he performs the act through trial and error.

For cognitive learning, it must be assumed the learner is able to respond at all levels of the cognitive hierarchy in Design Cluster One and in Design Cluster Two before he can respond to instruction for a goal classified at the Application level of Design Cluster Three. For example, before the learner can be expected to apply the phenomena discussed in one paper of the scientific terms or concepts used to his other readings, he must first extend or extrapolate these terms or concepts in their original context. This level of performance would, of course, also be dependent on lower-level prerequisites progressing downward in the hierarchy to the point where he has learned to recall specific bits of information, such as defining the terms used in the paper.

In the affective category of Appreciation of Design Cluster Three, before the learner can be expected to recognize that something has worth, or to develop a high degree of commitment to a value by his certainty about its worth, he must first show evidence that he actively attends to what is required and has demonstrated an interest in something. The performance characteristics for the Appreciation category in the acceptance of a value require that the learner first demonstrate his competency to perform at all levels of Interest in Design Cluster Two and of Awareness in Design Cluster One.

For example, it would be difficult to develop the learner's desire to speak and write effectively if he has not demonstrated that he is willing to respond in this way and finds some sort of pleasure in this type of response. In the same manner, in Design Cluster Three, it is essential for the learner to show a preference for a value, for example, by deliberately examining a variety of viewpoints on controversial issues with a view to forming opinions about them before his commitment to a value could be expected by devotion to those ideas and ideals that result from the opinions he has formed.

HORIZONTAL PERFORMANCE RELATIONSHIPS   A secondary goal can be considered by the horizontal relationships between the levels of the three domains within Design Cluster Three or in prerequisite Design Clusters. While related performance in other domains may occur, it is highly unlikely that instruction would be necessary or be efficiently designed for a horizontal relationship to levels higher than those described in Design Cluster Three.

In Design Cluster Three, performance at levels within the psychomotor Habitual Performance category may permit or even require a cognitive capacity to respond. At this level, it can be expected that the individual be able to use information out of its original context in the habitual performance of some motor task. For example, unless the learner demonstrates a larger cognitive capability than merely comprehending instructions in the performance of an act, the chances of that performance becoming habitual are diminished.

Performance at this psychomotor level may also have a relationship to some affective disposition of the learner. Habitual performance of an act would be an easier response to achieve if it could be assured that the learner ascribed some worth in performing the act out of habit. For the person who has no appreciation of golf, the confidence and degree of skill expected in performance levels in the Habitual Performance category would be much more difficult to come by.

Performance at levels within the Application category of the cognitive domain may have a horizontal relationship to levels of affective learning if it is expected that the learner will have an appreciation of information that is useful to him. For example, the learner's response to instruction in which it is expected he will predict the probable effect of change in a factor on a biological situation previously at equilibrium, may be easier to achieve if it can also be assured in design that the learner ascribes some value or worth to this intellectual ability or skill.

Performance at this cognitive level may also indicate a psychomotor ability to respond. For example, if the learner is expected to use some information given in a scientific treatise in his own work, it may be required that he demonstrate that he has the psychomotor ability to perform this kind of experiment out of habit.

Performance at levels within the affective Appreciation category may permit or even require a psychomotor ability to respond. At this level it can be expected that the learner could habitually perform an act when he commits himself to a value. For example, if it is expected that the learner recognize the worth of golf to demonstrate his appreciation of participatory sports, he could also be expected to have the psychomotor learned competencies that would be demonstrated in his confidence and some degree of skill in the sport.

Performance at this affective level may also indicate the necessity for a cognitive capacity to respond. For example, if the learner will be expected to examine a variety of viewpoints on controversial issues with a view to forming opinions about them, it may be necessary to expect that he be able to use information about these issues beyond the context in which the information was originally given to him.

EXTENDED PERFORMANCE EXPECTATIONS   Performance in the learning domains of Design Cluster Three will provide prerequisite levels to extend performance expectations of the learner to those levels in the categories of Design Cluster Four.

Demonstrated skill performance at the Habitual Performance category of cognitive learning in Design Cluster Three will provide the learner with the prerequisites to analyze or synthesize information at the Operations category of Design Cluster Four. For example, after sufficient habitual performance in swinging that golf club, the learner can be expected to master the performance of the act by swinging the club without first getting a mental picture of the sequence involved.

Demonstrated intellectual performance at the Application category of cognitive learning in Design Cluster Three will provide the learner with the prerequisites to analyze or synthesize information at the Operations category of Design Cluster Four. For example, after it has been demonstrated that the learner can apply scientific terminology in contexts other than those in which he was first acquainted with them, he has achieved the necessary prerequisites to analyze the components of this terminology, the way in which it manages to communicate, as well as the way in which the terminology is organized.

Demonstrated attitudinal performance at the Appreciation category of affective learning will provide the learner with the necessary prerequisites for the performance expectations of the Values category of Design Cluster Four. For example, as the learner commits himself to a value, he may encounter situations for which more than one value is relevant. This would necessitate the organization of values into a system, the determination of the interrelationships among them, and the establishment of the dominant or pervasive value.

The examples used to illustrate performance characteristics for Design Cluster Three were taken largely from those given in the Condensed Version of the *Taxonomy of Educational Objectives* for each domain of learning to enable the use of these taxonomies to be related to the concept of Design Clusters. It is recommended that more detailed study be made of the performance concepts in the Taxonomies of Simpson, Bloom and Krathwohl.

Instructional Design Cluster Four

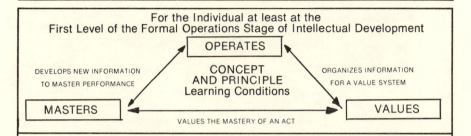

For the Individual at least at the
First Level of the Formal Operations Stage of Intellectual Development

OPERATES

DEVELOPS NEW INFORMATION
TO MASTER PERFORMANCE

CONCEPT
AND PRINCIPLE
Learning Conditions

ORGANIZES INFORMATION
FOR A VALUE SYSTEM

MASTERS

VALUES

VALUES THE MASTERY OF AN ACT

Intellectual Development Limitations
For the individual at least at the
Formal Operations (Level I) Stage of Intellectual Development

Primary Goal Performance Characteristics
MASTERS PERFORMANCE category of psychomotor goals:
  The learner performs a complex motor act that involves co-
  ordination.
OPERATIONS category of cognitive goals:
  The learner breaks down information and develops a new
  idea or material from the component parts.
VALUES category of affective goals:
  The learner begins to build his own value system.

Secondary Goal Performance Characteristics
Affective Disposition to the Primary Psychomotor Goal:
  The learner can be expected to value the mastery of the per-
  formance of some motor act.
Cognitive Capacity to the Primary Psychomotor Goal:
  The learner can be expected to organize new information into
  mastering the performance of an act.
Psychomotor Ability for the Primary Cognitive Goal:
  The learner can be expected to master the performance of an
  act in order to organize new information.
Affective Disposition to the Primary Cognitive Goal:
  The learner can be expected to value developing new informa-
  tion or a new form of communication.
Psychomotor Ability for the Primary Affective Goal:
  The learner can be expected to master the performance of an
  act to exhibit a value system.
Cognitive Capacity for the Primary Affective Goal:
  The learner can be expected to organize new information in
  building his own value system.

Sequence Strategy for the Psychomotor Goal

Before Instruction:

Prerequisite to psychomotor performance at levels in Design Cluster Four, the learner is expected to have demonstrated learned competencies at all levels up to those in Design Cluster Three:

PERCEPTION STEP: The learner should now be physically aware of objects, qualities and relations through his senses as they relate to the motor act.

SET STEP: The learner should now be prepared to perform the motor act.

GUIDED RESPONSE STEP: The learner should now have tried various ways of performing the motor act until he was successful.

MECHANISM STEP: The learner should now have achieved enough confidence and a degree of skill to perform the motor act out of habit.

For Instruction:

The psychomotor goal is classified at one of these levels in the COMPLEX OVERT RESPONSE STEP:

Level 10—RESOLUTION OF UNCERTAINTY

The learner can be expected to perform an act with limited coordination and without consciously thinking about the sequence of movements.

Level 11—AUTOMATIC PERFORMANCE:

The learner can be expected to perform a finely coordinated motor act with a great deal of ease and muscle control.

To Extend Instruction:

The learner has the prerequisites to extend instruction for performance described in Design Cluster Five.

CREATION STEP: The learner can now be expected to adapt or create a motor act to meet the requirements of a new situation or his personal characteristics.

Sequence Strategy for the Cognitive Goal

Before Instruction:

Prerequisite to cognitive performance at levels in Design Cluster Four, the learner is expected to have demonstrated learned competencies at all levels up to those in Design Cluster Three:

KNOWLEDGE OF SPECIFICS STEP: The learner should now recall specific bits of information.

KNOWLEDGE OF PROCEDURES STEP: The learner should now be aware of the ways specifics are dealt with.

KNOWLEDGE OF UNIVERSALS STEP: The learner should now recognize the major schemes and patterns by which information is organized.

COMPREHENSION STEP: The learner should now know what is being communicated and make limited use of the information or ideas.

APPLICATION STEP: The learner should now use ideas beyond the context in which they were originally given.
For Instruction:
The cognitive goal is classified at one of these levels in the ANALYSIS AND SYNTHESIS STEPS:
Level 14—ANALYSIS OF ELEMENTS
The learner can be expected to discriminate between the bits of information included in the idea.
Level 15—ANALYSIS OF RELATIONSHIPS
The learner can be expected to describe the connections between the bits of information in the idea, or the interactions between other ideas.
Level 16—ANALYSIS OF ORGANIZATIONAL PRINCIPLES
The learner can be expected to study the arrangement and structure of information that holds the ideas together.
Level 17—PRODUCTION OF A UNIQUE
             COMMUNICATION
The learner can be expected to construct new material in which he conveys feelings and experiences to others.
Level 18—PRODUCTION OF A PLAN OR PROPOSED SET
             OF OPERATIONS
The learner can be expected to develop a plan of work or propose a plan of operations.
Level 19—DERIVATION OF A SET OF ABSTRACT
             RELATIONS
The learner can be expected to derive new material by using abstractions to classify or explain ideas.
To Extend Instruction:
The learner has the prerequisites to extend instruction for performance described in Design Cluster Five:
EVALUATION STEP: The learner should now be expected to judge the value of material for a given purpose.

Sequence Strategy for the Affective Goal

Before Instruction:
Prerequisite to affective performance at levels in Design Cluster Four, the learner is expected to have demonstrated learned competencies at all levels up to those in Design Cluster Three:
RECEIVING STEP: The learner should now know that a concept exists and should now be willing to pay attention to it.
RESPONDING STEP: The learner should now actively pay attention to the concept—or at least have done something with or about it besides merely being aware of it.
VALUES STEP: The learner should now recognize that related concepts have worth as a value.
For Instruction:
The affective goal is classified at one of these levels in the ORGANIZATION STEP:

Level 10—CONCEPTUALIZATION OF A VALUE
The learner can be expected to see how the value relates to those he already holds or to a new one he is coming to hold.
Level 11—ORGANIZATION OF A VALUE SYSTEM
The learner can be expected to bring together a complex of values into an ordered relationship with each other.
To Extend Instruction:
The learner has the prerequisites to extend instruction for performance described in Design Cluster Five:
INTERNALIZATION STEP: The learner can now be expected to have organized values into some kind of internally consistent system and to have these values control his behavior long enough that he has adapted to behaving in this way.

Stimulus Design Requirements
Prerequisite Instructional Conditions:
Multiple Discrimination Learning is prerequisite to Concept and Principle Learning. The learner must have previously acquired the verbal and non-verbal connections representative of the class that describes the concept or principle and that distinguishes these stimuli from others not included in the class.
Conditions for Instruction:
Concept and Principle Learning: The stimuli are designed so the learner can combine two or more classes of stimuli into a concept and then sequence two or more concepts so the general principle is evident.
Extended Instructional Conditions:
Concept and Principle Learning is prerequisite to *Problem Solving Learning.* The learner is now ready to combine two or more previously acquired principles to produce a new, higher-order principle that solves a problem.

DESIGN LIMITATIONS BY LEVEL OF INTELLECTUAL DEVELOPMENT

The individual must have matured to at least the first level of the *Formal Operations* stage of intellectual development if he is to respond to the experiences or symbols designed as stimuli for Design Cluster Four. At this level of development, the learner can now also analyze, hypothesize, synthesize and display abstract, conceptual thinking. For instructional experiences in Design Cluster Four, it is highly unlikely that the learner would respond as desired if his intellectual development is at a lower level that the first level of the Formal Operations stage.

Performance Conditions for Design Cluster Four

PSYCHOMOTOR PERFORMANCE CHARACTERISTICS   In Design Cluster Four, the performance characteristics for manipulative or motor skills can be described at levels for the *Masters Performance* classification of psychomotor goals. At this category, the learner can be expected to perform a complex motor act that involves coordination.

For example, the learner's ability to clean and adjust a carburetor would be characteristic of the resolution of uncertainty in the learner and the task would be performed without hesitating to get a mental picture of its sequence. It might also be expected, for example, that the learner would perform a finely coordinated motor skill with a great deal of ease and muscle control. This might be seen by playing a recognizable tune on a violin.

COGNITIVE PERFORMANCE CHARACTERISTICS   In Design Cluster Four, performance characteristics for the development of intellectual abilities and skills are described at levels for the *Operations* classification of cognitive goals. At this category, the learner can be expected to break down information so the order of ideas is made clear and the relationships between ideas is explicit; or it can be expected that he put together ideas to formulate new information.

For example, the learner might be expected to distinguish facts from hypotheses in information. This would demonstrate his intellectual skill to identify the elements of a communication (characteristic of performance in the Analysis step of the cognitive hierarchy). He might also be asked to analyze the relationships between the parts of a communication by checking the consistency of hypotheses within given information and assumptions. Or, the learner might be expected to analyze the organizational principles of forms and patterns in literary or artistic works as a way of understanding their meaning.

The learner might also be expected to put together elements to form some sort of coherent whole as would be indicated by levels in the Synthesis step of cognitive learning. Performance expectations might be characterized by the learner's intellectual skill in writing, using an appropriate organization of ideas and statements. Or, the learner may be expected to propose ways of testing hypotheses; or to derive a set of abstract relationships by formulating appropriate hypotheses based on an analysis of factors involved and then to modify these hypotheses in the light of new factors or considerations.

AFFECTIVE PERFORMANCE CHARACTERISTICS   In Design Cluster Four, performance characteristics for the development of attitudes, values or adjustment are described at levels for the *Values* classification of affective goals. (At this level, instructional goals are classified beyond the development of interest or appreciation.) At this category, the learner can be expected to organize values when he encounters situations for which more than one value is relevant in order to build his own value system.

For example, the learner might conceptualize a value to form judgments as to the responsibility of society for conserving human and material resources. It might also be expected that the learner weigh alternative social policies and practices against the standards of the public welfare rather than the advantage of a specialized narrow-interest group.

Instructional Strategy for Performance Goals

Once the performance characteristics have been identified at a level in Design Cluster Four, it is possible to design the arrangement of response conditions for the sequence of instruction.

VERTICAL PERFORMANCE PREREQUISITES   Learner performance at each category of Design Cluster Four requires and assumes learner performance at all levels in that same hierarchy in all three previous Design Clusters. In addition, learner performance in each category of Design Cluster Four would require achievement at a lower level in that same category.

Before the learner can be expected to resolve uncertainty in the performance of a complex motor act for Design Cluster Four, it must be assumed that he has responded at all psychomotor levels of Readiness in Design Cluster One, at all levels of Attempted Performance in Design Cluster Two, and at all levels of Habitual Performance in Design Cluster Three.

For example, before he has reached the point where he can be expected to display a high degree of skill in cleaning and adjusting a carburetor, the learner must have progressed through the learning hierarchy to the point where he habitually cleaned and adjusted a carburetor—but in so doing, had to get a mental picture of all the steps involved.

For cognitive learning, it must be assumed the learner has responded at all levels of the cognitive hierarchy for the recall and recognition of knowledge of Design Cluster One; knows what is being communicated and can make limited use of the material as expected in Design Cluster Two; and has used abstractions in particular and concrete situations as expected in Design Cluster Three. Based on these performance assumptions, the learner can then be expected to respond to instruction for a goal at the Analysis level of Design Cluster Four.

For example, before the learner can identify the specific elements of a communication, he must first perform at all levels up to the point where he applies these elements in particular and concrete situations beyond the original context in which these elements were first displayed to him. In a like manner, in Design Cluster Four, before the learner can be expected to show an ability to plan a unit of instruction for a particular teaching-learning situation, he must first display some skill in communicating using an accepted pattern of the organization of ideas and statements.

At the affective levels in Design Cluster Four, before it can be expected the learner will respond to instruction in the Values category, it is assumed and required that he perform at all levels in the affective hierarchy to the level of Design Cluster Three where he commits himself to a value with a high degree of certainty about its worth. For example, before the learner can form judgments about the responsibilities of society for conserving human and material resources, the learner must first have demonstrated that he has committed himself to the value concept that conserving human and material resources *is* a responsibility of society.

Similarly, his judgment on the responsibilities of society for conserving these resources is itself prerequisite to the learner's disposition to bring together the whole complex of economic, biological and social relationships involved in this ecological value to formulate his own value system.

HORIZONTAL PERFORMANCE RELATIONSHIPS   A secondary goal can be considered by the horizontal relationships between the levels of the three domains within Design Cluster Four or in prerequisite Design Clusters. While related performance in other domains may occur, it is highly unlikely that instruction would be necessary or efficiently designed for a horizontal relationship to levels higher than those described in Design Cluster Four.

In Design Cluster Four, performance at levels within the psychomotor Masters Performance category may permit or even require a cognitive capacity to respond. At this level, it can be expected that the individual have the intellectual abilities and skills to work operationally with knowledge if he is expected to apply that knowledge in performing a complex motor act with a great deal of coordination. For example, it is expected that the learner analyze and sort out pertinent data from the instrument panel of an airplane if he is to master the piloting of that plane with the ease and coordination required.

Similarly, unless the learner can organize values into some sort of system, he may not be able to respond to instruction at this psychomotor level. For example, while it may be expected that the learner type with fully automatic skill and complete resolution of uncertainty, if he is unconvinced that this performance act has some worth to him—unless he has placed this performance into some sort of accepted value system—he is highly unlikely to develop anything further than habitual performance in his typing.

Performance at levels within the Operations category of the cognitive domain may have a horizontal relationship to levels of affective learning if it is expected that the learner formulate a value system in order to analyze information or to formulate new pieces of information or communications from various component parts. For example, the learner may be expected to look for sentence structure in a literary work, and then rewrite that work in terms of accepted standards. Unless those standards have been accepted by the individual in his own value system, performance at this cognitive level may not demonstrate learned competencies, but rather parroted reactions to instruction.

In a similar manner, cognitive performance at the Operations category may have a horizontal relationship that would permit the expectations of a psychomotor ability to respond. For example, if it is expected that the learner derive some abstract principle from some information given to him, these expectations may not be realized if the information requires some finely coordinated manipulative skill to analyze. The learner cannot analyze or compare his tonal quality with others in a violin recital without first being able to master the skill in playing a recognizable tune on that instrument.

Performance at levels within the affective values category may have a horizontal relationship to a psychomotor ability to respond. At this level it could be expected that the learner master the performance of an act in order to exhibit the formation of his own value system. Internal consistency and preference for safety rules as a value system may not be possible, for example, without some demonstrated competencies in the performance of the tasks or skills to which these rules apply.

Performance at this affective level may also indicate a horizontal cognitive relationship where the learner could be expected to analyze or organize new information in building his own value system. For example, it may be desired that the learner demonstrate that he can analyze information about various cultural ethnic groups before he can be expected to formulate an internally consistent value system about these groups.

EXTENDED PERFORMANCE EXPECTATIONS   Performance in any learning domain at the categories of Design Cluster Four will provide the prerequisite levels to extend performance expectations of the learner to the levels in those categories of Design Cluster Five.

Demonstrated performance at the Masters Performance category for psychomotor learning in Design Cluster Four will provide the learner with the prerequisites for the Creation of Performance category of Design Cluster Five. For example, after the learner has demonstrated his skill in playing a violin with a great deal of ease and muscle control, it can then be expected that he might be ready to adapt his performance in terms of a specific piece of music, or because his fingers are too short for normal fingering. He might also be expected to create a new pattern of bowing or tremolo for a special effect.

Demonstrated intellectual performance at the Operations category for cognitive goals of Design Cluster Four will provide the prerequisites for performance in Design Cluster Five where it could be expected that the learner make judgments about material in terms of internal or external standards. For example, after the learner can formulate an appropriate hypothesis based on an analysis of all factors involved, he has demonstrated prerequisite performance characteristics to enable him then to judge, by internal evidence, the accuracy of these and other hypotheses.

Demonstrated attitudinal performance at the Organization of a Value System level of the affective hierarchy in Design Cluster Four will provide the learner with the prerequisite learning for expected performance for the adjustment to a value system characteristic of performance to instruction sequenced in Design Cluster Five. For example, if the learner has formed a value system about society's ecological responsibilities by bringing together all of the complex economic, biological and social relationships involved, he could then be expected (as characteristic of performance at Design Cluster Five) to internalize this value system and, as an individual in society, be characterized by these ecological beliefs and values.

The examples used to illustrate performance characteristics for Design Cluster Four were taken largely from those given in the Condensed Version of the *Taxonomy of Educational Objectives* for each domain of learning to enable the use of these taxonomies to be related to the concept of Design Clusters. It is recommended that more detailed study be made of the performance concepts in the Taxonomies of Simpson, Bloom and Krathwohl.

Instructional Design Cluster Five

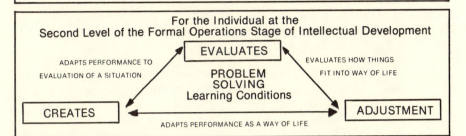

For the Individual at the
Second Level of the Formal Operations Stage of Intellectual Development

EVALUATES

ADAPTS PERFORMANCE TO
EVALUATION OF A SITUATION

PROBLEM
SOLVING
Learning Conditions

EVALUATES HOW THINGS
FIT INTO WAY OF LIFE

CREATES

ADJUSTMENT

ADAPTS PERFORMANCE AS A WAY OF LIFE

Intellectual Development Limitations
For the individual at the
Formal Operations (Level II) Stage of Intellectual Development

Primary Goal Performance Characteristics
CREATES PERFORMANCE category of psychomotor goals:
The learner devises a new way of performing a motor act to meet requirements of a new situation or of his own personal characteristics.
EVALUATION category of cognitive goals:
The learner makes judgments about the value of information for a given purpose.
ADJUSTMENT category of affective goals:
The learner has a hierarchy of values which form an internally consistent system to control his behavior.

Secondary Goal Performance Relationships
Affective Disposition to the Primary Psychomotor Goal:
The learner can be expected to internalize values to adapt or create new ways of performing an act.
Cognitive Capacity to the Primary Psychomotor Goal:
The learner can be expected to evaluate knowledge and information in order to adapt or create the performance of a motor act.
Psychomotor Ability for the Primary Cognitive Goal:
The learner can be expected to adapt or create performance in his evaluation of a situation or some information.
Affective Disposition to the Primary Cognitive Goal:
The learner can be expected to use his internalized value system to evaluate material or knowledge.
Psychomotor Ability for the Primary Affective Goal:
The learner can be expected to adapt or create the performance of motor skills to show that a value system characterizes his way of life.
Cognitive Capacity for the Primary Affective Goal:
The learner can be expected to evaluate how knowledge fits into the value system of his way of life.

Sequence Strategy for the Psychomotor Goal

Before Instruction:

Prerequisite to psychomotor performance at levels in Design Cluster Five, the learner is expected to have demonstrated learned competencies at all levels up to those in Design Cluster Four:

PERCEPTION STEP: The learner should now be physically aware of objects, qualities and relations through his senses as they relate to the motor act.

SET STEP: The learner should now be prepared to perform the motor act.

GUIDED RESPONSE STEP: The learner should now have tried various ways of performing the motor act until he has been successful.

MECHANISM STEP: The learner should now have achieved enough confidence and a degree of skill to perform the motor act out of habit.

COMPLEX OVERT RESPONSE STEP: The learner should now have combined simple actions into a complex motor act that involved sequence and coordination.

For Instruction:

The Psychomotor goal is classified at one of these levels in the CREATION STEP:

Level 12—ADAPTATION

The learner can be expected to adapt an action to meet specific requirements of a situation.

Level 13—ORIGINATION:

The learner can be expected to create new patterns of action to solve a specific problem.

To Extend Instruction:

It is assumed that instruction cannot be extended for performance beyond those levels described in Design Cluster Five.

Sequence Strategy for the Cognitive Goal

Before Instruction:

Prerequisite to cognitive performance at levels in Design Cluster Five, the learner is expected to have demonstrated learned competencies at all levels up to those in Design Cluster Four:

KNOWLEDGE OF SPECIFICS STEP: The learner should now recall specific bits of information.

KNOWLEDGE OF PROCEDURES STEP: The learner should now be aware of the ways specifics are dealt with.

KNOWLEDGE OF UNIVERSALS STEP: The learner should now recognize major schemes and patterns by which information is organized.

COMPREHENSION STEP: The learner should now know what is being communicated and make limited use of the information or ideas.

APPLICATION STEP: The learner should now use ideas beyond the context in which they were originally given.

ANALYSIS STEP: The learner should now break down ideas so that the order of information is made clear.

SYNTHESIS STEP: The learner should now put together ideas to form a whole.

For Instruction:

The cognitive goal is classified at one of these levels in the EVALUATION STEP:

Level 20—JUDGMENT IN TERMS OF INTERNAL
         EVIDENCE

The learner can be expected to evaluate the accuracy of material from such evidence as logical accuracy, consistency, and other internal evidence.

Level 21—JUDGMENT IN TERMS OF EXTERNAL
         CRITERIA

The learner can be expected to evaluate material with reference to other selected and remembered criteria.

To Extend Instruction:

It is assumed that instruction cannot be extended for performance beyond those levels described in Design Cluster Five.

Sequence Strategy for the Affective Goal

Before Instruction:

Prerequisite to affective performance at levels in Design Cluster Five, the learner is expected to have demonstrated learned competencies at all levels up to those in Design Cluster Four:

RECEIVING STEP: The learner should now know that a concept exists and should now be willing to pay attention to it.

RESPONDING STEP: The learner should now actively pay attention to the concept—or at least have done something with or about it besides merely being aware of it.

VALUES STEP: The learner should now recognize that related concepts have worth as a value.

ORGANIZATION STEP: The learner should now organize values when he encounters situations for which more than one value is relevant in order to have built his own value system.

For Instruction:

The affective goal is classified at one of these levels in the INTERNALIZATION STEP:

Level 12—GENERALIZED SET

The learner can be expected to have internal consistency in his system of values at any given moment.

Level 13—CHARACTERIZATION

The learner can be expected to completely internalize a value system into his way of life.

To Extend Instruction:

It is assumed that instruction cannot be extended for performance beyond those levels described in Design Cluster Five.

Stimulus Design Requirements

Prerequisite Instructional Conditions:
Concept and Principle Learning is prerequisite to Problem Solving Learning. The learner must possess a critical mass of the principles that are to be put together to achieve the solution to a problem.

Conditions for Instruction:
Problem Solving Learning: The stimuli are designed so the learner can generalize two or more previously acquired principles for a new, higher order principle that can be used to solve a problem.

Extended Instructional Conditions:
Achievement of performance at the Problem Solving level of learning constitutes the theoretical top limit of the hierarchy of stimulus design. The learner is now ready for more complex problem-solving learning to sharpen his learned competencies.

DESIGN LIMITATIONS BY LEVEL OF INTELLECTUAL DEVELOPMENT

The individual must have matured to the Formal Operations stage (Level II) of intellectual development if he is to respond to the symbols or experiences designed as stimuli in Design Cluster Five. At this level of development, the learner can now also imagine, evaluate, and his reasoning is generalized. For instructional sequences in Design Cluster Five, it is highly unlikely that the learner would be able to respond as expected if his intellectual development is at a level lower than the second level of the Formal Operations stage.

Performance Conditions for Design Cluster Five

PSYCHOMOTOR PERFORMANCE CHARACTERISTICS   In Design Cluster Five, the performance characteristics for manipulative or motor skills can be described at levels for the *Creates Performance* classification of psychomotor goals. At this category, the learner can be expected to devise a new way of performing a motor act to meet requirements of a new situation or of his own personal characteristics.

The learner might be expected to adapt an action in terms of his own unique attributes or of the situation in which he finds himself when he must perform the act. For example, a person who has just learned to fly might be expected to adapt his performance skills to the particular characteristics of different aircraft. Where it is expected that the learner will create new patterns of action in solving a specific skill problem, a mason might create a new way to lay brick to meet the specifications of a circular school building.

COGNITIVE PERFORMANCE CHARACTERISTICS   In Design Cluster Five, learner performance characteristics for the development of intellectual abilities and skills are described at levels for the *Evaluation* classification of cognitive goals. At this category, the learner can be expected to make judgments about the value of information or methods for a given purpose.

For example, performance characteristics of the learner's intellectual ability to judge material by internal evidence would be seen when he assesses the general probability of accuracy in reporting facts from the care and attention given to the exactness of statements, documentation or proof in a communication. He might also be expected to judge by external criteria, displaying his intellectual skill, comparing a work of the highest known standards in its field with other works of recognized excellence.

AFFECTIVE PERFORMANCE CHARACTERISTICS   In Design Cluster Five, goals for affective learner performance are limited to the development of personal adjustment at the levels for the *Adjustment* classification of goals. (At this level, affective performance characteristics are beyond those expected in the development of attitudes or values as well as those characteristics described in the development of interest or appreciation.) At the Adjustment category, the learner can be expected to have a hierarchy of values that form an internally consistent system to control his behavior and by which he is characterized as a person in a society.

For example, the learner may be expected to give internal consistency to the system of attitudes and values so that he might be characterized by his ability to judge problems and issues in terms of situations, purposes, and consequences involved rather than in terms of fixed, dogmatic precepts or emotionally wishful thinking. At the top level of affective performance, the goals are so encompassing that they tend to characterize the person almost completely. For example, the learner might be expected to develop his personal and civic life according to a code of behavior based on ethical principles consistent with democratic ideals.

Instructional Strategy for Performance Goals

Once the performance characteristics have been identified at a level in Design Cluster Five, it is possible to design the arrangement of response conditions for the sequence of instruction.

VERTICAL PERFORMANCE PREREQUISITES   Learner performance for each category of Design Cluster Five requires and assumes learner performance at all levels in that same hierarchy in *all* previous Design Clusters. In addition, learner performance in each step of Design Cluster Five would require performance at the lower level in that step.

Before the learner can be expected to adapt his performance in terms of the specific requirements of a situation, he must first perform a finely coordinated act with a great deal of muscle control. This performance would, in turn, require the learner to respond to all levels of Readiness to Perform for Design Cluster One; all levels of Attempted Performance for Design Cluster Two; all levels of Habitual Performance for Design Cluster Three; and to respond at all levels of the Mastery of Performance of Design Cluster Four. Only then can instruction be designed with any degree of confidence that the learner will adapt or create performance as described in Design Cluster Five. For example, before it can be expected that the learner will adapt his flying performance skills to the particular characteristics of different types of airplanes, he must first demonstrate prerequisite performance by flying the plane in which he learned with a great deal of automatic and coordinated skill and muscle control.

For cognitive learning, it must be assumed the learner will develop a set of abstract relations either to classify or to explain particular data or phenomena in the performance characteristics at a level in Design Cluster Four before he can be expected to judge material or information by internal evidence, characteristic of performance described in Design Cluster Five. For example, before the learner can judge the accuracy of the reporting of facts from the way these facts are presented in some communication, it is expected that he would first synthesize and analyze the elements of that communication to recognize abstract relationships.

For the adjustment and internalization of values expected for affective learning at Design Cluster Five, it must be assumed that the learner has organized a value system as might have previously been expected by the performance described in Design Cluster Four. For example, if it is expected that the learner judge problems and issues in terms of situations, purposes and consequences involved, then it must be expected that his value system previously established would not force him to make this judgment in terms of fixed, dogmatic precepts or emotionally wishful thinking.

HORIZONTAL PERFORMANCE RELATIONSHIPS   A secondary goal can be considered by the horizontal relationships between the levels of the three domains within Design Cluster Five or in prerequisite Design Clusters.

In Design Cluster Five, performance at levels within each of the categories of learning can have a horizontal relationship to all levels of learned competencies in the other domains. Just as in Design Cluster One where the simplistic nature of the characteristics of performance made horizontal relationships between the domains difficult to distinguish so, too, at Design Cluster Five, the highly complex relationships between domains make clean discriminations virtually impossible.

Performance at levels within the psychomotor Creates Performance category may permit a cognitive capacity to respond. At this level, it could be expected that the learner evaluate knowledge in order to adapt or create the performance of an act. For example, judgments about his characteristics of flying, made either in terms of internalized standards or by criteria set by other pilots, may be necessary before the new pilot can be expected to adapt his patterns of flying to the characteristics of different aircraft.

At this psychomotor level, it could also be expected that the learner internalize values or adjust his personal way of life in some way in order to create the performance of a motor act. For example, it could be argued that by definition the creation of some manipulative or motor act is dependent on an internalized value system about the worth of the act. Creating new ways of expressing one's self does indeed reflect an internalized value system about self-expression.

Performance at levels within the Evaluates category of the cognitive domain have a horizontal relationship to levels of affective learning. It could be expected that the learner internalize values in order to evaluate knowledge or information. For example, almost by definition, judgment by internal standards assumes some sort of internalized system of values that forms the criteria against which the learner can make the cognitive response of evaluation.

Similarly, performance at levels within the cognitive Evaluates category may indicate a horizontal relationship to levels of psychomotor learning. At this level, it could be expected that the learner would adapt the performance of an act in the evaluation of a situation. For example, in evaluating the effectiveness of several different pieces of communication describing how to perform some motor act, the learner may have to adapt his own performance of that act in each way described in order to formulate qualitative judgments about the effectiveness of each set of directions.

Performance at levels within the affective Adjustment category of Design Cluster Five may permit or even require a cognitive capacity to respond. This would be seen where the learner would be expected to evaluate how knowledge fits into his adjusted way of life. For example, if the learner is expected to be characterized as a person by his internally-consistent value system, it is almost assumed that he have the cognitive intellectual skills to evaluate his value system according to known and accepted standards.

It might also be expected that performance at the affective Adjustment category would have a horizontal relationship to a psychomotor ability to respond. The demonstration of holding a value system may have to be shown by the learner's ability to adapt or create the performance of some overt act. For example, the existence of an internalized value system about participatory sports can only be seen when the learner actually adapts his own performance, or creates a new pattern of performance in that sport to demonstrate that a value system has become a way of life for him.

EXTENDED PERFORMANCE EXPECTATIONS   Since the categories of Design Cluster Five represent a theoretical top limit of performance expectations as the direct result of instruction for each of the domains of learning, there is represented an arbitrary terminal level where instruction is not sequenced to a higher level. But the skill and intellectual and attitudinal performance of the individual can be further refined and expanded into a more sophisticated psychomotor ability, cognitive capability or affective disposition.

The examples used to illustrate performance characteristics for Design Cluster Five were taken largely from those given in the Condensed Version of the *Taxonomy of Educational Objectives* for each domain of learning to enable the use of these taxonomies to be related to the concept of Design Clusters. It is recommended that more detailed study be made of the performance concepts in the Taxonomies of Simpson, Bloom and Krathwohl.

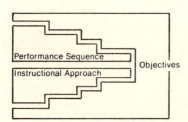

Performance Sequence
Instructional Approach
Objectives

Instructional Approach

The approach to instruction is determined by the requirements identified in the instructional classification of the goal.

FRAME OF REFERENCE FOR THE APPROACH TO INSTRUCTION

This design function should begin from the frame of reference established by acknowledging any restraints imposed on the determination of the best way possible to reach the learner with instruction.

Restraints may be imposed by restrictions against using some certain approaches already identified as the best way to reach the learner. This should be considered then in establishing a frame of reference from which to begin this design function. For example, if it has been determined necessary to reach the learner directly, without any other instructional intervention, the design effort may be restrained if it is required that all instructional efforts for the school be channeled through the classroom teacher.

Approach to Instruction

The intermeshing of the identified elements of the instructional intent and the instructional classification of the goal defines which approach to instruction can best be used to reach the learner. A specific approach to instruction must be relevant to the individual as well as to the instructional setting in which it is intended to be used. The approach maps out a precise strategy to best reach the individual learner.

Each approach strategy has quite rigid tolerances that cannot be violated without sacrificing the integrity of the design scheme. However, within any given single experience for an individual, it is possible to include more than one instructional segment, each of which may be developed with a different approach. For example, in a brief television program, instruction can not only provide a new course of study for the classroom teacher in one segment; but in a subsequent segment in the same program, provide the teacher with the material to implement this new course of study. The same program could also devote another segment to direct interaction with the learner to start instruction that will be carried on by conventional instruction later in the classroom. However, each of these segments should be designed as a separate entity, and put together later with appropriate transitional devices.

For each of the following ways to approach instruction, not only will the structure of the stimulus design be different; but since each approach tries to reach the learner differently, each will require a slightly different statement of objectives, structure, and responsibilities for testing the results.

Approaches to Mediated Instruction

THE DIRECT EXPERIENCE APPROACH

If the primary intent in instruction is to reach the learner directly, then instruction is designed so the learner can respond directly, without other instructional intervention.

Give Prerequisite Learning: Give initial exposure to instruction for learning experiences that are prerequisite to planned future instruction.

Develop Expository Learning: Develop additional exposure to instruction for learning experiences that build on previous learning and lead to planned future instruction.

Present Terminal Learning: Present the total exposure for complete units of instruction that are autonomous learning experiences.

THE COURSE OF STUDY GUIDELINES APPROACH

If the primary intent in instruction is to change what the teacher does in conventional instruction to reach the learner, then mediated instruction is designed so the learner can respond to the classroom teacher whose teaching has been given direction by a mediated course of study.

Implement Imposed Guidelines: Augment a teaching structure to follow where the course of study is imposed by some academic administrative authority.

Reinforce Existing Guidelines: Extend a teaching structure to use with a course of study that now exists in other mediated forms.

Create New Guidelines: Formulate a teaching structure for a course of study that does not now exist in any usable form.

THE SUPPLEMENTAL MATERIAL APPROACH

If the primary intent is to guide what the teacher uses to reach the learner, then instruction is designed so the learner can respond to the classroom teacher after mediated instruction has provided material to use with an established course of study.

Mediate Inaccessible Material: Mediate material that exists in forms that are not accessible for direct use in the conventional classroom because of size, location, expense, and so forth.

Translate Undesirable Material: Translate material from its original format that is not desired to be used directly with the learner because it is potentially dangerous, frightening, offensive, etc.

Display Otherwise Unavailable Material: Display material that is not readily available for direct use by the classroom teacher because it is consumable, requires extensive preparation, etc.

THE ENRICHED RESOURCES APPROACH

If the primary intent in instruction is to influence indirectly the conditions of the learner, then instruction is designed so the learner can respond to the classroom teacher after mediated instruction has complemented the total educational program.

Enhance Motivational Resources: Enhance the motivation of the learner with resources that will create more appropriate opportunities for learning.

Expand Experiential Resources: Expand the learner's experiences with resources that will increase opportunities for learning.

Extend Environmental Resources: Extend the learner's environment with resources that will broaden opportunities for learning.

The Direct Experience Approach

For the Direct Experience Approach, instruction is designed to reach the target population without any other instructional intervention. Efforts to effect learning gains can be accomplished by direct experiences for the learner. Evidence of increased learning gains will be shown by the measurement of specific behavioral responses made by the individual.

The strategy to achieve specific learning gains would involve selecting ways to approach instruction by giving initial exposure to new content—developing additional exposure to content already familiar to the learner—or by presenting the total exposure of content to the individual exclusively through the mediated instruction.

GIVE PREREQUISITE LEARNING EXPERIENCES   If the major design emphasis is to supply input for later conventional or mediated instruction, then instruction should initiate adequate preparatory learning. For example, a learner must know numbers and numerals in isolation before they can be combined into even elementary mathematical functions. Initial exposure to number symbols for the recognition of number form and value can be designed. This instructional sequence would prepare the learner for later conventional or mediated instruction in higher mathematical functions.

DEVELOP EXPOSITORY LEARNING EXPERIENCES   If the major design emphasis is to expand present instruction in order to supply input to later conventional or other mediated instruction, then the instruction designed should advance appropriate continuous learning. For example, after initial explanation of a literary form used in poetry (such as alliteration, onomatopoeia, or rhymed couplets), the learner should have additional exposure to these and other poetic formulas found in literature. This exposure can be designed for continuous learning that has been initiated (and will be extended) in the classroom with or without the intervention of other mediated instruction.

PRESENT TERMINAL LEARNING EXPERIENCES   If the major design emphasis is to provide complete instruction that may or may not be based on previous mediated or conventional instruction, then the instruction designed should provide comprehensive self-contained learning. For example, the learner may require knowledge of the use of the slide rule for a planned learning experience in architecture. An instructional sequence can be mediated to provide the complete explanations and practice in using the slide rule as an autonomous, self-contained learning experience.

Course of Study Guidelines Approach

For the Course of Study Guidelines Approach, instruction is designed so the learner can respond to the classroom teaching structure that is given direction by mediated course of study guidelines. Efforts can facilitate teaching by providing guidelines to be followed in conducting conventional classroom instruction. Assessment of student responses that have been guided by the classroom teacher will evidence increased teaching effectiveness in the Course of Study Guidelines Approach.

The strategy to increase teaching effectiveness would include selecting ways to approach instruction to implement imposed guidelines prescribed by state or system administrative requirements—to extend or reinforce guidelines for a course of study existing in other media (such as the textbook or State Regent's exams) that is already being used—or to create new guidelines in those areas where adequate help to structure the conventional classroom teaching situation does not exist.

IMPLEMENT IMPOSED GUIDELINES   If a compulsory course of study is imposed by some academic administrative authority, mediated instruction can facilitate a teaching structure with ways to augment these imposed guidelines. Often a state department of education, for example, will come out with a new course of study in a subject area that is recommended for all schools in the state. More rapid and universal implementation of this imposed curriculum can be effected by presenting these prescribed guidelines to all schools in a controlled, sequential manner through a series of radio or television broadcasts.

REINFORCE EXISTING GUIDELINES   If additional organization is required to facilitate teaching, mediated instruction can extend established guidelines to reinforce a course of study that already exists in the various other media available to the classroom teacher. For example, in some schools, innovative curriculum directors may want to tamper with the universal course of study determinant (the textbook) the designing mediated instruction to rearrange the published scope and sequence. Perhaps it is desired to augment the text with curriculum material specifically designed to meet local instructional needs. This might be seen when it would be expected to add a unit in state history to the course of study established on a United States History textbook.

CREATE NEW GUIDELINES   If a course of study is required to facilitate teaching, but is nonexistent, the design effort can structure a new teaching pattern by developing new course of study guidelines. For example, if no course of study exists for a differentiated curriculum for the gifted or talented students, mediated instruction could be designed to provide guidelines for the teacher to use to create a curriculum for a truly "gifted" program rather than allowing an "accelerated" program to be provided for these students—a program that most likely would be dependent only on the initiative and imagination of the classroom teacher.

The Supplemental Material Approach

For the Supplemental Material Approach, instruction is designed so the learner can respond after material has been mediated to implement an instructional process. Efforts to supplement a course of study with instructional material should result in a growth in the scope of the instructional process. Any such growth can be evidenced by an evaluation of the extent of the teacher's use of this supplemental material.

The strategy to increase the scope of the instructional process would involve ways to approach instruction to mediate material that the teachers would use if it were accessible for use; to translate material that, by its inherent nature, is not desired for direct use; or to display material that teachers do not have available for direct use.

MEDIATE INACCESSIBLE MATERIAL   Teachers may be expected to use material they cannot have. The design effort can mediate material that is not accessible for direct use in such a way that teachers will be able to use the material. For example, the instructional material required may be a demonstration of the democratic process in action. A field trip to the State Capitol during a legislative session would not only be a nerve-racking experience for the teacher, but at best only a cursory exposure to the democratic process for the learner. By compressing time and space, the instruction can break through the veneer of the legislative process seen on a senate floor. This will then provide more substantive material for the teacher's use in a much more accessible way than attempting to parade 30 fourth-graders into the legislative smoke-filled caucus chambers several times a day or during the late evening hours.

TRANSLATE UNDESIRABLE MATERIAL   Teachers are often expected to use material they are unwilling to have because of the inherent nature of the material itself (such as potentially dangerous, offensive, or relatively expensive or fragile material). The design effort can translate, from its original form, that material not desired for direct use. This should be done in such a way that teachers will be willing to use the mediated material.

For example, the teacher may not want to expose the students to an actual demonstration of the combination of certain chemical elements such as sodium and water. However, if this demonstration is translated to a mediated format, the experience is more likely to remain in the instructional process. Or, the teacher may be expected to use an oscilloscope in a planned sequence to have the learner visually discriminate pitch and tempo in music. Most fourth-grade classrooms are going to be deprived of this learning experience unless the material is mediated for use.

DISPLAY UNAVAILABLE MATERIAL   Teachers may also be expected to use material they do not have. The design must then guide the development of material that teachers will want to use that is not now available for direct use. For example, the course of study may require that teachers use prepared demonstrations of certain phenomena in the Inquiry Approach to science. These demonstrations can be displayed for the teacher's use in some mediated form. In this way, the classroom teacher does not have to spend the previous day preparing these demonstrations for the consumption of the learners during the first period of the next day.

Enriched Resources Approach

For the Enriched Resources Approach, instruction is designed so that the learner can respond after resources have been mediated to enrich or complement the educational program in which the individual learns. This can be accomplished by making available resources that will complement learning opportunities. Evidence of an enriched educational program can be obtained by observing the effect of these complementary resources on the learner.

The strategy to add a fuller dimension to the educational program would include selecting ways to approach instruction to enhance the motivation of the learner—to extend the environment of the learner—or to increase or expand the learner's experiences. To some extent, instruction using this approach more closely approximates the intent in the use of technology to inform, enrich or entertain, described earlier (see pages 10-12).

ENHANCE MOTIVATIONAL RESOURCES   The individual may be expected to have an appropriate motivation for learning to satisfy the instructional intent. Mediated resources can create motivation for enhanced learning opportunities. For example, a learner may reluctantly enter into a study of classical literature unless, perhaps, through the design of instruction, dramatic resources can show that Rabelais, Balzac and even Shakespeare wrote some "dirty stories."

EXPAND EXPERIENTIAL RESOURCES   The individual may be expected to have sufficient experiences in order to satisfy the instructional intent. Mediated resources can increase experiences for expanded learning opportunities. For example, a learner may never have been exposed to a policeman in other than arrest and enforcement situations. The design of mediated instruction can expand the learner's experiences by providing opportunities to show that policemen have functions that contribute to society in other than arrests.

EXTEND ENVIRONMENTAL RESOURCES   The individual may be expected to have an adequate environment for learning to satisfy the instructional intent. Instruction can be designed to provide resources to enlarge the environment for extended learning opportunities. For a school in suburban areas, for example, the learners may have relatively few opportunities to see the environmental conditions of urban or rural ghettos. It would be possible to extend opportunities for learning by mediated resources to enlarge, even vicariously, the social environment of these children. Mediated instruction could provide the learner with the resources to extend even further his cultural environment, by exposing him to another group's way of life.

Other Operational Approaches

Electronic technology can be used for other purposes than instantaneous mass-replicability across space and through time. The specific design strategy in the approaches related to instruction describing the uses of electronic media may vary greatly. Some are recognized here to distinguish their uses and structures from those with which these design procedures are principally concerned.

THE OBJECT-DISPLAY APPROACH   Instructional media can also be designed as a display device in an instructional setting where the structure prevents direct teacher or learner confrontation with items or processes. Use of this operational approach is generally confined to meeting specific in-house presentations for learner performance in response to a "front row" view of the phenomenon displayed.

THE SELF-CONFRONTATION APPROACH   Often it is necessary to use the media of technology to meet specific administrative goals related to instruction. The operational strategy for the Self-Confrontation Approach is to display student- or teacher-skill performance for individual self-criticism or collective group analysis.

THE PEOPLE-EXTENDER APPROACH   It is often desired, when media are used to reach learners in a widely dispersed geographic area, to extend the influence of people to all individuals in the total population. An example of this approach is most readily apparent in the recording and dissemination of talks by resource people who cannot visit every school in the system. However, it also includes the use of media to extend administrative and supervisory personnel by bringing teachers' meetings and so forth to the people in the schools rather than bringing all the people of the schools to the teachers' meetings.

Objectives

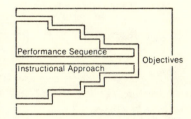

Performance Sequence
Objectives
Instructional Approach

For each anticipated response, a specific objective must be written that will show evidence of progress toward a goal or to show evidence that the goal has been reached.

FRAME OF REFERENCE FOR FORMULATING OBJECTIVES

This design function should begin from the frame of reference established by acknowledging any restraints imposed on writing a specific objective for all levels in the sequence of performance leading to the goal.

Restraints to design may be imposed by using existing behavioral objectives which do not relate to a specific approach or are not sequenced in a hierarchy to reach a goal.

It may also be determined that empirical evidence, set against some internal criteria of acceptance, will be required to show that learning has occurred. Hopefully the response stated in the objective would be universally recognized as evidence of learning. This restraint can be seen more in affective instruction where some overt indicators of the more covert attitudes must be accepted as evidence of learning. However, this restraint is common to other kinds of learning too. The ability to translate a paragraph of Balzac—established as the criterion of success by a curriculum committee—may not be universally accepted as fluency in French. However, if this restriction is placed on design, it should be considered in establishing the frame of reference from which this design function can begin.

Objectives for Instruction

The designer is obligated to look at the total learning process from the learner's point of view and not only at the design of instruction for mediation. Moreover, all areas and levels of learning must be assessed against the expectations of the community of what should happen in school. In over a decade, traditional uses of instructional media have rarely been asked to be accountable. Therefore, vague objectives to supplement and enrich an educational system have been relegated to these media. This system itself has not been held accountable for specific learner performance. In the blind rush to innovate by insisting that behavioral objectives

147

be written for all instruction (whether mediated by the classroom teacher, or electronically by radio or television) there has resulted only an abundance of highly specific yet trivial performance expectations stated by teachers, and by instructional technologists as well.

In discussing "Instructional Objectives in the Affective Domain" for the January 1970 issue of *Educational Technology*, Mary B. Harbeck cautions that the use of performance objectives, stated in terms of specific behavioral responses, does provide a measuring device for assessing effectiveness. This practice does not guarantee that the quantity and the quality of instruction will improve. Many teachers, according to Harbeck, who are currently learning to write and use performance objectives, have difficulty in choosing worthwhile goals toward which to work. Much has been written about the "trivial" nature of performance objectives. It is easy to distort unconsciously the concept while trying only to state it more specifically (Harbeck, 1970).

What should result in instructional design are objectives that guide the display of stimuli for a measurable result. If the learner fails to achieve the objective, then the instruction needs to be revised to make it more effective.

An individual is more likely to *respond* to instruction in which he is an active participant in learning. He is more likely to *react* to an educational sequence in which he is a passive receptor of teaching. Responding implies performance of a predetermined nature. Reacting implies achievement of a random nature. If the designer is to be held accountable for effective and efficient instruction, it is essential to be concerned more with measurable responses.

Objectives must be written to show achievement only of what was attempted in design. They must be stated in a form that will allow objectivity in applying them to design and testing the results of instruction.

Types of Objectives

In his foreword to Robert F. Mager's book, *Preparing Instructional Objectives*, John P. Gilpin specified that educational units, whether large or small, should be prepared in response to these questions: "What is it that we must teach?" "How will we know when we have taught it?" and "What materials and procedures will work best to teach what we wish to teach?" These questions can form a criterion to illustrate the more conventional types of objectives (Gilpin in Mager, 1962).

Academic Objectives

In more conventional approaches to instruction found in educational systems, the basic types of academic objectives can be classified in three general categories: Content Objectives, Means Objectives, and Behavioral Objectives.

CONTENT OBJECTIVES   Content Objectives use only part of Gilpin's structural criterion and ask simply, "What is it that we must teach?" These objectives can be assessed on a measured amount of teacher output. Often these Content Objectives are stated in such a way that no learners need to be present to achieve the desired outcome. For instance, the objective may be stated to expect that the teacher "cover the period between the American Revolution and the Civil War." This could very well (perhaps even most efficiently) be done by the teacher in complete isolation from any student.

MEANS OBJECTIVE   Means Objectives ask not only, "What is it that must be taught?" but add also, "What material and procedures will work best to teach what must be taught?" Means Objectives are most often expressed by those caught up in the "audiovisual mystique." They can be assessed by a measured amount of output assisted by teaching aids. Means Objectives such as "To show the film, *Territorial Possessions of the United States*," are pointed to with a great pride of accomplishment by the active audiovisual director who assumes that the film was shown to students even though it was not specified in the objective. Even assessment procedures that would ask, "Did the pupils like the moving pictures?" are beyond the testing obligation for that Means Objective.

BEHAVIORAL OBJECTIVES   Behavioral Objectives add the criterion of measurement, "How will we know when it has been taught?" It is with the addition of this element that the Behavioral Objectives are written to show evidence of some sort of planned achievement of a predetermined content presentation assisted by the proper media and methods. But formulating teaching from Behavioral Objectives also assumes the presence of a learner. This then alters the structural criteria of the educational unit beyond the framework suggested by Gilpin.

Operational Objectives

It cannot always be assumed that teaching is synonymous with learning. To design instruction relevant to the individual and to the environment in which he learns, it is necessary to prepare learning experiences (rather than teaching units) in response to the questions: "What is it that we want the individual to *learn?*" "How will we know when he has *learned* it?" What materials and procedures will work best to create conditions in which *learning* can occur?" It is also necessary then to relate more directly to the learner's needs by asking, "*Why* must it be learned?" From this revised criterion, operational objectives for instructional design can be formulated.

In this design that allows for a divergence of approach, it is necessary to formulate distinct objectives that will give evidence of performance in whatever approach is taken to instruction. Thus, objectives must not only be written for all levels of anticipated responses of the target population after exposure to instruction, but each approach to instruction requires the statement of objectives from a different point of view.

In any approach, the objectives should state precisely what should happen when the goal is reached or when progress toward the goal is being made.

LEARNING OBJECTIVES   Objectives in the Direct Experience Approach must specify an individual's response to show specific learning gains. Objectives for this approach must, therefore, be written to show the effectiveness of instruction mediated for the individual as direct learning experiences.

An objective for the Direct Experience Approach to instruction would be stated so that a specific learner response to the mediated experience could be measured or observed directly to see if instruction was adequate for the desired level of learner performance. For example, it may be expected that as a direct result of viewing a television lesson, the learner recall specific facts about the causes of the Civil War. It would be inappropirate to state an objective that would guide instruction to be used also by the classroom teacher as a course of study or to demonstrate good teaching procedures. While this may happen, it is not the primary intent of instruction and thus should not be reflected in the statement of the objective.

Objectives for the Direct Experience Approach must be written for evidence of the effectiveness of the mediated instruction in reaching the learner directly. In this example, the rationale of the objective can be given to the learner to let him know in advance what is expected of him and why.

TESTING CONDITIONS	When given a visual illustration as a recall cue.
RESPONSE	The learner will write from memory a descriptive sentence about the marketing principle for farm management illustrated in each step of the flow of an agricultural commodity from product planting to consumer purchase.
CONDITIONS FOR THE LEARNER	After the flow of an agricultural commodity from product planting to consumer purchase is shown and identified for him in a mediated segment that compresses time and space,
CRITERIA	descriptions may be in the learner's own words. All steps should be described in terms of their relationship to the sequence, and two-thirds of the steps should contain the learner's view of their accepted implication to farm management.
RATIONALE	What happens in agricultural marketing is important to the way you will manage a farm. We will show you what happens to several farm products from the time they are planted to the time they are brought in a store. After you have seen this sequence of events, we will ask you to state in your own words the importance of what happens at each step in the process.

TEACHING OBJECTIVES   Objectives in the Course of Study Guidelines Approach must specify how the learner will respond to what the classroom teacher does to show evidence of how the mediated instruction has given direction to a course of study to increase teaching effectiveness. Objectives for teaching must, therefore, be written for evidence on how effective the mediated course of study guidelines were to change what the teacher does to reach the learner.

For the Course of Study Guidelines Approach, an objective would be stated so that the teacher's use of the mediated course of study could be assessed. The response of the students, as a result of the modified teaching structure, would indicate if instruction were adequate to increase teaching effectiveness for the desired level of learner performance. For example, the current classroom procedures may not have adequately structured a course of study in local history. Increased student participation in local government as a result of new instruction given by the classroom teacher might then be accepted as evidence of increased teaching effectiveness as the result of using the mediated guidelines.

In stating the objectives, the instructional intervention of the classroom teacher should be recognized. The statement should not seek to give direction for the design of instruction that could circumvent the classroom teaching structure. Ojbectives should be written to guide instruction that will effect change in the individual because of what the classroom teacher would be helped to do in conventional instruction.

Objectives for the Course of Study Guidelines Approach must be written to show the effectiveness of the mediated instruction in giving direction to a course of study for classroom teaching. In this example, the rationale of the objective can be given to the classroom teacher for advance information about what is expected and why.

TESTING CONDITIONS	When asked to follow mediated guidelines to get a predetermined learner response,
RESPONSE	the classroom teacher will follow the mediated information describing the Nebraska Unicameral Legislature to structure a situation in the classroom so learners will describe the basic differences between this one-house system and the two-house system used in all other states;
CONDITIONS FOR THE TEACHER	after the scope and sequence for teaching this unit has been given to the teacher in a mediated form,
CONDITIONS FOR THE LEARNER	and the process by which a bill becomes a law has been illustrated through the processes of both types of legislatures.
CRITERIA	The teachers will use the guidelines as suggested if they had none to follow before, so their learners will describe from memory at least three differences in the processes in a unicameral legislature.

RATIONALE	Because nothing now exists to help you implement the required course of study in Nebraska History, guidelines will be developed for you to follow. By following these guidelines, you should be able to structure your teaching to present whatever comparative information is necessary for your students to achieve the objective that states, "The learner will describe the basic differences between Nebraska's Unicameral Legislature and the two-house system used in all other states."

SUPPLEMENTING OBJECTIVES   Objectives for the Supplemental Material Approach must specify how the learner will respond to what the classroom teacher uses to show evidence of how the mediated instruction has provided material for an established course of study. Objectives for the Supplemental Material Approach must, therefore, be written for evidence on how effective the mediated material was to change what the teacher uses to reach the learner.

An objective for the Supplemental Material Approach to instruction would be stated in terms of the expected use of the mediated material by the classroom teacher. The ultimate responsibility is one step farther removed from the response of the learner. Here, the concern is how the teacher uses material in the instructional process of an established course of study to get the response from the learner. Objectives should not be stated to expect to measure a direct learner response because of all the variables of teacher use and course of study structure that intervene between the mediated instruction and the actual confrontation between the material and the learner. Although seemingly couched in ambiguity, objectives could be stated in such a way as to specify that if the learner were exposed to this material, *in its proper use in the instructional process*, he most likely would respond in this way.

Objectives for the Supplemental Material Appraoch must be written to show the effectiveness of mediated instruction in providing material to be used with an established course of study. In this example, the rationale of the objective can be given to the classroom teacher to inform in advance what is expected and why.

TESTING CONDITIONS	When asked to use mediated material in an established course of study for a predetermined learner response,
RESPONSE	the classroom teacher will include this mediated material in the scope and sequence of a science course so the learner will make inferences about the specific gravity of various liquids,
CONDITIONS FOR THE TEACHER	after a demonstration related to the established science curriculum has been given in a mediated form for the learner to

CONDITIONS FOR THE LEARNER	observe objects of the same weight and size descend at varying rates in containers of different liquids.
CRITERION	The mediated demonstration will be used by teachers to allow access by their students as frequently as needed for the student to infer that the rates by which the objects descend is a function of the specific gravity of the liquid, not of the object.
RATIONALE	Observing the experiment where objects of the same weight and size descend at varying rates in containers of different liquids is necessary for your students to make inferences about the specific gravity of various liquids in your Inquiry Approach to Science. Since we do not expect you to build this demonstration yourself, and since we know very few of the devices are available in the system for you to use when you want it, we will make a film loop of it available to you to use on the classroom projector you do have. In this way, you should be able to use the material in your teaching to achieve the learner objective that states, "The learner will make inferences about the specific gravity of various liquids after repeated observation of the demonstration in which objects of the same weight and size descend at varying rates in containers of different liquids."

COMPLEMENTING OBJECTIVES   Objectives in the Enriched Resources Approach must specify how the learner will respond indirectly to the instruction to show evidence of how the mediated instruction has complemented the total educational program of the learner. Objectives for the Enriched Resources Approach must, therefore, be written for evidence on whether or not the mediated instruction indirectly influenced the conditions of the learner to enable him to respond.

An objective for the Enriched Resources Approach to instruction is perhaps the most difficult to state in precise response terms because design responsibilities are so far removed from directly effecting a change in the individual. It is possible to state an objective that will guide instruction so that it would be possible to observe an individual's use of mediated resources. However, any actual behavioral change may result from the impingement of many other factors. It is possible to observe a change in the actual learning environment as a result of instruction in the Enriched Resources Approach. What may have to be assumed by empirical judgment is that these changes contribute in some way to the desired learning.

Objectives for the Enriched Resources Approach must be written to show the effectiveness of the mediated instruction in complementing the total educational program. In this example, the rationale of the objective can be given to the classroom teacher to inform in advance what is expected and why. In the Enriched Resources Approach, however, objectives can also be written for the individual learner as well as the classroom teacher.

TESTING CONDITIONS	When resources are stored for retrieval access by students or their teacher and used so
RESPONSE	the educational program will be expanded to include mediated resources in classical music for learners to seek out classical compositions to compare with current popular tunes,
CONDITIONS FOR THE TEACHER	after learners have been motivated in the conventional instructional program and have been made aware that these mediated resources exist,
CONDITIONS FOR THE LEARNER	and the resources illustrate enough classical music from which the rhythms and melodies of many popular tunes have been adapted.
CRITERIA	The teachers should allow learners to seek out these resources to make proper comparisons on their own initiative.
RATIONALE	Creating situations in your classroom for today's students to appreciate fine music can be difficult, at best, with the limited experiences your students have had with the classics. Your students may be expected to respond to instruction to achieve an objective in which it is stated: "The learner will actively seek your classical music compositions and draw proper comparisons with popular tunes." To provide a common base of experiences for all of your students from which you can work toward achieving this objective, we will provide your school with these classics for you to use in your own classroom situation, or encourage students to use on their own.

The basic format for objectives should follow what has become the traditional "Magerian Form." That is, the form of an objective, suggested by Robert F. Mager, should always include a response component, a conditions component, and a criteria component. To his "Magerian Form" has been added the component of a rationale. It may also be desired to add the component of the criterion test item to the statement of objective itself at this point. However, for these design procedures, testing will be considered as a distinctly separate function (see page 215).

Response Component

Mager has defined *response* as that terminal act expected of the individual to evidence learning (Mager, 1962).

Thus, it must be determined what specific response will be accepted as evidence of the achievement of the objective. The response is derived from the performance characteristics described at the level in the learning domain at which the objective is written.

NATURE OF RESPONSE Responses may be active, clearly demonstrable or they may assume a more passive nature more easily inferred than demonstrated. For example, in the statement of the instructional goal, it might be expected that the learner be interested in all functions. For the response at this level, it might be expected that the learner, when presented with several alternatives, may indicate a policeman as one choice of those who could be of help to him if he were lost. An active response of selecting a policeman from among other choices in prepared material might be indicated in the objective to demonstrate cognitive learning. The learner, for instance, might be expected to select the policeman from a series of photographs.

However, evidence of the affective, secondary goal may be shown by a more passive response. Interest in the nonenforcement functions of a policeman may have to be inferred to show evidence of the learner's disposition to want to notice these nonenforcement functions. Or, some sort of overt indicators of the more covert attitude would have to be determined. For instance, what kind of visible response would indicate that the learner was interested in the functions of policemen? Or, what active indicators can be seen to satisfy the requirements of a more passive disposition in the learner?

OCCURRENCE OF RESPONSE Responses may occur during or immediately after exposure to instruction. They may also be delayed for days, even weeks, after instruction. For example, if the learner is expected to indicate, from a series of photographs, a policeman as one person who could help him if he were lost, the photographs could be provided for an immediate response directly after instruction. On the other hand, the learner may be expected to notice and identify nonenforcement functions of an actual policeman in a real situation. Then the response must obviously be delayed until the individual is confronted with a policeman engaged in nonenforcement activities in the community.

STATEMENT OF THE RESPONSE COMPONENT The objective must state what response is desired in verifiable terms. The response component defines desired individual or environmental changes. The indications of the response must be stated, using carefully selected terms that enable it to be demonstrated or inferred. The key element in this component is the selection of active verbs that describe visible actions. The learner, for example, might be asked to list, state, identify, summarize, solve, classify, prepare, evaluate, etc. Each of these may indicate a different level of response in the hierarchy of learning used to reach the goal.

This response verb must be so specific and so demonstrable, that there is no room at all for individual interpretation, if all conditions are known. Ambiguous verbs such as "construct" should be avoided. In psychomotor sequences, "construct" may indicate a clearly visible response. But, what would the learner do when he is expected to "construct" the steps of agri-cultural food production at the synthesis level of cognitive learning? Verbs such as "understand," "appreciate," and "like" should be avoided at all costs.

Quite often objectives will be written for a response that would indicate that "the learner will be able to list five causes of the Civil War." Just be-cause the learner *is able to* make this list doesn't mean that he *will*. At any given point in time, anyone is able to jump through a glass in a window—but they don't. What the learner *is able to* do is not as easily observed as what he *actually does*. It is highly recommended in stating *all* objectives to avoid using the phrase, "is able to." When writing the very specific cri-terion objectives, the deletion of this phrase is required. Criterion tests, by definition, must *measure* every response. The studied use of the phrase in the more general terminal objectives may be permitted—if it is understood that all the responses the learner "is able to" perform could actually be demonstrated if desired. This point is somewhat belabored here to stress the importance of being quite specific about what is expected of the learner. While it has been said in these design procedures that the response is not necessary for learning to occur, if the response can't be seen or measured, no one is ever going to know if learning has occurred.

Conditions Component

According to Mager, the objective will be further clarified by stating the *conditions* that will be imposed on the learner when he is demonstrating his mastery of the performance described in the objective. The objective will be more specific if it describes the situation (givens, allowances, restric-tions) under which the learner will be expected to demonstrate performance (Mager, 1962).

TESTING CONDITIONS   Because of the nature of the learner, his environment, or the material to be learned, certain restrictions may be in-herent in the situations under which the response is expected to occur. For example, the learner will only observe nonenforcement functions of the policeman where there is a policeman engaged in nonenforcement func-tions for the learner to observe. In a similar manner, unless the classroom teacher can create conditions to allow the learner to report nonenforce-ment functions of the policeman (other than those he has been exposed to in instruction), the affective response indicating a disposition to be inter-ested in policemen cannot be inferred.

CONDITIONS OF THE LEARNER   It may also be necessary to limit the conditions under which the response will be expected to occur by formulating such conditions as a part of the objective. One of the key structured conditions will reflect the approach to instruction used in de-sign. In the Direct Experience Approach, this conditions component can state that the mediated instruction is presented directly to the learner without other instructional intervention. However, for the Course of Study Guidelines Approach, not only must it be stated what the situation will be in which the learner will respond, it also has to be stated what the situation will be in which the mediated guidelines will be followed.

Similarly, in the Supplemental Material Approach, the conditions must state what is the situation in which the material will be used as well as the situation in which the learner will respond. This would also be true in stating the conditions for an objective written for the Enriched Resources Approach. Here, not only is it necessary to define the situation in which the learner will respond, but also the situation in which the resources will be used before the learner can respond.

It may also be necessary to build in restrictions in order to minimize variables or to control the situation under which the response will be made. For example, if the learner is expected to indicate from a series of photographs a policeman as a person who might help him if he were lost, it may be necessary (or desired) to specify what the other choices in the photographs should be. For instance, it may be desired to structure restrictions by specifying that the individual will respond as expected when presented with several photographs, some of which are obviously correct choices of assistance (which would include the policeman), and others that are doubtful choices. What would be looked for is his selection of the preferred choice—the policeman—not his rejection of the other alternatives.

STATEMENT OF THE CONDITIONS COMPONENT The conditions decided on must be stated in the objective. Conditions can be stated in relation to educational outcomes, external or environmental factors, inputs or operational contexts, and management factors. They may be expressed as operative limits, constraints or specifications that must be managed, met or maintained. Characteristics of this component of an objective is the selection of word or phrase modifiers that clarify or limit the action to be taken. The conditions component also serves to assure reliable interpretation of intent by elaborating on the characteristics of the relevant or critical response factors. For example, the key modifying phrase most often stated (and more often implied) in the design of mediated instruction is, of course, "After exposure to the mediated instructional experience. . . ." This must then be followed by other conditional modifiers such as, ". . . and given a series of nine photographs that depict. . . ."

Criteria Component

In the statement of objectives, written according to Mager's formula, the acceptable performance must be indicated by describing the *criterion of success*. By stating at least the minimum acceptable performance for each objective, there will be a standard against which to test the effectiveness of instruction (Mager, 1962).

The minimum level of performance that will be accepted as evidence of learning tells how well it is expected that the learner perform to reach the level in the learning hierarchy at which the objective is written.

ABSOLUTE CRITERIA   Absolute criteria of acceptable performance define prespecified standards against which the individual's response can be measured. Ideally, of course, the aim is to have all learners achieve all objectives. Since this is not realistically possible in all situations, some compromise standards are necessary. For example, it may be expected that the learner will achieve six out of ten stated objectives to evidence acceptable learning. But, three objectives critical to actual performance in a real situation must be among the six.

In achieving individual objectives, an absolute criteria of acceptable performance may also be given. For example, it may be determined arbitrarily that the learner who can answer 60 out of 100 problems in simple subtraction would have shown evidence of acceptable learning of the concept taught. Any absolute standard should reflect variances of student mood, attitude and environmental conditions in actually responding to instruction. Thus, the 100-percent achievement is desired but not realistic.

RELATIVE CRITERIA   Relative criteria of acceptable performance specify performance expectations of the learner as measured against the performance of other learners or of student norms. For example, it might be expected that the learner score at least in the third quartile of national norms on the *California Achievement Tests*. Or, it might be expected that after instruction, the learner increase his Reading Comprehension score on the *Iowa Tests of Basic Skills* by at least 2.8 grade equivalents in two years.

STATEMENT OF THE CRITERIA COMPONENT   The objectives must contain a criterion statement that defines standards used to verify incremental progress toward the achievement of the specified outcomes. For example, when presented with several alternatives, the learner may be expected to indicate a policeman as one choice of those who could be of help to him if he were lost. The learner might then be given a sheet containing pictures of several people and asked to draw a circle around those who could help him. The criteria of success could then be established by stating that the policeman would be selected from photographs six out of eight times the learner was given the opportunity to respond.

All statements of objectives *must* contain a statement of absolute criteria and they *may* contain a statement of relative criteria.

Rationale Component

The objective must also contain a statement of rationale that justifies and personalizes the desired behavioral outcome, communicates the intent of the organized design effort, provides an incentive for involvement and encourages the learner to participate toward the achievement of the specified outcome. This component places the objective in the frame of learner reference.

STATEMENT OF RATIONALE COMPONENT   The conventional statement of objectives clarifies what the learner is being asked to do, but does not necessarily provide any clues as to why he should do it. The rationale for instruction is an objective, for example, may contain a statement of justification such as this: "Many children from low-income neighborhoods have already formed negative attitudes toward the law in general and police in particular. Even the child from a law-abiding family hears and sees enough in his neighborhood to know that a policeman usually means trouble. Hence, if the child ever found himself in a situation in which he needed to seek assistance from someone, a policeman would not be an immediate choice. Therefore, it is necessary for the child to know a policeman does other things than to arrest people and is one of those persons to whom he can turn if lost."

Structure

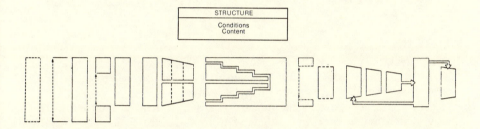

STRUCTURE
Conditions
Content

Each objective is looked at individually to develop a structure for the experience that is compatible with the approach and the sequence selected.

A structural framework is necessary for the display of symbols or experiences as stimuli in instruction. This structural framework is determined by starting with the terminal conditions that describe where to end instruction—what the target population is expected to be like when the objective has been achieved. Then the entry conditions are identified to tell where to begin instruction. These conditions are implied in the objective that tell what the target population has been exposed to in instruction to make him as he is. The enabling conditions can then be identified by what has to be done to enable the learner to respond. By thus identifying only the essential content, this structural framework prevents instruction from being overloaded by attempting to do too much in the time available.

Structure

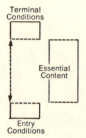

Terminal Conditions

Essential Content

Entry Conditions

Implied in each objective are entry conditions that tell where to begin instruction. Where to end instruction is described by what the terminal conditions should be like when the objective is achieved. The essential content necessary to achieve that objective is then described by those conditions that will enable the learner to make the response.

FRAME OF REFERENCE FOR THE STRUCTURE OF INSTRUCTION

This design function should begin from the frame of reference established by acknowledging any restraints imposed on selecting only the content essential to achieve each of the objectives written.

Restraints to design may be imposed that would restrict instruction from being structured so that the content would be selected to include only that essential to elicit the desired response. Often, other related but not essential content may be desirable in the learning experience, and design must, therefore, begin from that frame of reference. For example, it may be desired that the learner recall all functions of a policeman when he has been exposed to law officers only in arrest and enforcement situations. Requirements including descriptions of the paraphenalia appended to the uniform may be nice for a small child to know but would probably not help him respond as expected.

Structural Design Conditions

The instructional experience should be structured to achieve the stated objective by modifying the conditions that now exist to approximate those that are expected to exist. In a very real sense, the structural framework requires the response conditions in the sequence of instruction now to be combined with the instructional conditions in the approach to instruction to tell what to include as essential content for the desired response to occur.

TERMINAL CONDITIONS   The terminal conditions describe where instruction should end in the segment being designed. These are the conditions, described in the objective, that should exist after the response has been made.

For example, in the objective it may be expected that the learner will distinguish between the many functions of a policeman and those specifically familiar to the child of arrest and enforcement. The terminal conditions would describe the entire set of instructional situations and responses that should exist after instruction.

The statement of terminal conditions may not vary too much from the statement of objectives. The terminal conditions for the objective illustrated above might describe that this discrimination between various functions of policemen could be made in simulated conditions in the classroom (rather than on the streets where such functions would actually be observed). The learner could be given lists or descriptions from which he should make the distinctions. Or, the learner could be asked to describe in his own words these functions (depending on the level at which the goal has been set and for which the objective has been written).

ENTRY CONDITIONS   The entry conditions describe where to begin instruction. These are the conditions that now exist in the learner and in his environment to get the desired response. More often than not, the entry conditions are described in the instructional classification of the goal.

For example, if it has been assumed (or it has been determined) that the learner is now familiar with policemen only in arrest and enforcement activities, and he has never been made aware of other less authoritarian functions, a baseline has been established from which instruction can then be designed. Other factors of what the learner brings with him to the instructional experience may also help establish the entry conditions for design. It might have to be known whether the learner can define terms, or whether he has the appropriate mind-set or attitude even to try to describe other police functions for him to retain the information.

ENABLING CONDITIONS   The enabling conditions describe what is essential to include as content in the mediated experience. The enabling conditions will tell how the specific approach selected should be structured to create the terminal conditions from the existing entry conditions.

For example, the terminal conditions may be described by how the learner should discriminate functions of policemen. It has been determined the learner has been exposed to policemen in arrest and enforcement situations (but is disposed to know more about policemen). The enabling conditions should then give additional exposure for the learner to nonenforcement functions of policemen. This should then result in increasing his knowledge from the sole concern with arrest functions to the expected discrimination of other functions as well. These other functions would have to be shown, described and illustrated so the learner can recognize and recall them when asked.

That content *essential* to reach the terminal conditions from the existing entry conditions must be included. The experience *may* contain other content elements, if they do not detract from the essential content and relate to or reinforce the learned experience. It would not help, in this case, to show the learner that some policemen walk beats while others patrol in squad cars or on motorcycles. It would also not help achieve the objective most efficiently to dwell on enforcement functions with which the child is already familiar and which are a part of his learned competencies identified in his entry level.

If these nonessential elements are included, it must be recognized immediately that they are there for less specific informational, enrichment or entertainment functions and are *not* part of the instruction that will be tested. They may even be irrelevant stimuli that could work against the achievement of the objective. If too many of these nonessential elements compete against the essential content, the learner may be confused about what he is expected to learn.

Actual attempts to modify the existing conditions to those described as the terminal conditions will be distinctively different for each approach to instruction used in design. To use these procedures in an actual design effort, only the conditions described for the approach selected in design should be followed.

Structure for the Direct Experience Approach

Where it is possible to reach the learner directly with mediated instruction, direct learning experiences can be structured to achieve the objective.

STRUCTURE OF APPROACH TO GIVE PREREQUISITE LEARNING EXPERIENCES   Direct experiences can be structured to achieve an objective in which it is specified that the learner will have adequate initial exposure to instruction for learning experiences that are prerequisite to a planned sequence of instruction. The rationale for instruction may, for example, indicate "principles of agricultural marketing are essential to farm management for the target population in a largely rural area." The objective would be written then for initial exposure to the concept of marketing for an understanding of the interrelationships between the market and the farmer. This objective might state that, "Given a specific agricultural product, the learner will trace its history from planting to consumer purchase."

The terminal conditions described in the objective illustrated here, for example, would expect the learner would have either written or told about all of the steps some agricultural product has to go through before it is finally purchased by someone in a store. It is assumed this will prepare the learner for a larger unit of instruction in which he would be expected to apply agricultural economics on his own farm.

It is known or assumed the learner has no previous information that would relate all marketing problems to agricultural production. The entry conditions would then identify how familiar the learner is now with most of the elements in isolation from an interrelated function. It might also be assumed that the learner associates farm management with conservation, not product marketing. Thus he has not been exposed to this concept in his formal instruction.

It might be helpful, though, if the learner could define the terms associated with agricultural marketing. These factors may have to be assumed as the level of readiness for the initial exposure to the concept of farm management. However, they most likely are not in the present performance capabilities of the learner and might have to be included in the instruction designed.

The enabling conditions determine what is required to be included in instruction for the prerequisite content information. It is either assumed or determined by measurement that the learner has not been exposed to the chain of events in marketing an agricultural product. The content would then be structured to sequence this chain of events in an order and manner to so familiarize the learner with the total sequence, that he will recall and interpret the events in his own words. Information about contour plowing or the merits of organic versus inorganic fertilizers would *not* be essential to include as content to develop this concept of farm management. While they might be nice to include, they should not be thought of as helping the learner achieve the objective.

STRUCTURE OF APPROACH TO DEVELOP EXPOSITORY LEARNING EXPERIENCES

Direct experiences can be structured to achieve an objective in which it is specified that the learner will have appropriate additional exposure to instruction for learning experiences that are continuous in a planned sequence. The rationale for instruction may, for example, indicate that immediate and automatic recognition of number value from written numerals is necessary before the learner can perform elementary computational tasks. Then, in the objective for additional exposure to number concepts (to build on his known ability to recognize written numbers) it would be expected that the learner translate written forms to number values. This objective might be stated: "Given a list with ten printed numbers and ten quantities of various objects, the learner will correctly match the number with the illustration containing that amount of objects."

In the terminal conditions described in the objective, it would be expected that the learner will directly respond to additional exposure to content with which he is already somewhat familiar. The learner, for example, would be expected at least to have matched the written number with print representations of objects in that quantity. He is *not* expected to count out actual objects in the amount of a printed number shown to him, only to match the predetermined quantities he sees in a print form.

The entry conditions exist in the extent to which the learner has now reached some level of learned competencies by previous exposure to the content. Before he can match the printed numbers with representations of objects, he must first recognize a printed number and distinguish that from an alphabetic symbol. He must also recognize objects pictured so that he can readily tell when more than one is shown. There may be other aspects of learning that the individual should display before he is ready for instruction that will guide him in associating quantity with numbers. The total range of entry conditions is not limited by the examples used here.

The enabling conditions determine what content will have to be presented as additional instructional experiences. It is known that the learner can identify numbers. It is also known that he can recognize objects. What has to be done in the mediated experience is to display something for the learner so he can see the relationship between the two. Eventually the learner may have to combine these groups of objects or number values in computational skills.

However, it is *not* required (or even desired) to include discrimination of the objects in this segment of instruction to enable the learner to achieve the stated objective. This selection of essential content appears so obvious that the procedures to structure the enabling conditions seem almost like an academic exercise. However, in going through this procedure it may be found that the entry conditions might restrict the display of objects to only those familiar to the individual in this specific target population, because the learner might become more interested in *what* these unfamiliar objects are than he would be in *how many* there are.

STRUCTURE OF APPROACH TO PRESENT TERMINAL LEARNING EXPERIENCES

Direct experiences can be structured to achieve an objective in which it is specified that the learner will have complete exposure to instruction for learning experiences that are autonomous and complete within themselves. The rationale for instruction may, for example, indicate that "because children are often outside playing during the early summer months, communication with them about potentially dangerous weather conditions is not always possible through mass media. Therefore, it is important that they recognize these conditions." Thus, the objective for complete exposure to instruction about weather conditions for the learner to identify those that may be potentially dangerous might be stated: "While observing film of various weather conditions, the learner will indicate all of those that would most likely indicate possible tornado conditions."

The terminal conditions are described in the objective where it is expected that the individual directly respond to complete exposure to the content without any other instructional intervention. The terminal conditions for the objective illustrated here would expect the learner to have identified motion pictures of impending tornado conditions. He is not asked to tell what to do in a tornado. He is simply asked to recognize the weather conditions on the film that would indicate the possibility of a tornado.

For the entry conditions for complete exposure to the content, it must be determined if the learner is ready, in other intellectual and instructional development, to receive this instruction without spending a lot of time defining terms he already knows in other contexts. In the example used here, the entry conditions would start with the identification of all of the visual components of an impending tornado. It would then have to be determined if the learner has looked at weather enough to be aware of changing conditions and also if he is able to recognize motion pictures of conditions and also if he is able to recognize motion pictures of conditions that he might be familiar with in a real life situation in nature. Then, it must be determined how many of these visual components he can now recognize in this context. The rest become a part of instruction.

The enabling conditions require that all essential content elements that the learner does not now have a command of, be included. For example, it may be determined that tornados more frequently occur along the leading edge of a rapidly moving cold front. The *essential* elements to be included as enabling conditions would not be an explanation of frontal movements. It would describe how these fronts actually appear in nature. Recognition of the leading edge of stratus and cumulonimbus cloud formations would be of more essential value than would recognition of the configuration used to indicate this front on a weather map. On the other hand, one sure sign of an impending tornado is a funnel cloud. It is highly unlikely that an individual in a target population, influenced by mass media, would not be familiar with the sight of an actual funnel cloud. The question then, would be how essential is this aspect—already familiar to the learner in his entry behavior—to treat in instruction?

Structure for the Course of Study Guidelines Approach

If it is not possible to reach the learner directly with mediated instruction, and there is no established course of study in the content area, it may be desired to structure guidelines that will facilitate teaching for a learner response.

To design guidelines to facilitate teaching, the terminal conditions are expressed in terms of what is required to increase teaching effectiveness to get learner responses.

Facilitating a new, prescribed or existing course of study for increased teaching effectiveness will require the knowledge, for the entry conditions, of how well the current classroom teaching structures are now used.

The selection of elements to facilitate a teaching structure as the enabling conditions will be based on the difference between the specific increase in teaching effectiveness expected with the mediated guidelines and the known or assumed effectiveness now realized with existing structures.

STRUCTURE OF APPROACH TO IMPLEMENT IMPOSED GUIDE-LINES   A mediated course of study can be structured so the learner will respond to the use of a required teaching structure which augments a course of study imposed by some administrative agency. A sample rationale for this approach to instruction is that state law requires teaching of state history to every student before he can graduate. Thus, teachers must follow the guidelines in Nebraska History imposed by the State Department of Education. The objective for a specific segment to help augment these prescribed guidelines might be stated: "After having been presented with comparative information by the classroom teacher who has been guided by mediated guidelines in the prescribed course of study, the student will describe the basic differences between Nebraska's Unicameral Legislature and the two-house system used in all other states."

In the illustration used above, the terminal conditions would include the use of mediated guidelines by the classroom teacher to structure the pattern of teaching so that the students could discriminate between two-house legislatures and Nebraska's Unicameral system.

The entry conditions for this way to approach instruction exist in how well the classroom teaching structure can now follow the imposed course of study. For example, many state guidelines are so couched in ambiguity and generalities that they give very little pragmatic direction to the scope and sequence for the classroom teacher. If a study of Nebraska History is prescribed, and guidelines do exist, the starting point to augment a pre-scribed, and guidelines do exist, the starting point to augment a prescribed course of study would be the extent to which the current guidelines are effective in directing patterns of teaching.

Thus, from the broad statement of intent about the study of Nebraska History, the enabling conditions can build from the teacher's current use of those state-imposed guidelines and relate a structured scope and sequence not only to the instructional needs for which the course of study exists, but also to the learner needs to make this field of study relevant to the individual.

STRUCTURE OF APPROACH TO REINFORCE EXISTING GUIDE-LINES

A course of study can be structured to achieve an objective in which it is specified that a learner will respond to the use of a reinforced teaching structure to extend a course of study that now exists in other mediated forms. For example, it may be difficult for teachers to integrate contemporary aerospace education into an existing science course of study. Guidelines may touch upon contemporary aerospace aspects, but too often in cursory detail. Thus, an objective may specify that, "Upon receiving classroom instruction facilitated by a mediated structure to extend a course of study in science, the learner will explain in his own words how the sudden loss of capsule pressure in Russia's Soyuz 11 spacecraft could cause the death of the three cosmonauts."

A course of study may now exist in the textbook or in published system or state guidelines for the teacher to use. It can be expected from the statement of this objective that in the terminal conditions, the teacher be prepared to extend patterns of teaching to include contemporary events and developments which have occurred since the publication of the guidelines. These events may have changed or rendered inadequate the use of existing guidelines.

Classroom teachers might have difficulty in integrating the headlines of today into the scope and sequence of yesterday's course of study. How much help the teacher needs in extending an existing course of study with other elements will establish the starting point, or entry conditions, to extend and reinforce these established structures into greater content depth and for increased performance capabilities.

Based on the knowledge of what now exists in the science or aerospace course of study, those elements essential to achieve the expectations of relating the material to current space history will determine the structural components of the course of study guidelines to be mediated for use in extending an existing teaching structure.

STRUCTURE OF APPROACH TO CREATE NEW GUIDELINES

A mediated course of study can be structured to achieve an objective in which it is specified that the learner will respond to the teacher's use of a new structure that develops a course of study where one does not now exist. Based on the rationale that expected cognitive responses to initial exposure to instruction in sex education, teaching to this rationale may not be possible because of the lack of a course of study in the content area. The objective might be stated: "The learner will identify common contraceptive devices after class discussion in a teaching situation that has been created and is given direction by new mediated guidelines."

As can be seen in this example, just having the mediated guidelines will be of no benefit if the teacher does not use them to get a desired learner response. Hence, the full description of the terminal conditions would include the way it would be expected the teacher will have used the mediated guidelines to enable the students to make the desired response about common contraceptive devices.

In establishing a starting point in instruction for the development of a new set of course of study guidelines, it should be determined how much structure is really needed by the teachers. It may be known that no guidelines now exist for teaching in this content area, and little curriculum help is given in other media. Thus, the critical element for the entry conditions would appear to be how receptive to the new course of study the teacher is now to determine how much direction will have to be given.

The enabling conditions should describe a new teaching structure for the classroom teachers to use for the desired learner responses. This structure can be developed from the base of knowledge and organization about the content area teachers now have and use in the conventional instruction. A course of study that can be used to lead toward the desired response (concerning types of contraceptives, for example, as a part of the larger sex education course of study) should so structure what the teacher does in the classroom that all students will respond to the teaching as expected.

Structure for the Supplemental Material Approach

If it is not possible to reach the learner directly with a mediated instructional experience, and an adequate course of study does exist, it may be desirable to mediate material to supplement the instructional process for the teachers to use to get the desired learner response.

The extent of the teacher's use of material mediated in the Supplemental Material Approach will describe the terminal conditions expected for the anticipated growth in the instructional process.

Entry conditions are identified on the basis of the knowledge of what material is now used for learner responses in the instructional process.

For the enabling conditions, the selection of what mediated material will be used to implement a course of study can be based on the difference between the expected scope of the instructional process and the material existing that is used now for instruction.

STRUCTURE OF APPROACH TO MEDIATE INACCESSIBLE MATERIAL Mediated material can be structured to achieve an objective in which it is specified that the learner will respond when teachers are able to use material that has been made accessible to them. For example, to develop an appreciation of the democratic process in action, it may be necessary to have access to legislative procedures in enacting a bill into law.

The mediated material, then, would be the set of procedures and human reactions rather than some thing or object. The rationale for instruction might state that "Knowledge of the way a bill becomes law will give the learner a cognitive base upon which he can begin to build a system of values to demonstrate his appreciation of the democratic process." Then, in the objective, it might be stated: "The steps involved from the introduction of a legislative bill into its final enactment as law will be so demonstrated that the learner will recall from memory the injection of the human factors at each step in the required process."

In treating the legislative process in the structure of experiences to achieve the stated objective, it is necessary that the entire legislative process be shown. This would necessitate compressing time and space to show events that happen throughout the procedures. But the terminal conditions that should exist after instruction would be a situation in which material is available to show the whole legislative process in a manageable way.

The entry conditions in this way to approach instruction are defined by the real world resources which now exist but which because of their size, location, expense, etc., are not accessible to the classroom teacher for direct use in the instructional process. The open and public legislative procedures of enacting laws, for example, are there for the teacher to use if the teacher wants to take the time and expend the energy to spend several months on the Senate floor, in the committee rooms, and in the nooks and crannies where trade-offs are made. Although available, it is not really accessible for use in a formal instructional process. The legislative process is lengthy, involving several months at many different locations. It is next to impossible to have access to the entire process. Thus teachers are not able to use it as material for an instructional process.

In this case, for example, not only must this legislative process be mediated for the teacher to use as enabling conditions, but a dramatic vignette rather than a description is implied in order to show the human element. In mediating this material to make it more accessible for teachers to be able to use, it is also necessary to plan ways in production to compress time and space.

Also implied in the objective would be the description of the complete legislative process involved from the time a bill is introduced to the time it becomes law. However, in the objective, the entry point for the description of the process is the introduction of the bill into the legislature. Descriptions of *why* the bill is introduced may be nice to include (and may be inferred from descriptions of later steps) but to achieve this objective, the information is not essential in order to show evidence of the kind and level of learning stated.

STRUCTURE OF APPROACH TO TRANSLATE UNDESIRABLE MATERIAL

Mediated material can be structured to achieve an objective in which it is specified that the learner will respond when the teachers are willing to use and do use material that is made desirable. The instructional classification of the goal may indicate an instructional deficiency in material to detect sources of radiation in objects. Because this material is both expensive and potentially dangerous to the learners, teachers may not be willing to include it in the instructional process. Teachers might also be unwilling to expose themselves to radiation seven classes a day. Exposure to his material may be necessary, however, in an instructional experience to develop the knowledge of the use of radioisotope technology in medicine.

In the objective, then, it might be stated: "In order for the learner to demonstrate how radioactive tracers can be used to detect bone disease, the procedures and cautions in handling radioactive material must be described before actual use." In the rationale for this instruction it would be hoped that mediated material can not only reduce potential danger to the learner but can illustrate what might happen if something goes wrong.

In the terminal conditions, it will be expected that material be made desirable in such a way that teachers will be willing to use it to get expected learner response in the existing instructional process. For example, the terminal conditions for this objective would include a thorough demonstration of handling a radioactive substance so that the techniques as well as the potential danger were adequately shown in a mediated form, and so that teachers were then willing to use it in the instructional process.

The entry conditions are defined by the material that now exists for use in the instructional process but because of the fact that it may be inherently dangerous, frightening, offensive, etc., it is not desired by the classroom teacher for direct use with students. So, even if the radioisotope equipment may be in the classroom for later use in instruction, its use now may still not be desired because of some potential danger in the use of radioactive substance to the teacher and to the student.

The enabling conditions require the structure of a mediated instructional experience that translates existing material from its original form to be desirable for the teachers to be willing to use. Either by translating the use of radioactive material with the radioisotope equipment to a simulator, or by showing the real equipment's use in a film or videotape, it can be provided to the classroom teacher for use in the instructional process in a more desirable form.

STRUCTURE OF APPROACH TO DISPLAY UNAVAILABLE MATERIAL

Mediated material can be structured to achieve an objective in which it is specified that the learner will respond when teachers want to and do use material that is made available. It may be found, for example, that instruction requires the use of prepared apparatus to demonstrate the specific gravity of various liquids in an Inquiry Approach to science. The required demonstration may not be included in the instructional process because the material for the experiment is not available for direct use in the classroom; or, it may be found that the material is not available because teachers don't know how to prepare the demonstration.

In the rationale for this instruction then, it may be stated that "Before the learner can make inferences about the specific gravity of various liquids, he must have the opportunity to observe (as often as necessary) the demonstration where objects of the same weight descend at varying rates in containers of different liquids." The objective might then be stated: "In order for the learner to observe the phenomenon of the effect of specific gravity on solid objects, the demonstration (as mentioned above) must be readily available for the teacher to use in the instructional process."

While ultimately, for example, it is expected that the learner identify that the varied rates at which solid objects descend in liquids are functions of the specific gravity of those liquids. However, for this instructional experience, the terminal conditions would be limited to making this demonstration available for teachers to want to use in order to get the desired response. It is also implied in the objective that the material should be available for individualized and repeated use. This factor would provide a criterion element for the later selection of an appropriate medium for the instructional experience.

The entry conditions may describe that the material is difficult for the classroom teacher to obtain or use. It would be assumed, in the example given above, that exposure to this demonstration is required to move the learner through the instructional process. If the material is unavailable or impractical to use, the instructional process would be seriously impeded. Thus, the expected cognitive learning to the additional exposure to the content area may not be realized. This may also result in the eventual lack of prerequisite learning to advance the individual toward the ultimate intent of instruction in this school of thought in science.

Thus it would be required, in the enabling conditions, for example, to mediate the demonstration on specific gravity so that teachers will use it in the instructional process. The mediated demonstration should also be readily available for repeated use by the teacher for the students. It would *not* be appropriate to this approach or to this objective to go into detailed instructions on how to prepare this demonstration. It is not expected that either the teacher or the students do so. (If teachers *were* expected to replicate the experiment, the whole design concern would shift to the Direct Experience Approach where instruction would be treated as a complete learning experience for a target population of classroom science teachers.)

Structure for the Enriched Resources Approach

If it is not possible to reach the learner directly with mediated instruction and an adequate, well-supplemented instructional process in an established course of study now exists, it may be desired to mediate resources that will complement the educational program in which the learner can respond to instruction.

The terminal conditions for the design of resources in the Enriched Resources Approach will specify the extent to which it is desired that the educational program be complemented for fuller, more enriched learning opportunities.

Each of the ways of complementing learning opportunities in the educational program will require knowledge of how resources are now used. This will define the entry conditions for instructional design.

The selection of the resources to be mediated as the essential content to satisfy the enabling conditions will be based on the difference between the extent it is expected to give a more complete dimension to the educational program and the nature of the resources that are known (or assumed) to exist now in the educational program.

STRUCTURE OF APPROACH TO ENHANCE MOTIVATIONAL RESOURCES

Resources can be structured to achieve an objective in which it is specified that the learner will be better able to respond to instruction after exposure to resources that will enhance his motivation. For example, the instructional needs may suggest that all students recognize form and style in classical music so they will be more disposed to "appreciate fine music."

However, in the school, teachers must contend with a generation where music is a way of life and is not only heard but felt through that "electronic appendage to their left ear." Such a teacher is going to have problems introducing Beethoven, even wearing a "Schroeder" T-shirt to class. Thus, an objective to structure experiences to create motivation for classical form in music might be stated: "The learner will be exposed to enough classical music from which the rhythms and melodies of many popular tunes have been taken that he will actively seek out additional classical compositions to compare."

The terminal conditions are what is described in the objective that should happen to enhance the motivation of the learner. In this example, it is assumed that comparisons of familiar classical tunes used in popular music will create a positive approach tendency in the learner to seek out more classical music. It would *not* help to achieve this objective to show the learner a performance of "Jesus Christ, Superstar" and contrast its form with Wagnerian opera. This is not to say there is no place for this instructional experience, only to say that it is not the terminal condition that must be created as specified in *this* particular objective.

The entry conditions are defined by how appropriate the motivational resources for the individual now are. While, for example, the learner has probably heard classical music themes which he related to pop music, often the range is limited, and familiarity is the extent of the experience. He is not ready (motivated) to go out and listen to more classical music to see what is familiar to him.

The enabling conditions should be structured to select resources that will enhance or create motivation in the learner. In instructional design for this objective, for example, it might be decided that the selection of the contemporary treatment of the classics, perhaps by synthesizers, would be an appropriate resource to create the motivation to seek out other classical music forms.

STRUCTURE OF APPROACH TO EXPAND EXPERIENTIAL RESOURCES

Resources can be structured to achieve an objective in which it is specified the learner will be better able to respond to instruction after exposure to mediated resources that will expand his experiences. For the young learner who is expected to know what to do and to whom to go for help if he were lost, for example, the concept of being lost and needing help might be so beyond his range of experiences that no instruction could be entirely effective.

It would not be too wise for the teacher to take this child downtown and abandon him, even though this would expand his experiences in preparation for the planned instruction. What would, perhaps, work better would be to simulate the conditions of being lost without frightening the child, while at the same time expanding his experiences to what *might* actually occur in real life. An objective to thus expand a child's experiences might specify that resources be presented for the educational program so that "The learner will recognize what it is like to be lost so that if the actual situation ever occurred, he would recall aspects from a less frightened state of mind."

The terminal conditions are descirbed in the objective for this way to approach instruction where it is expected that some experience of the individual be expanded. This may be an objective leading toward a larger sequence of instruction, stated because it is desired that all learners begin an instructional event from the same basic common ground of experiences. Thus, in the example given above, the terminal conditions would be a simulated or vicarious experience of being lost that is not frightening to a young learner.

The entry conditions are defined by how sufficient the current experiences of the individual are. The child in the previous example has never been lost and it is assumed has never known anyone who has been lost, to share their experience. Thus, the whole concept of not knowing where he is is so strange to him that instruction about what to do when he is lost is beyond his range of readiness.

An attempt in Project ASERT to treat this concept in a television lesson met with some unexpected entry conditions. It was found, after several attempts to test the results of the program with young viewers, that many times from the child's point of view, he is not the one who is lost. He may not know where his parents or his own neighborhood may be, but he does know where *he* is. He's right *here*—wherever that may be. The concern with these children may not be with being lost but with not having somebody know where they are.

So, without examining the conditions that are now within the range of experiences for the target population, the whole intent of instruction could be approached from assumed conditions that don't really exist.

In the enabling conditions to expand the experiences of a child who has never been lost, a simulated experience of another child of his age who is lost might be shown to him on a television program. To attempt to convey some of the emotional aspects, a highly subjective camera could exaggerate the aspects that would be quite frightening for him to experience in person. While he might get completely wrapped up in the experience while viewing the television program, he can be jarred back to the comfortable and familiar reality of the classroom at any time. Thus, it might be possible to extend his experience to include an aspect of life he could never have under controlled situations except through some mediated or simulated form.

STRUCTURE OF APPROACH TO EXTEND ENVIRONMENTAL RE-SOURCES   Resources can be structured to achieve an objective in which it is specified that the learner will be better able to respond to instruction after exposure to mediated resources that will extend his environment. For example, in a community where the economy is based largely on meat-packing industires, many children may not have had the opportunity to see what goes on at the other end of the food chain.

If this were the rationale for instruction, the objective might be stated: "Since exposure to aspects of rural ranch life is an essential prerequisite to the learner's ability to name the relationships of other economic environments to the economy of meat-processing plants in his own community, after viewing a televised description of a ranch, the learner will recall from memory how cattle are prepared on ranches for their ultimate disposition at the meat-packing plant."

The terminal conditions are described in the objective where it is stated how the environment of the individual should be after it has been extended. For example, it would not only be necessary to have extended the learner's environment to include selected aspects of a cattle ranch, but it may also be necessary, according to the way the objective is stated, to have so pictured the ranch life for the intended target population that the relevant aspects of it have been committed to memory for recall.

The entry conditions are defined by how adequate the environment of the individual is now for learning. For example, it may be known that the learner's urban environment is now adequate only for being told about cattle on ranches in the abstract, or is distorted by seeing cattle drives and ranches on "Gunsmoke" or "Bonanza."

The enabling conditions describe what is required to select resources to extend the environment for adequate learning opportunities. It may be necessary, for example, to give a complete picture of a cattle ranch to extend the learner's environment beyond his own local community. It is *not* necessary to describe slaughtering and rendering, for the learner is most likely familiar with these functions in his own community.

Display

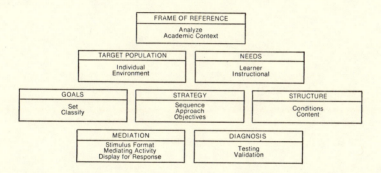

After the direction given by setting goals is developed into specific units of instruction, the experiences can then be translated into a mediated form for display to the target population. Essential content has to be re-shaped into a specific stimulus. These stimuli then have to be arranged in a format with other stimuli as an appropriate instructional experience. This composite experience can then be translated into some mediated form. The mediated instruction can be displayed for the individual learner to respond to, under controlled conditions.

Mediation

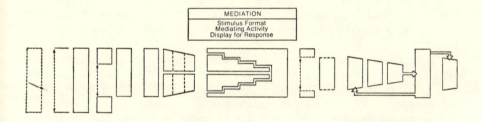

MEDIATION
Stimulus Format
Mediating Activity
Display for Response

In preparing the actual segment of instruction for display, the mediating activity should reflect consideration of how a stimulus can best be treated to get the desired response.

An analysis of the enabling conditions should be made to break down the task into manageable units of instruction that will be translated into some mediated form. The enabling conditions which have been identified to create the conditions specified in the objectives from the conditions that now exist have determined the essential content of the mediated experience. It should then be possible to conduct a task analysis of this essential content to determine just how it will be displayed to the learner so that he can respond as expected.

Stimulus Format

An analysis of the essential content should be made to break it down into specific stimuli that will be translated into some mediated form.

FRAME OF REFERENCE FOR ANALYZING THE STIMULUS FORMAT

This design function should begin from the frame of reference established by acknowledging any restraints imposed on reshaping the essential content as a specific stimulus that can be translated into some mediated form.

Restraints may restrict the breaking down of the structure of the mediated experience into units manageable enough to be translated into some mediated form. Instead of analyzing the stimulus-response components of the instructional experience to structure a manageable unit of instruction, it may be necessary to work from the frame of reference established by a previous decision to use a given medium. If, for example, it has already been determined that television must be used to mediate instruction, it would be a waste of design energies (and would probably result in design frustrations) to analyze the stimulus-response components of the instructional task for a more appropriate medium.

Stimulus Sequence

The approach to instruction that will be used to reach the learner is based on known conditions in the instructional environment. However, the process of translating content elements into specific response stimuli can be sequenced in design to relate to the performance level at which the objective is classified. A different kind of stimulus design is indicated in the sequence according to the Design Cluster at which the instruction is designed.

Conditions for Learning

Robert M. Gagné has observed that few things are so intriguing to wonder about as the development of human behavior. The adult human being, according to Gagné's observations, becomes a marvelously adaptable, completely functioning person within a complex cultural society. Somehow he is able to achieve this level of competency from the humble beginnings as a highly dependent, relatively incapable, newborn infant.

This biological maturation characteristic shared by all human beings in the process of growth and development can account for only a part of this unique human ability. The development of human skills, reasoning and values are generally recognized to depend for their development on the events called "learning" (Gagné 1965). Gagné concludes, therefore, that if human learning outcomes can be structured in a hierarchical order, so too can there be a sequential order to the instructional conditions in the design of stimuli to which the individual is exposed for his expected response.

To establish the conditions for instruction, Gagné has advanced a hierarchy of the "Types of Learning" based on the multiplicative application of the Stimulus-Response (S-R) theory of learning.

Although variations of this Stimulus-Response theory are widely debated (and disputed) in the academic community, these confrontations are usually made from the base of the almost universal acceptance by learning theorists of the viability of the basic S-R model to explain human learning development.

At the risk of over-simplification, in S-R theory, the learner is presented with a stimulus (S)—usually through some mediating channel—to which he makes a response (r). The stimulus may be verbal, visual, or simulated experiences or symbols. The response may be overt or covert, immediate or delayed, internalized or conditioned, remembered or forgotten, observed or ignored, rewarded or punished. The feedback from the response, in a closed-loop system, should determine the nature of the stimulus for the next increment in the instructional sequence.

The hierarchy of the "Types of Learning" was advanced by Gagné as a set of principles arising from generalizations (rather than as a theory) to distinguish classes of performance change. It can also be used to discipline design in the selection, sequencing and structure of stimuli that will be required to achieve the desired response described by the Design Cluster at which the objective is classified.

Stimulus Design

The hierarchical structure of the design strategy can be used to determine the specific design requirements for stimuli that will provide the conditions to bring about the desired type of learning. To use the strategy of the Design Clusters, the eight types of learning advanced by Gagné have been synthesized into five categories of conditions for stimulus design. (See diagram on page 97 for a graphic display of the relationship of these instructional conditions to each of the Design Clusters.)

Stimulus Design Requirements of the Conditions for Instruction[1]

Type 1—Signal Learning: The individual learns to make a general, diffuse (and often involuntary) response to a signal as a stimulus.

The stimulus must be designed to provide for a conditioned response.

Type 2—Stimulus-Response Learning: The learner acquires a precise response to a discriminated stimulus.

A discriminated stimulus must be designed to provide for the desired voluntary response.

Stimulus-Response Learning *may* require, as a prerequisite, learner performance in the conditions for Signal Learning.

Type 3—Chaining: The learner acquires a chain of two or more stimulus-response connections.

If a chain is being learned, an external cue must be designed for each link even though these cues may become unnecessary later.

Chaining requires, as a prerequisite, learner performance in the conditions for Stimulus-Response Learning.

Type 4—Verbal Association: Verbal Association is the learning of chains that are verbal, and is so closely associated with Chaining Learning (one being verbal and the other non-verbal) that the two are often considered as a single type.

Stimuli must be designed to present the verbal units in the proper sequence and, as is true for non-verbal chains, external stimuli must be designed that furnish the cues for the proper order of the verbal chain.

Verbal Association requires, as a prerequisite, Chaining, although the two are so closely associated, both are often said to have the same immediate prerequisite of Stimulus-Response Learning.

Type 5—Multiple Discrimination: The individual learns to make any number of different identifying responses to as many different stimuli that may or may not resemble each other in physical appearnace.

If multiple discrimination is to be accomplished, the design of stimuli to be discriminated must allow for them to be displayed so that correct connections can be differentiated from incorrect ones.

Multiple Discrimination requires, as a prerequisite, learner performance in the conditions for Verbal Association and other Chaining.

Type 6—Concept Learning: The learner acquires a capability of making a common response to a class of stimuli that may differ from each other widely in physical appearance.

If concepts are being learned, a suitable variety of objects or events representing a class must be designed as stimuli.

Concept Learning requires, as a prerequisite, learner performance in the conditions for Multiple Discrimination.

Type 7—Principle Learning: In simplest terms, a principle is a chain of two or more concepts. Principles represent the relationships that must be made among concepts.

If principles are being learned, the design of stimuli to which the learner must attend must apply somehow to present the stimulus object to which the principles apply.

Principle Learning requires, as a prerequisite, learner performance in the conditions for Concept Learning.

---

[1]Adapted from: Gagné, Robert M. *The Conditions of Learning*, New York: Holt, Rinehart and Winston, Inc., 1965.

Type 8—Problem Solving: **The learner is expected to somehow combine two or more previously acquired principles to produce new capability that can be shown to depend on a "higher order" principle and can be used by the learner as a part of his repertoire of capabilities to solve problems.**

The design of the stimulus for the learner must display the problem situation by presenting all of the previously learned principles that are required to achieve a solution to the problem.

Problem Solving requires, as a prerequisite, learner performance in the conditions for Principle Learning.

Instructional conditions for the display of symbols or experiences to which the learner must attend can be designed with specific response stimuli and arranged in a sequential order according to the level at which learner performance is expected. The level is derived from the Design Cluster selected to guide the design of instruction.

INSTRUCTIONAL CONDITIONS FOR DESIGN CLUSTER ONE

If the performance sequence concentrated efforts to formulate the objectives in Design Cluster One, the selection and design of the stimulus should be made according to the requirements of *Stimulus Response* Learning. In the conditions for Stimulus-Response Learning, the stimulus is designed so the learner can make a simple response to a single stimulus. In the mediated instructional experience, conditions should be provided for the repetition of the stimulus-response connections. In the stiuation where the mediated experience will be used, conditions should be provided to apply reinforcement immediately after the response is made.

INSTRUCTIONAL CONDITIONS FOR DESIGN CLUSTER TWO

If the performance sequence concentrated efforts to formulate the objectives in Design Cluster Two, the selection and design of the stimulus should be made according to the requirements of either *Chaining* learning or *Verbal Association* learning. In the conditions for Chaining or Verbal Association, the stimulus is designed so the learner can acquire two or more stimulus-response connections in a sequence of verbal or non-verbal units. In the mediated instructional experience, conditions should be provided to rearrange the stimulus-response links of the chain in their proper order. In the situation where the mediated experience will be used, conditions should be provided for the immediate confirmation of the correct response to each link and to the chain as a whole.

INSTRUCTIONAL CONDITIONS FOR DESIGN CLUSTER THREE

If the performance sequence concentrated efforts to formulate objectives in Design Cluster Three, the selection and design of the stimulus should be made according to the requirements of *Multiple Discrimination*. In the conditions for Multiple Discrimination, the stimulus is designed so the learner can discriminate the common traits among stimulus-response connections regardless of their physical appearance in order to recognize a class of stimuli. In the mediated instructional experience, conditions must be provided to present stimuli to emphasize their distinctiveness. Additional repetition may have to be provided to reduce interference among individual connections. In the situation where the mediated experience will be used, conditions should be provided for, to confirm the correct response when the correct identifying discrimination is made.

INSTRUCTIONAL CONDITIONS FOR DESIGN CLUSTER FOUR

If the performance sequence concentrated efforts to formulate the objectives in Design Cluster Four, the selection and design of the stimulus should be made according to the requirements of *Concept* Learning or of *Principle*. In the conditions for Concept and Principle Learning, the stimulus is designed so the learner can combine two or more classes of stimuli into a concept and then sequence two or more concepts so the general principle is evident. In the mediated instructional experience conditions should be provided for a presentation of a suitable variety of stimuli to represent the concept class, each stimulus having a connection with a common response. In the situation where the mediated experience will be used, conditions should be provided to present a novel stimulus that is also a member of the class of stimuli presented in the mediated experience to verify consistency of correct responses.

INSTRUCTIONAL CONDITIONS FOR DESIGN CLUSTER FIVE

If the performance sequence concentrated efforts to formulate objectives in Design Cluster Five, the selection and design of the stimulus should be made according to the requirements of *Problem Solving*. In the conditions for Problem Solving, the stimulus is designed so the learner can generalize two or more previously acquired principles for a new, higher-order principle that can be used to solve a problem. In the mediated experience, conditions must be provided to present a situation that evokes recall of previously learned concepts or principles. In these conditions, the learner should also be informed of the performance expected and be provided guidance to direct his thinking without stating the "higher order" principle being sought. In the situation where the mediated experience will be used, conditions should ask the learner to "demonstrate" in a concrete instance his ability to solve problems.

Stimulus Components

If, as Gagné maintains, learning is largely dependent on events in the environment with which the individual interacts, then it is necessary in the design of instruction to create conditions that are appropriate to the way in which the individual should relate to the complex patterns of behavior expected in society.

In instructional design, there is no control over all elements of the academic environment. However, there is control over the display of symbols or experiences during instruction. Instructional conditions describe the way that a mediated segment will become a part of the total instructional experiences of the learner through the array of stimuli to which he is asked to attend.

The actual segment of instruction will be structured around only those components that are essential as stimuli to elicit the desired response. It is at this point in design that the symbols or experiences that have been identified as the elements of the essential content to which the learner must be exposed are now thought of as stimuli to get the desired response.

In the programed course in instructional design, "The Instructional Technology Workshop," performance is defined for task analysis as a meaningful unit of behavior. A meaningful unit of behavior has an identifiable stimulus that will cause an identifiable response with an identifiable consequence.

When a task analysis is being conducted to break down units of instruction into a more manageable form; both the stimuli and responses must be identified. The responses are identified first primarily because it is easier; what the learner does (his response) is usually readily observable. Then, the stimuli must be identified in order to determine what is going to cause this response to be made. Identifying the response first—while easier in the context of instructional design—has rarely been done in the past. Identifying the stimulus first is more comfortable to teachers accustomed to more traditional ways of doing things.

A task analysis is conducted, then, to determine exactly which stimuli will cause the response to occur. Other elements contributing to, clarifying or giving added dimension to these key elements can then be planned for with all of the creative intuition and artistry the designer or his producers can command.

KEY STIMULI For each microsegment of the instructional experience, the learner must discriminate and respond to a key stimulus. For example, if the learner is expected to name a dinosaur from a picture, the key stimulus would be a picture of that dinosaur, not the actual dinosaur itself. If, on the other hand, the learner was expected to match the pictures of four dinosaurs with their correct names, the key stimuli would be both the pictures and the list of names. However, in many instructional experiences, it may not be possible for the learner to discriminate the key stimulus, especially early in the instructional sequence. Often, some help must be given to him to discriminate the key stimulus and to clarify the critical response.

PROMPTING STIMULI A prompting stimulus serves to help the learner recognize the key stimulus and make the critical response. In instruction, it is often necessary to ask questions, to outline procedures, or to perform some task that will indicate to the learner what it is he should actually respond to and to clarify how he will be expected to respond.

A very simple prompting stimulus would be seen where the teacher would hold up a picture of a brontosaurus and say to the learner, "This is a picture of a brontosaurus. Now what is the dinosaur in this picture called?" In this over-simplified example, both the stimulus and the learner's expected response have been clarified. Had the teacher held up the picture and said, "This is a brontosaurus; what is this dinosaur called?" neither the stimulus nor the expected response would have been clarified. The learner may think brontosaurus, is the brand name of the paper on which the picture is printed. In instruction, care must be taken in using a prompting stimulus to direct the learner's attention to the actual *key* stimulus and to clarify the critical response that is expected of him. Variations of this use of prompting stimuli are a normal part of conventional teaching.

Prompting stimuli should be treated in such a way that the learner does not come to rely on them and, as quickly as possible, responds as expected to the key stimulus. There are times, however, when prompting stimuli remain as an aid in the learned experience long after instruction has ended. The pre-takeoff procedures a pilot must follow are usually committed to memory very quickly in his flight training. Yet, the use of a preflight checklist—as a prompting stimulus to discriminate what instrument he should look at and what response he should make to the indication on that instrument—is recommended by many flight schools even for the most experienced pilots.

Caution should be exercised in using prompting stimuli. Some parents, when teaching their children to read, will (out of a state of frustration) say a word that the child is struggling to sound out from the printed form. Eventually, the child could learn to respond to his parent's prompting for unfamiliar words rather than to the written symbols themselves.

MEDIATORS   The learner may have to rely on some other stimulus-response elements that will enable the correct response to be made to a complex stimulus. Therefore, some mediators (that may be either internal in the learner or external to the learner) may have to be provided to help the learner make the critical response to the key stimulus. For example, many of us have learned to differentiate which months have 30 days and which have 31 by the mnemonic "Thirty days hath September, April, June and. . . ." When asked to respond to the key stimulus of saying today's date when yesterday was October 30, most of us would have to first refer to this "internal mediator" before we would be able to make the critical response.

External mediators are perhaps more frequently used in higher levels of instruction. If, for example, the critical response expected of the learner is to name the square root of a number, the learner could actually calculate this value by going through a complex sequence of using the formula to extract square roots. This process is actually an internal mediator to get the critical response (the square root value) from the key stimulus (the number from which the square root is to be extracted). However, an external mediator could be provided in the form of a square root table. Then, once he has discriminated the key stimulus as the number from which the square root is to be extracted, he would then locate that number on the table (which is the external mediator) and find the entry that would help him make the critical response—in this case naming the square root value.

The distinction between prompting stimuli and mediators is often confused. The precise discrimination is not as important as the function in the instructional task. A prompting stimulus directs the learner's attention to the key stimulus and gives him clues as to how he is expected to respond. A mediator is a series of stimulus-response units that must be learned before the individual can make the critical response to the key stimulus. Prompting stimuli are not learned as a part of the instructional experience but are used as aids within instruction. The use of mediators is often included in the total scope of learned experiences for which instruction is designed.

Stimulus Format

The format of the actual segment of instruction will be structured in a sequence of responses to specific stimuli that have been identified to enable the learner to achieve the objective.

STIMULUS-RESPONSE PAIRS   Each performance task is made up of stimulus-response units. For example, if someone were asked to write his name on a form, a stimulus would be the spoken command and the response would be writing the name. However, it is also possible to break down this performance task into smaller stimulus-response units. It is assumed that the stimulus, "Write your *name*," will result in the learner's response to recall what a name is and not an address or telephone number. It is expected that the learner will respond with his name (and not someone else's) to the stimulus, "Write *your* name." Also, there is a complex set of stimulus-response units involved with *"Writing* your name," including even the basic manipulative characteristics of stimulus-response units involved in holding a pencil.

The question arises, then, just how far should the task analysis break down the instructional event into stimulus-response units for instructional design? There is no precise prescriptive rule. As a rule of thumb, however, the task analysis should break down the instructional task into units that are large enough to work without ambiguity, but small enough to be manageable in design.

It will help to determine the extent of the task analysis for instructional design if it is remembered that any performance task is usually made up of a sequence of stimulus-response units. The size of the task for instructional design would be based principally on the number of *essential* stimulus-response elements, that are not now a part of the individual's learned competencies.

STIMULUS-RESPONSE CONNECTIONS   Each performance task within the instructional experience requires a response to be made to some stimulus input. Each response that makes up a task normally resulted in some consequence which, in turn, acts as the stimulus for the next response. Thus, after each response has been identified, its consequence may be used to help identify the next stimulus. For example, if a typist encounters a word in a written copy and questions its spelling, she looks for the word in a dictionary. In this example, the written word she encounters in the copy is the stimulus, and her response would be looking up the word. Seeing the correct spelling of the word as a consequence of finding it would be the stimulus for the next response of either typing it as it appears in the copy or making a correction (General Programmed Teaching, 1972).

Often the consequence of a response is a confirmation that it was correct.

STIMULUS-RESPONSE STRATEGY   Before the critical response can be made, it is often necessary to break down the performance task into dependent responses to prerequisite stimuli. Many tasks consist of a sequence of stimulus-response pairs that must follow in a certain order or the task cannot be completed. This is because the consequence of one response acts to provide the stimulus for the next response. If the consequence does not occur, the next response cannot be made.

A chain can be readily identified in the task analysis as a sequence of stimulus-response pairs with certain common characteristics. For example, if a man strikes a match, then lights his pipe, this performance involves a chain of stimulus-response units. The man cannot light his pipe before he strikes the match, therefore the consequence of the response of striking the match is the lighted match. That then becomes the stimulus for the next response of lighting the pipe.

Or, a student may write a column of figures, then add them up. If it is assumed that the learner cannot add these figures in his head, then this performance task is a chain, and the instructional segment must contain elements to show not only how to add up figures in a column, but also how to write figures in a column that can be added without the chance of digits appearing in the wrong place.

In another example used in the Instructional Technology Workshop by General Programmed Teaching, a boy throwing a ball and then sitting down, would *not* be a chain. The boy could very well sit down and then throw the ball. He could even sit down without throwing the ball. One element is not dependent on the other. Thus, if this task were reflected in instruction, both actions (sitting and throwing) would have to be treated as separate instructional segments rather than as components of the same performance task.

STIMULUS-RESPONSE SEQUENCE   If the stimulus-response chains are identified as component elements of the instructional task, or where individual stimulus-response pairs are prerequisite to later response elements, the sequence of these stimulus-response components will determine the actual format of the segment of instruction.

This format may involve *linear sequencing*. In this structure, all stimulus-response components are sequenced in the proper order to move from the simple to the complex or from the familiar to the unfamiliar, etc. For example, if there is a chain of stimulus-response units involved in a performance task, it would be most logical to structure instruction so that each unit is learned in sequence for the consequence of each response is in effect the stimulus for the next response. But, even if a stimulus-response chain is not involved, even single stimulus-response pairs may be prerequisite to later stimulus-response pairs. For example, it would be desirable to define terms before using these terms in an instructional situation.

It is also possible, at times, to use *nonlinear sequencing* in the structural format of the instructional segment. In this structure, for example, the stimulus-response pairs are arranged to present the learner with all elements necessary to demonstrate some intellectual skill or to draw on any information needed to piece together elements himself in a nonlinear arrangement of instructional stimuli.

STIMULUS-RESPONSE ARRANGEMENTS   In the arrangement of stimuli for the instructional format, the *Cognitive-Conflict* theory may be applied. Here, the learner is confronted with several alternative explanations and the cognitive conflict that results must be resolved by thought process. The use of cognitive conflict as a display format is in itself in conflict with some learning psychology that states, "Never teach a child something wrong." There is, however, an essential difference between that psychology and the theory of cognitive conflict, as explained by Robert R. Buell, where the learner is told to look for the wrong things. He knows there are wrong elements; he isn't being taught wrong elements as if they were right. The learner's task is to work on the information, assimilating and accommodating it to his previous knowledge (Buell, 1970).

Another approach to a nonlinear arrangement of stimuli for the format is termed the *affect wave*. Numerous learning theorists have postulated that learning occurs as a function of the reduction of a tension state. In the display of stimuli for mediation, the affect-wave arrangement of stimuli would use a format to generate mild, highly directional tension states with questions, statements of requirements, deliberate ambiguity, and then to provide directional cues for the learners to follow in reducing the tension state.

There are many other theories and schools of thought on the sequence and arrangement of instruction in a nonlinear fashion. The two mentioned here were used to illustrate how stimuli can be arranged in the format of instruction in ways other than beginning at the beginning and ending at the end.

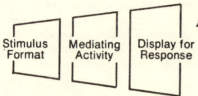

Mediating Activity

Stimulus Format | Mediating Activity | Display for Response

It is essential to decide on an effective mediating activity to present the selected stimuli to cue the desired response.

FRAME OF REFERENCE FOR TRANSLATING INSTRUCTION FOR MEDIATION

This design function should begin from the frame of reference established by acknowledging any restraints imposed on the selection and treatment of the appropriate medium by which instruction will be displayed to a target population.

Predetermined factors of production may limit the way the information or experiences can be displayed to the learner. For example, instruction may have to be designed around the restraint imposed by television broadcast schedules. Often, the length of each segment must be adjusted to conform to a 29-minute time block allotted it on the schedule sheet. Seldom does this conform to the actual time it will take to complete the instructional experience.

In more general terms, it will have to be known how much direction must be given to those responsible for production. It may be enough, for example, to specify that the target population is a four-year-old child. However, it may be necessary to further specify what that means—to specify more precisely what a four-year-old is like—and how that will affect the treatment of the content for the target population.

Mediating Activity

Once the structural elements and format have been determined, a specific mediating activity can be selected. For example, it may be decided now that some objectives in the instructional task will more likely be achieved by displaying stimuli through electronic media such as television, while other objectives in the same instructional task might be more effectively achieved by displaying stimuli in the supplemental print or nonprint material that will be designed to reinforce or complement the televised segment. For instance, if in the objective it is required that the learner make certain inferences about the characteristics of a chemical reaction shown to him, the instructions on how he is to proceed may well be presented in printed student guide material, while the reaction itself is shown on television. Then, the student may be provided the actual elements to replicate this reaction on his own in the classroom.

It is not uncommon to see displayed on television verbal material that would have been better mediated in print. It is important to determine the most efficient mediating mode if instruction is to be held accountable for efficiency as well as for effectiveness in achieving the objectives.

Mediating Conditions

Deciding on the conditions to mediate instruction for the objectives in the instructional task is essential for an efficient mode of display for the symbols or experiences to serve as stimuli to cue a response. The assignment of media priorities does nothing more than decide how something will be most efficiently displayed to the target population. Theoretically, the mode of display has not yet been determined at this point in design. Only now, in the application of these procedures without restraints imposed, is it decided if production will be with material for television or for the overhead projector.

Robert E. Stepp has advanced a technique to select media for instruction for the acoustically-handicapped child that would apply as well to assigning media priorities for any target population. In advancing this technique, Stepp (1970) says:

> The array of instructional materials available today is vastly different from what was used ten years ago. Even during the short span of another decade, the variety of learning resources and the accessibility of these learning resources will make drastic changes in instruction. The process will shift heavily toward the independent acquisition of knowledge by the student and will move away from dependence on his teacher for the major presentation of instruction. In other words, learning will become more a responsibility of the student. The teacher in this type of educational environment will become the learning mentor, serving as a guide, counselor, and director of the learning experience.

Stepp also maintains:

> Instructional media are no longer "aids" to teaching; nor are they devices employed exclusively by teachers in their presentations. Instructional media are now, or should be, an integral part of all learning tasks. The second point is that instructional media are the communication modes of the younger generation. They feel as comfortable with a camera as the older generation does with a pen. The computer will be as commonplace to them as the typewriter is now. This awareness of new frontiers in educational technology opens many avenues of creative expression for students and expands the instructional strategies possible.

In the initial step to assign media priorities, Stepp asks:

> What reference is being made to what the learner is doing during the process of learning? What learning activities or experiences must the student have in order to learn? Is he sitting? listening? reciting? writing?

marking X's in a workbook? Drawing lines between diagrams? Matching pictures? Filling in blanks? Is he an-
swering true or false? Saying yes or no? Giving other
one word replies? What are the learner's contributions
to the learning task? How demanding are these requirements? How involved is he? Is the instructional activity
appropriate to the learning situation?

Thus it is first necessary to define what activities the learner will be engaged in his exposure to instruction.

Instructional resources offer unique contributions toward acquisition of information, development of concepts, realistic simulation of experiences, performance of
skills, and actual involvement in the learning experience.
These contributions will vary according to the functions
required of the media, and the extent of involvement will
be dependent on the type of learning activity which is to
be performed by the student:

Activities Leading to Learning

**Thinking, Inquiring, Discovering, Speaking, Discussing, Conferring,
Editing, Listening, Aural Discrimination, Interviewing, Audio Record-
ing, Reporting, Reading (words, symbols, pictures), Writing, Outlining,
Constructing, Creating, Designing, Drawing, Sketching, Painting,
Lettering, Labeling, Diagramming, Graphing, Charting, Mapping,
Visual Storyboarding, Photographing, Filming, Videorecording, Edit-
ing,
Collecting, Classifying, Displaying, Showing, Manipulating, Demon-
strating, Observing, Watching, Witnessing, Experimenting, Research-
ing, Problem Solving,
Dramatizing, Role Playing, Acting, Singing, Dancing, Pantomiming,
Traveling,
Imagining, Visualizing, Organizing, Summarizing, Accounting, Com-
puting, Testing, Judging, Evaluating**

(Stepp, 1970)

From the above list and more activities that the reader
might add may be selected the experiences that will provide for the learner the type of involvement appropriate
and essential for the student to learn and perform the
learning task.

In his procedures, Stepp maintains that although the selection of the
mode for display of symbols is secondary to the specification of goals and
objectives in instruction, the prescription of the precise media is as significant as any decision made.

Instructional Media Leading to Learning

Textbooks, Supplementary Books, Reference Books, Indexes, Documents, Dictionairies, Encyclopedias, Newspapers, Magazines, Clippings, Duplicated Materials, Programed Materials (self-instructional)

Graphs, Charts, Diagrams, Illustrations, Maps, Globes, Flat Pictures, Posters, Cartoons, Comics

Photographs, Slides, Filmstrips, Transparencies, Microfilm, Microcards, Stereographs, Radio, Recordings (Tape and Disc), Motion Pictures (8mm and 16mm), Television, Videotape, Electronic Video Recordings

Puppets, Models, Mock-ups, Collections, Specimens, Realia, Instructional Displays

Consumable Supplies, Construction Materials, Free and Inexpensive Sponsored Materials

And . . . the classroom teacher.

(Stepp, 1970)

Stepp feels that surely from this vast assortment of communicative media, it is possible to achieve any objective desired. The instructional technologist may not have access to the precise medium needed in each case. One of the major tasks is to constantly and consistently collect and assemble the required learning resources. Circumstances may necessitate compromises resulting in the substitution of one medium for another but this situation should not continue year after year as it has been the case in so many schools in the past.

However wide the range of media from which to choose, instructional designers are cautioned not to pretend media choices they don't have. The instructional technologist, according to George L. Hall, does not begin his instructional design task with an unfilled order blank before him on which he will list the precise media resources he wants and can afford. Almost invariably, he begins with an inventory list that enumerates the resources already available. He may add or substract, but for the most part he is constrained to make do with what he has.

The skill of the instructional technologist will be evidenced by the efficient array of these existing elements. He will look beyond his inventory list only if what he has is woefully insufficient and if what he needs is readily obtainable. Therefore, he will not compare "the media" in the abstract; he will assess only those already available in the instructional situation (Hall, 1970).

The term "Learning Resources" can be distinctively associated with instructional design for technology. The term identifies the resources and material that a school must have for instruction. Stepp has listed these "Learning Resources" as those of which the designer should be aware:

Considerations for the Selection of Learning Resources For the Instructional Task

For Display:	Chalkboard, bulletin board, flannel board, posters, hook 'n loop boards, exhibits.
For Audition:	Speech, audio recordings (reels, cassettes, card discs) auditory training units, radio.
For Symbology:	Charts, graphs, maps, diagrams, cartoons, comics.
For Iconography:	Slides, filmstrips, pictures, study prints, illustrations, television.
For Observation:	Films (16mm and 8mm), television videotape recordings, electronic or laser recordings.
For Coordination:	Overhead transparencies, texts, manuals, workbooks.
For Simulation:	Models, mock-ups, programed learning material, computer-assisted instruction.
For Application:	Demonstrations, performance, field trips, realia.
For Creation:	Multimedia student production and response modes.
For Environment:	Classroom, laboratory, library, study carrel, church, home, community, mass media.

(Stepp, 1970)

Hall has maintained that the choice of a medium to perform instructional functions must follow a projected comparison of its relative efficiency in the prevailing situation. That is,

> Selection is actually made relative to other media that are available within the multi-various psychological, cost, physical, temporal and instructional constraints actually present in the instructional situation. The instructional technologist must take strictly into account the need to balance cost-effectiveness against learning effectiveness. He "trades off" one against the other to achieve an optimum input-output relationship: an acceptable learning gain for a specific student group at an acceptable expenditure of money, personnel, facilities, time, media, etc. (Hall, 1970).

Stepp's approach recognizes it is often very difficult to separate the instructional process into discrete activities and thus a varied approach to media may be necessary. This means selecting and using any and all media required to display each specific instructional task. This is true no matter how large or small the increment of the task may be. Stepp bases his choice of display devices for the instructional process on the design of the task and the materials at hand.

Mediaware Leading to Learning

Boards of Education

Chalkboards, Flannel Boards, Peg Boards, Electric Boards, Bulletin Boards, Hook 'n Loop Boards, Magnet Boards, Game Boards.

Iconographic Devices
Slide Projectors, Motion Picture Projectors (16mm & 8mm) Overhead Projectors, Microprojectors, Television Sets, Filmstrip Projectors, Opaque Projectors, Microscopes, Projection Screens.

Auditory Devices
Record Players, Tape Recorders (reel-to-reel, cartridge, cassette), Radios (AM, FM) Audio Card Players and Recorders, Language Laboratories, Public Address Sound Systems, And . . . the Classroom Teacher.

Production Devices
Lettering Sets, Dry Mount Presses, Transparency Printers and Developers, Photographic Copiers, Still Cameras, Motion Picture Cameras (16mm & 8mm), Television Cameras, Video Tape Recorders, Paper Cutters, Slide Copiers, Duplicators (Spirit, Mimeography, Electronic), Graphic Arts Tools and Instruments, Microphones, Audiotape Recorders, Typewriters.

Self-Instructional Devices
Slide Viewers, Filmstrip Viewers, Listening Posts and Stations, Cartridge Load Film and Still Projectors, Cassette Load Audio Recorders, Reel-to-Reel and Cassette-Load Video Recorders, Reading Pacers and Controllers, Programed Teaching Machines and Texts, Computer Terminals.

(Stepp, 1970)

Assigning Media Priorities

A prime factor in assigning priorities to those media available is the instructional activity selected to satisfy the instructional intent that will fill learner needs. Stepp advances the idea that activities may require verbal, visual, tactile, or simulated experiences for the learner.

MEDIA FOR VERBAL EXPERIENCES   The instructional task may require narrative, expository or other verbal experiences for the learner. Stepp recommends these instructional activities and media possibilities for consideration if instruction can be developed by some form of oral-aural discourse:

Verbal Experiences

ACTIVITIES

Speaking	Reading
Listening	Recording
Writing	

MEDIA POSSIBILITIES

Lectures	Pamphlets
Discussions	Correspondence Courses

Books	Programed Instruction
Periodicals	Records and Radio
Manuals	Tape Recordings

(Stepp, 1970)

MEDIA FOR VISUAL EXPERIENCES

Not all ideas are verbal in nature. If the instructional task includes visual activities, don't talk about it; show the learner what is meant. For visual ideas, these instructional activities and media possibilities should be considered:

Visual Experiences

ACTIVITIES

Diagramming	Photographing
Sketching	Viewing
Animating	Recording
Reading	

MEDIA POSSIBILITIES

Charts	Bulletin Boards
Graphs	Flannel Boards
Maps	Films (8mm & 16mm)
Transparencies	Television
Photographs	Video Recordings
Slides	Visitations
Filmstrips	Books and Printed Media

(Stepp, 1970)

MEDIA FOR TACTILE EXPERIENCES

Stepp also maintains there is no reason to read about something or to observe situations depicting it if learning results could efficiently be achieved through actual participation. Tactile experiences may be difficult to mediate. However, they should be considered as a part of the total instructional experience of the learner. From these activities, the one required for the learner may be found for the design of instruction:

Tactile Experiences

ACTIVITIES

Handling	Assembling
Practicing	Arranging
Demonstrating	Classifying
Constructing	

MEDIA POSSIBILITIES	
Models	Realia
Mock-ups	Demonstrations
Specimens	Construction Tools

(Stepp, 1970)

MEDIA FOR SIMULATED EXPERIENCES   If the learner's need indicates an instructional activity that simulates a real experience, the environment or facilities created must be determined by the degree of learner involvement expected.

Simulated experiences often involve simultaneously the verbal, visual and manipulative (tactile) categories. But, simulated experiences may function more efficiently and more effectively because of the design of the medium used or the nature of the instructional task. Forms of instructional media that offer opportunities for simulation have been classified by Stepp as follows:

Simulated Experiences

ACTIVITIES

Verbalizing	*Visualizing*	*Manipulating*
Interacting	Observing	Dramatizing
Conversing	Witnessing	Performing

MEDIA POSSIBILITIES
8mm films in cartridges (silent and sound)
Television programs
Radio programs and audio-tutorial
Magnetic and video recordings
Programed learning materials (teaching machines)
Multimedia units or kits
Audio recordings
Dial-access auditory training systems
Computer systems
Mediated instructional programs
Electronic systems

(Stepp, 1970)

No instructional medium or simulation can completely replace real life situations. In designing instruction, Stepp urges that every possible opportunity should be provided to experience first-hand situations. Sometimes, however, the vicarious experience has greater impact because of its direct focus on only relevant stimuli. On other occasions, mediated instruction serves a unique function by preparing the learner for his real experience, or when following up activities of these real experiences.

It must be known where mediated experiences are more valuable than real life experiences and when the reverse is true (Stepp, 1970). Then, a detailed analysis of both the target population and the instructional task will help to arrive at this conclusion.

There is no decisive evidence that a child learns better from exposure to one medium over another. What he does learn from is the treatment of instruction in the medium. Therefore, priorities for mediation can be assigned on the basis of efficient uses of available media.

Instructional media—especially electronic media, such as radio and television—have remained peripheral to the educational program because they have not usually been assigned an integrated role in the instructional process. Assignment of media priorities, integrated into a learning structure, however, may mean a complete restructuring of the attitude toward and the use of mediated instruction. John Goodlad cautioned against the continued use of electronic technology to supplement and enrich what teachers are already doing when he said, "If educational radio and educational television come into the school and say, 'Look, this is an extension of you. This will permit *you* to extend yourself further. Learn how to operate the equipment. Learn the rhetoric of audiovisual education,' then we have only further burdened the teacher" (Goodlad, 1969). Is so doing, we may also have further entrenched technology on the periphery of the instructional process.

In their survey of the research in instructional television, Godwin Chu and Wilbur Schramm found it is much harder to find evidence of impact and success where television is being used in a small way, tentatively, and for supplemental efforts rather than for direct experiences. This is not to say, they conclude, that television cannot be used effectively for curricular supplement; only that it is harder to find satisfying evidence of impact when it is so used (Chu and Schramm, 1967).

If media priorities are assigned to display stimuli to achieve each of the objectives in the instructional task, the design of mediated instruction instead of being tangential to the learning structure is assigned an integral function to reach a specific goal *instead of* some other instructional element such as the classroom teacher or the textbook. Then, if the mediated stimulus display is removed, it must be replaced by some other instructional element or the whole structure will collapse or will be dangerously weakened. In this way, media will receive a higher priority in the academic system without destroying the integrity of the humanistic qualities of learning.

Media Functions

In preparing the actual sequence of instruction for display to the target population, the nature of the instructional task will help determine what function the media should play in the display of experiences to the learner.

TO DISPLAY   A medium can function to display objects or places for prolonged or detailed study. For example, if the learner is expected to evaluate the characteristics of a piece of sculpture, the mediated segment can function to display the object for analysis and evaluation—hopefully for as long as it takes for the learner to complete his study of it.

TO ORGANIZE   A medium could also function to organize a variety of situations to provide continuity of thought and action. For example, if it is expected in the instructional task that the learner classify a phenomenon in the series of events that make up any particular situation, the medium can function to display these events in such a way as to show the continuity of each individual phenomenon to the total situation.

TO CRYSTALIZE   The function of the medium can be concerned with the display of prompting stimuli or mediators that either clarify the key stimuli or provide clues for the learner as to what response is expected. In this context, the medium can function to crystalize abstractions with more concrete referents. For example, if the learner is expected to explain the social responsibilities of a democracy, the medium can function to display this abstraction by showing very concrete examples of accepted types of social responsibilities seen in the immediate environment of the individual.

TO VISUALIZE   A medium can also function to visualize concepts for observation and study. For example, if the learner is expected to distinguish between the verbal concepts of height and width, the media functions in instruction will be to visualize the discriminative differences between height and width so that the learner will be able to make the distinction in his response.

TO SIMULATE   A medium can also simulate actual events in which the learner is an active participant. For example, for an instructional task in a foreign language segment in which the learner is expected to actively respond to statements or questions asked in the language by the mediated teacher, the function of the medium is to display the stimuli in such a way that the learner becomes a part of the dialog, not a passive observer of a mololog.

TO STIMULATE   A medium can stimulate interaction with or participation in an actual event. For example, for an instructional task in which it is expected that the learner actually perform an exercise during his exposure to mediated instruction in Physical Education, the function of the medium would be to display some activity in such a way that the learner will make the active response and attempt the exercise as expected.

Media Techniques

Specific techniques, suited to the medium selected and to the function it is to play in instruction, must be selected for the display of a composite instructional experience.

TREATMENT   The actual presentational mode can be determined by the treatment of symbols or experiences as stimuli in the medium selected.

In the display, the stimuli might be treated in an *iconic presentational mode* for the display of symbolic representations of the real thing. For example, where the instructional task requires the learner to observe the operational sequence of a four-cycle gasoline engine, it might be determined that the presentational mode for the treatment of this concept would be better displayed for the learner in a simple, animated graphic rather than showing the cycle in the clutter of an actual engine.

Or, it may be determined that the *realia presentational mode* would be more appropriate to the display of the actual objects that will function as stimuli. For example, where the instructional task expects that the learner will identify what happens in a specific chemical reaction, a mediated display of the actual chemical reaction is almost dictated where the actual reaction would be dangerous or offensive to the learner.

DISPLAY   The degree of learner involvement in the actual use of symbols or experiences as stimuli can help determine what technique will be used to display the stimuli in the mediated experience.

Techniques that allow the individual to be exposed, as a third-person observer, to an event that is taking place would require an *objective display*. For example, based on an analysis of the target population, and of the objective, where it is expected that the learner identify functions of a policeman other than enforcement and arrest, it may be desired to show a child depicted as being lost and as found and returned to his parent by a policeman. The learner would then simply observe the vignette taking place.

To allow the individual to become a part of an event, *subjective display* techniques are called for. For example, it may be desired to involve the learner by displaying the events in such a way that he feels he is actually part of the situation shown. In the design and production of television segments, for instance, simply lowering the height of the camera to view a situation from the point of view of a four-year-old (rather than from the convenience of a six-foot cameraman) will add a subjective element even to the objective display of the event taking place, and will increase the potential of learner involvement and identification.

PACING   The initial consideration of pacing techniques in a mediated segment of instruction should determine whether an immediate or a delayed response is expected. Other aspects of the learner and of the instructional task will also affect the total pacing of mediated instruction.

If, in the instructional task, it is expected that the learner respond during exposure to instruction, *intermittent pacing* can be used. If, for example, it is expected that the learner repeat foreign language phrases after they are first given by the mediated teacher, then the pacing of the segment will have to allow time for these responses to be made.

If, however, the anticipated response is not expected to occur until after exposure to the mediated segment, then *continuous pacing* is required to prevent premature responses. For example, if the learner is expected to do something after being shown what and how in the mediated segment, the pacing will not only have to lead toward a response after the total sequence of the act is explained, but must also be paced to prevent the learner from responding before all directions and explanations are given.

Pacing in instructional television, for example, has ranged from the ponderously pedantic treatment of a teacher-by-the-blackboard to the rhythmic, vivacious tempo in "Sesame Street." The reasons to use these pacing techniques are so conditional—depending on the characteristics of the target population and on the situation in which instruction will be used —that no prescriptive specifications can be suggested. For the purpose in these procedures, it is only recommended that the pacing be appropriate to the instructional task and to the population it seeks to affect.

Media Structure

A specific structural format should be developed that incorporates display techniques best suited to the way in which the medium will display the symbols or experiences as stimuli for the target population.

FORMAT   The specific format for the arrangement of stimuli in the mediated segment will depend largely on empirical judgments of what will work best to communicate the content to the target population.

In the format, the chronological or deductive approach of *sequential* development can be used. For example, if the learner is expected to list, in sequence, the steps that must be followed in the building of a house, then it would be appropriate to display these steps in their chronological order.

On the other hand, the logical or inductive approach of *nonsequential* development may be more appropriate to the intended target population or to the specific instructional task. For example, to achieve an objective where it is expected that the learner formulate a conclusion about the relative worth of a culture value system, a chronological approach to the growth of that culture may be totally inappropriate. It may well be better to provide, in a nonsequential arrangement of relative importance, the elements of this culture to enable the learner to use inductive reasoning about its worth.

RESOLUTION   The resolution of instruction will depend largely on whether expositiory presentation is planned to be used or if inquiry or discovery learning is planned.

It is possible to display the stimuli so that all conclusions are *resolved* as a part of the segment itself. For example, if the learner is expected to identify the correct application of a mathematical formula to a practical situation, the procedures as well as the correct answer would be an appropriate part of instruction for complete closure and resolution of all conclusions.

On the other hand, it may be necessary to arrange the stimuli in such a way that some or all conclusions are not resolved but are left *open-ended*. If the learner, for example, is expected to extrapolate a conclusion from existing evidence, the stimuli could be displayed to lead to a conclusion (or to several conclusions) that must be reached after exposure to the mediated segment.

IMPLEMENTATION   The actual implementation of the form of the mediated segment of instruction must take into account all design restraints to production as well as the characteristics of the medium that has been selected for use.

Individual segments of instruction for each objective can now be combined into a sequence for a specific performance level. Each of the sequences is then combined into a composite instructional experience in which each performance level leading to the goal is fully developed.

Time and space priorities will also determine the final appearance of the mediated instruction. It may be essential to identify the number of segments required in each mediated sequence, the desired length of the individual segments as well as the length of the total instructional experience. Then, the transitional devices that will be required between these individual segments can be designed and produced. For example, it may be determined that the target population is capable of responding to instruction leading toward the achievement of four objectives in one television experience. Each objective has been formulated and treated as a separate instructional segment, and they must now be combined into an articulated sequence in a single 30-minute television program.

It is also desirable, many times, to identify specific elements of instruction that should *not* be mediated as a part of the experience to which the learner will be exposed. This aspect of design goes beyond the imposed media restraints. For example, if in trying to show that a policeman is really a pretty nice guy, for a learner who has always associated policemen only with arresting his father, it would be well to specify for production that elements associated with arrest (such as handcuffs, the gun, and the nightstick) be minimized in the display of the situation, either by removing them from the policeman, or turning him in such a way that they are hidden from view.

Display for Response

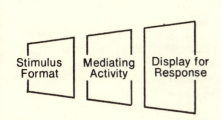

Stimulus Format | Mediating Activity | Display for Response

In order to achieve the desired response, the control over the conditions under which the instruction is displayed to the target population is an essential element of design.

FRAME OF REFERENCE FOR DISPLAYING INSTRUCTION TO THE TARGET POPULATION

This design function should begin from the frame of reference established by acknowledging any restraints imposed on the control of the conditions under which instruction will be displayed to the target population.

It should be possible to specify the exact conditions under which the mediated instruction should be displayed to the learner. However, restraints in a frame of reference from which to begin this design function are most likely to be imposed for this function. For example, where direct instruction may be desired for linear sequential use, design may have to begin from the frame of reference established by instructional media being seen only as an enrichment tool.

The facilities of the physical environment may have to remain as they are now, thus preventing planned change in the conditions that will influence the individual's access to mediated instruction. For example, if it is not possible to budget for additional pieces of equipment, the design must be accomodated to the existing hardware.

Display to the Target Population

In order to have confidence that instruction will be used as it has been designed, the control over the conditions under which the specific target population is exposed to instruction should become a function of design. However, in reality there is seldom absolute control over these conditions. Those elements over which little or no control is possible must be considered in the interpretation and the diagnosis of the results in testing.

Instructional Equipment

In the design of instruction to be mediated, it is often assumed that the learner will have ready access to that instruction. It must be known, however, what access the learner has to instructional hardware; what media exist in a usable condition in the schools; how the professional personnel in the classroom can and should manage the learning situation.

INSTRUCTIONAL MEDIA   It should be established first that there is the required hardware to permit efficient use of mediated instruction. The extent of the hardware currently available for use in the schools will, to some degree, affect the total design effort as well as it will affect the basic decision to mediate instruction. For example, despite a well-documented need for mediated instruction in a school located in a high crime rate section of a metropolitan area, it may well be discovered that vandalism and theft so consistently reduce the inventory of media equipment in the school that it is not practical to plan instructional experiences dependent on the use of media hardware. Or, the inventory of a specific medium may be so low that design for that mode would see relatively little use or would involve large expenditures to equip the schools to benefit from instruction designed for that medium.

Even where adequate inventories of equipment can be seen in the schools, it is almost a banal observation to report that most equipment gathers dust on a custodian's closet shelf. Therefore, there is the obligation not only to identify the extent to which media are now being used for instruction, but to discover why some equipment is *not* being used. For example, it may be reported that "everyone" has a television set but "no one" uses television in the classroom. This report on the extent of the use of that medium may make designers cautious in developing mediated instruction for television. However, an analysis of this situation might reveal that the medium is not being used only because it has not provided meaningful and relevant mediated experiences in the past.

High concentrations of the use of specific type of hardware, such as videotape cassette units, in the schools may affect the design by imposing the restraint that one medium be selected over others that may be more appropriate but less available.

The condition and repair of the media equipment available also is an important concern in instructional design. Mass concentrations of poorly adjusted television sets, projectors with burned-out lamps, or overheads dimmed by the collection of melted grease pencils may not always mean these media are available for use in instruction.

ACCESS TO INSTRUCTIONAL TECHNOLOGY   Since mediated instruction will be designed to be used largely for individual students in a classroom situation, the specific access to hardware items available must be known. Efficiency in the design of instruction for mediation will often require the use of electronic media to convey information across space and through time. The often capricious and temperamental nature of an electronic signal compounds the concerns in instructional design.

Since most electronic hardware must be used to serve many schools to maintain a relatively efficient cost-effectiveness ratio, it must be determined how many buildings can actually be served within the coverage area of the electronic hardware used. As most television engineers will hesitantly admit, the fact that a school building falls inside the Class B signal contour on the map is no indication that a signal can be received in that school.

While an electronic signal may be available in a school, the number of receiving devices within the building will determine what access there will be to mediated instruction in each individual classroom. Access to televised instruction in a school with four television receivers—all in the lunch room or teachers' lounge—is not the same as the access in a school with four receivers permanently installed in each of its classrooms. There is also relatively little practical access to a receiver that is transported from classroom to classroom if there are no antenna connections handy. There is also no practical access to television sets that are connected into a central distribution system that someone forgot to turn on.

The size and structure of the classroom unit will also influence the learner's access to media hardware. For instance, surveys that discover a single computer terminal to serve 1200 students may force decisions to be less reliant on computer-assisted instruction to meet basic design problems. Even under apparently ideal conditions of small class size and the proper operating condition of a television receiver, for example, the learner may not have access to it. The set might be placed on a stand six feet off the floor while first-graders (who are used to lying on their stomachs with noses pressed against a cathode ray tube at home) gather around, storytime fashion on their neat little rugs, to view ITV on a set they can't see.

PERSONNEL FOR INSTRUCTIONAL TECHNOLOGY   The qualifications of educational personnel in the use of media equipment will influence the way the academic environment is managed for mediated instruction.

Regardless of the nature and extent of media equipment inventories, at some point in time this equipment will have to be operated by someone in the academic environment. While instructional media are still largely considered peripheral to teaching, specialized formal training still appears to be the most reliable indicator (short of actual observation in every classroom) of the teacher's ability to manage the conditions for learning.

In the design of instruction, there has been a prevailing belief that a correlation exists between the number of course hours a teacher has taken in audiovisual techniques in college preparation and the ability to create the conditions for the use of instructional media. In the surveys of Nebraska schools conducted for Project ASERT, it was found that over 70 percent of the teachers who used the Project ASERT programs had not been exposed to television courses in their college teacher-training programs, or had even used television in their student teaching. Yet, learning gains of students (measured admittedly on a small, but representative sample of the total viewing audience) did not yield any evidence to support a statistical correlation between learning gains from media and media training of teachers (Cavert, 1968).

The nature and extent of formal in-service media training will help determine how current the educational personnel are with the new media use techniques and instructional philosophy.

In an effort to market a product that has seldom been comprehensively designed for consumer use, many efforts in recent years have been devoted to extensive in-service media training workshops for teachers. These efforts have resulted in a proliferation of glossy utilization guides. However, these guides have been characterized by outlining techniques to use media in the classroom without subjecting teachers to the trauma of having to change their established patterns of teaching.

Project ASERT surveys reported that over 85 percent of the teachers using the programs had not been exposed to any kind of in-service training in the use of instructional television. While these statistics provided information on the extent of in-service training of the educational personnel in the use of instructional television, they provided no clues as to the nature of the training they did have (Cavert, 1968). Therefore, surveys should include the extent and the nature of existing as well as desired in-service training deemed essential for personnel at all levels in the system.

Instructional Environment Conditions

No matter how carefully mediated instruction is designed, if the learner cannot be exposed to it under favorable conditions, little confidence can be placed in achieving the desired results.

PHILOSOPHY TOWARD INSTRUCTIONAL MEDIA   Comparing the stated philosophy toward the use of mediated instruction with the actual use will provide a useful index for the conditions under which the mediated instruction will be used. It must be recognized immediately that student, teacher and administrator attitudes toward instructional technology are largely based on the predisposition of previous experience with more conventional uses of media. The reported use of instructional media in the schools often bears little correlation to their actual use in the academic structure.

The expressed philosophy of the school administrative personnel reflects the atmosphere within the school toward the use of instructional media. This philosophy can verify the approach to instruction accepted in the school. Therefore, it is important to see if school administrators will accept the use of media in each approach to instruction which can be used in design: to provide direct learning experiences for individual student; to provide curriculum guidelines for their classroom teachers; to provide material to supplement the instructional process; or to provide resources to complement the total educational program.

However, these terms must be carefully defined in any survey instrument used to get this information. Respondents to both the 1967 and the 1968 surveys conducted for Nebraska's Project ASERT did not recognize the full potential of instructional television. The only distinction they made in the use of television was between direct instruction and programs to supplement and enrich some vague antecedant (Cavert, 1968). If the school philosophy reflects preference for an instructional approach different from the one used in design, someone must be convinced to accept the approach used before instruction will have any direct effect on the learners in that school.

The observed attitudes of the educational personnel toward the use of instructional media will indicate, with a little more accuracy, which approach to instruction will most likely be accepted in the school. Quite often the stated attitudes of educational personnel will mirror administrative philosophies, while the actual use is a more accurate index of attitude. For example, Project ASERT surveys conducted in over 2,000 school districts in Nebraska revealed that of the 67 percent of the teachers who felt that television should provide enrichment experiences, 36 percent actually used television for direct teaching. Of the 35 percent of the teachers who felt that television could also supplement their efforts in the classroom, almost a third actually used the programs as autonomous experiences, complete within themselves (Cavert, 1968).

Therefore, it should be made quite clear what approach to instruction has been used in design to encourage its proper use in the classroom. Instruction designed to provide curriculum guidelines for the classroom teacher would be of relatively little value if used as complete, direct learning experiences for an individual learner.

POLICIES ON USE OF INSTRUCTIONAL MEDIA   The institutional policies will affect the confidence that mediated instruction will be used as intended.

Instruction can be designed to be consistent with the policies of the institution which supports the total design effort, or efforts can be first directed to change that basic policy. It is not unusual to encounter an expressed policy that teachers can use no more than one television program in any given week. This policy usually reflects the belief that no more time than that should be taken away from the immediate task of teaching. Unfortunately, instructional television braodcast schedules more often than not reflect a servitude to this belief. A great deal can be learned about the role assigned to mediated instruction by looking at how the decisions are made for its use.

If decisions to use any form of mediated instruction are made by administrative mandate, information about the use of this form of instruction would be better communicated directly with school administrative or curriculum supervisory personnel. Discretionary use, dependent on the decisions of each classroom teacher, often finds mediated instruction in conflict with special assemblies, the music consultant's weekly junkets to the school, or even with the scheduled biennial maintenance of the media equipment. But, if the choice to use instructional media is made by the classroom teacher, communication on the intended use must be made directly with the classroom teacher. While information can be designed to communicate directly, getting it to the teacher often poses a much greater logistical problem. Libraries of teachers' guides and weekly information sheets are often stacked high in principals' offices—never distributed to the classroom teacher.

Target Population Conditions

Mediated instruction may not yield the same results when used with a target population other than the one for which it has been designed. Therefore, it must be made clear precisely for whom the instruction was designed. Hopefully, this will prevent disappointment in the results if it is used for another target population. It is then important to specify exactly what conditions for use were planned in design. Many teachers, for example, have provided feedback to instructional television producers that the programs were too fast for their slow students and too slow for their fast students. What is not known from this feedback is how well the television programs did for those students that were neither slow nor fast. However, specifying conditions *expected* to be present for use not only guides the conscientious classroom teacher, but also provides a hedge for the designer when reporting what results to expect.

SELECTION OF THE TARGET POPULATION   Specific characteristics of the individual in the target population should be made known to decide how exposure to mediated instruction can best be accomplished. If instruction has been designed for a specific target population, it should be used only for that specific target population. Therefore, the characteristics used to narrow the total learner population to a specific target group for design should also be made known for use. In addition, it is usually necessary to provide some kind of identification criteria so the classroom teacher knows which students actually possess those characteristics identified in the target population.

PREPARATION OF THE TARGET POPULATION   Mediated instruction will work with any degree of confidence only when used for the target population under the conditions specified in design. To be most effective, the experience must be a part of the total integrated composite of activities in the instructional setting of the learner.

Instruction is quite often dependent on activities that must be conducted in the classroom to provide the identified *prerequisite conditions* before exposure to the mediated segment. With mass-replicability technology such as radio and television, this prerequisite level often must be assumed rather than actually measured or observed. This presupposes a working knowledge of the step-by-step nature of the learning strategy used to design the instructional sequence. Therefore, the nature of the activities to be conducted by the classroom teacher should be made known to the teacher.

In more traditional approaches to television, for example, information would be given on the nature of "pre-program" activities to be conducted by the classroom teacher to prepare a group for viewing. In these procedures for instructional design, information should be provided to help the teacher know how to prepare an individual for learning.

For classroom use, the entry level characteristics that are expected must not only be stated, but precise instructions on determining the entry level of the target population should be provided. It is also important to identify what must be done to assure that every individual is at the level identified before exposure. Where instruction seeks to effect change in a learning environment, specific conditions are assumed to exist prior to the intervention of the mediated segment. For example, efforts may be to provide demonstrations of certain chemical or physical phenomenon to be integrated into an existing curriculum. Entry conditions may specify that the classroom teacher has structured the scope and sequence of instruction leading up to the mediated demonstration.

As opposed to "follow-up activities" to reinforce more traditional approaches to mediated instruction, it is often expected that *conditions to extend learning* beyond the level provided in the mediated segment will be created by the classroom teacher. This also presupposes the classroom teacher is equipped to function as a manager of the environment in which this learning can occur.

However, the nature of existing patterns of behavior of classroom teachers must be known if the emphasis in design will be based on the assumption that these conditions can and will exist. For example, in the Project ASERT surveys it was found that over a third of the teachers who were to use the Project ASERT television programs usually conducted no activities to prepare their classes for viewing. Classroom activities to follow up the television programs were reported by well over 80 percent of the teachers. Although these data were reported on existing patterns of classroom conditions associated with more traditional approaches to instructional television, on the basis of the analysis of this information, it was recommended that design for the use of Project ASERT programs reflect the fact that the teachers appear to be more at ease in working with students *after* they have been exposed to mediated instruction than in structuring conditions to prepare students for learning before exposure (Cavert, 1968).

The terminal response may often be designed to provide prerequisite entry behavior to other extended learning. Thus, specific activities can be conducted in the classroom to extend instruction to higher levels after exposure to the mediated sequence. Hence, it is not only important to specify what terminal conditions are expected from exposure to mediated instruction, but also to specify what other learning or environmental changes can result from the base provided by the mediated instruction.

In the design of stimuli for each of the Design Clusters used to sequence instruction to reach the goal, conditions are suggested to reinforce the mediated stimuli in the actual environment where instruction will be used (see pages 181 to 184). Creating these conditions in the classroom may be essential in integrating the instruction into an articulated pattern for the learner. It will also be important, if the instruction is designed to depend on communication to the classroom teacher, that any communication (print or nonprint) must be tested as a functional part of the total instructional effort.

FACTORS OF CLASSROOM USE   The conditions for selective exposure to selected segments of instruction will also affect the confidence in the results of instruction. Thus, it should be possible in design to describe ways of providing for the *selected use* of only that instruction appropriate to a *selective* group of even the target population.

Diagnosis

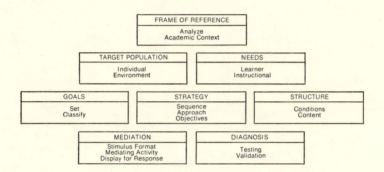

Test results provide feedback to reshape instruction if the response does not occur as expected. When the planned response is made, the diagnosis provides feed forward to advance instruction to the next level. When there is enough confidence in the test results to guarantee more universal findings, instruction is validated.

Diagnosis

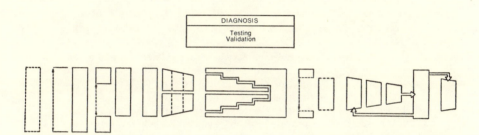

Testing and validation will provide the designer with information about how effectively and consistently the instruction produced the desired results.

When Leon M. Lessinger was the Associate Commissioner for Elementary and Secondary Education at the U.S. Office of Education, he observed that the federal involvement in the education of under-achieving poor children was symptomatic of widespread public concern about the results of education. Lessinger maintained this concern was as a demand that our schools become accountable for results.

Writing for the March 1970 issue of *Educate*, Lessinger said: "With the advent of major federal financial support, people increasingly ask of their schools, What are we getting for our money? Traditional answers in terms of resources used, teachers available, and buildings provided are no longer sufficient. The public wants to know if the young people can read, can get and hold a job, can successfully compete at a higher level of education. This calls for accountability for results—a demand for changes of such size and influence that the results can only be characterized as revolutionary" (Lessinger, 1970).

Lessinger then offered these challenges to educational design: If schools are to be accountable for results, a new approach to their basic mission is necessary. In the first place, the focus must shift from teaching to learning. Second, the schools must cease to merit credit solely for their ability to screen and sort in a rutted roadbed toward college or the discard pile. Third,

213

a technology of instruction based on specific learning objectives must be built. And finally, a rational relationship should be established between costs and benefits (Lessinger, 1970).

Many who seek to discredit the application of systems procedures to education and instruction feel that subjecting a child to batteries of tests and psychometric observations will only further dehumanize education. But it is not the child that is being tested. Rather, it is the effectiveness of the learning system coming under scrutiny in a systematic approach to instructional design. It is (or should be) apparent that if the objectives or goals are not realized, it is, more often than not, the system that has failed to provide adequate situations in which the individual can learn. With adequate instructional design, there is a great range of learning that can occur within the capacity of the intellectual maturity of the learner.

Thus, it is necessary to test not only how well the individual is doing in progressing toward goals, but how well the design effort itself has done in establishing realistic goals.

In talking about developing attitudes toward learning, Robert F. Mager advanced a two-fold approach to instructional diagnosis that will provide the data required to defend adequately any case for accountability for results. Mager says,

> There are two kinds of evaluation to be considered. One is an assessment of whether our students appear as willing to approach our subject at the end of our influence as they were when it began. The other is the assessment of how well we have been doing. In other words, one is the evaluation of results and the other is the evaluation of process. Results evaluation tells us something about how well we have done: process evaluation tells us how we might do better (Mager, 1968).

In recent years results evaluations have been associated with summative testing; process evaluation with formative testing.

Therefore, in instructional design it may be possible to be held accountable both for how well the target population is doing in reaching realistic goals and for how well the entire design effort is doing in creating the conditions where movement toward this end can take place.

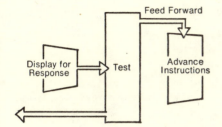

Feed Forward

Display for Response → Test → Advance Instructions

Testing

Testing provides feedback information to reshape instruction if the critical response does not occur. When the planned response does occur, testing provides feed-forward to advance instruction to the next level.

FRAME OF REFERENCE FOR CONDUCTING INSTRUCTIONAL DIAGNOSIS

This design function should begin from the frame of reference established by acknowledging any restraints imposed on using testing to provide feedback information to reshape instruction and to provide feed-forward information to advance instruction.

The chief use of testing may be to discriminate learners, determining norms for grading; this clearly restrains efforts to make the primary role of testing the improvement of instruction. For example, test results showing all students achieved the stated objective may not satisfy the requirements for the distribution of grades along the normal curve.

In the pure application of these design procedures, both formative and summative testing should be conducted at all critical phases. However, this aspect of design may be restrained if predetermined assumptions about the entry level, progress toward the goal or achievement of the goal are allowed. For example, the design of instruction may depend on the known learned competencies. If this entry level is assumed, rather than actually determined by measurement, it is not known whether the learner was not ready for instruction if the goal was not reached or whether instruction was not needed because the goal was too easily reached.

It may often be required that existing standardized tests be used to assess the results of instruction rather than individually designed tests, based on what was intended to be done only in a particular segment of instruction. Standardized tests might not measure what instruction intended to do. Thus, their use would give a distorted and useless view of the effectiveness of the instruction designed.

Testing should be accomplished under the actual conditions of intended use. However, it will more often be the case (especially in the formative stages of design) that testing will have to be conducted under simulated conditions. For example, if a series for televised instruction is being designed, each segment may be shown to a representative sample of the target population and changes made in production until the desired response is made. It would be impossible to isolate the effect of each version of the televised instruction if segments in all stages of development were shown to the same sample of the target population.

Testing

Psychometry in the systematic design of instruction will verify the degree to which the stated objectives were achieved by the target population. But, testing is for instruction diagnosis rather than for the discrimination of learners for grading.

There is almost universal dislike for assessing learner progress by frequent paper-and-pencil tests. This attitude may well have been caused by poor test design and rigid disciplinary controls associated with examinations of this sort in the past. There are no hard data to support the contention that frequent assessment of learner progress toward a goal in any way adversely affects learning. On the contrary, efforts in programed instruction and its further sophistication in computer-assisted instruction have demonstrated repeatedly that frequent assessment of learner progress, coupled with immediate communication of results to the learner, increases the efficiency of a learning situation.

Testing Responsibilities

In establishing any testing procedure for the results of instruction, it is important to know what was sought to be done and for whom. Thus, the responsibilities for testing will vary according to the approach to instruction taken in design.

For example, if all design efforts were directed to provide teaching material to supplement a course of study, measuring only individual learning gains might be beyond the scope of immediate testing responsibilities. The design effort should have been directed, in this example, only to create material to supplement the instructional process so that each classroom teacher would use the material in his or her own way to guide student responses. Ultimately then, the teacher's efforts would result in the desired learning gains. Since producing this learning was not a direct responsibility in design, it should not be a direct responsibility in testing.

In psychometry for instructional design, testing responsibilities are limited to finding out if objectives were achieved—if instruction made the learner respond as expected, under the conditions specified, to the degree of accuracy stated or implied (and for reasons that made sense to the learner). It has been said that a well-formulated objective is its own test. The statement of the objective should so specify what is required to show evidence of achievement that there is little room for ambiguity.

Testing in the Direct Experience Approach

The testing responsibilities in the Direct Experience Approach are limited to a measurement of learner responses to show evidence of specific learning gains after direct exposure to instruction.

What is important in testing for direct learning experiences is to isolate, as much as possible, the effect of the designed instruction. Pretesting may indicate that the individual cannot respond as expected in the statement of objective before exposure to instruction. However, after exposure to mediated instruction, it is important to know if his response is a direct result of the mediated instruction designed. Other elements in the classroom or the environment may have caused the response to occur. Often, it is impossible to tell what caused the response to be made with absolute certainty.

There are statistical ways to indicate the probability that the correct responses could have occurred at random, or if one target group (who may have learned the experience from other sources) is different from another. Often it is necessary, especially when restrained by time and financial resources, to say that exposure to the mediated segment of instruction *most likely* produced the response if most students who were exposed to the instruction responded as intended while most students who were not exposed to the instruction did not.

For instance, it is highly unlikely that all students in typical sixth-grade classroom will have all of the characteristics of a target population. Therefore, a profile of the target population should be communicated to those responsible for the conditions under which mediated instruction will be used. It will also be necessary to provide specific help to determine those characteristics ascribed to the target population. Under ideal conditions, *only* those individuals identified as the target population will be exposed to instruction. In some nongraded, rural, one-room elementary schools in Nebraska during the Project ASERT effort, for example, target population students clustered around a television receiver turned to a corner of the classroom for viewing, and listened to the audio portion of the program with earphones connected to a "listening station."

For the objective in which it is stated: "Given a specific agricultural product, the learner will trace its history from planting to consumer purchase," it is the responsibility to test only how accurately the student can list all the steps important from planting to purchase. Different tests may be administered with different agricultural products as the variable. This would test for consistency of response to see if the individual has learned the principle, not just memorized the steps for the product given in the instruction.

Another objective may be stated: "Given a list with ten printed numbers and ten quantities of various objects, the learner will correctly match the number with the illustration containing the amount of objects."

Testing responsibilities seem to be quite clearly outlined in this example. To show evidence that the learner can translate written numerical symbols to number values, matching the items to written symbols on a paper-and-pencil test is accepted as evidence that he has learned the concept. If the individual has responded as expected, it can also be assumed that the treatment of the content material in mediated instruction was appropriate to create the desired learning gains.

However, there are other testing aspects not prescribed in the objective, for which there is also a design responsibility. Because the characteristics of the target population are known, the selection of items used for identification should be familiar to this child. It is not the testing responsibility to measure recognition or discrimination of objects. It would not be appropriate to this target population, for example, to show a group of pocket watches. The learner in this target group probably has never seen a pocket watch. And, the number that the hands point to might introduce an irrelevant prompting stimulus for a response that might be correct to the learner, but not the one expected in design. It would also not be appropriate to show a group of three octopuses, for the learner might try to match the 24 arms rather than the three bodies. But these alternative tests are not uncommon in conventional as well as in mediated instruction.

This testing error is more frequently seen when attempting to match the initial letters of items with written alphabetic symbols. Would an illustration of a pocket watch cue the response in a young child of the letter "C' (for clock), "P" (for pocket watch), "W" (for watch), "T" (for time), "N" (for noon) or "A" (for antique)?

Testing in the Course of Study Guidelines Approach

The testing responsibilities in the Course of Study Guidelines Approach are limited to assessing the fact that the guidelines are mediated so teachers can actually use them to change what is done in the classroom. Implied in the responsibilities for testing in the Course of Study Guidelines Approach is an assessment of whether the resultant change in the classroom teaching actually helps students learn better.

Ultimately the responsibility for design in this approach to instruction is to test how much the mediated course of study guidelines actually increased teaching effectiveness. Unless other standards are imposed by some academic structure, increased teaching effectiveness is seen by how much better the students learn from what the teacher does. Therefore, there is implied an interrelated two-fold responsibility to assess the effectiveness of mediated guidelines: First, are they mediated so that teachers actually can and will put them to use; second, does the resultant change in the classroom teaching actually help students learn better. Thus the assessment of increased teaching effectiveness is conducted by testing both learner response and teacher use.

For example, an objective may be stated: "The student will describe the basic differences between Nebraska's Unicameral Legislature and the two-house system used in all other states when presented with comparative information by the classroom teacher in a prescribed course of study that has been implemented by mediated guidelines." A direct measurement of student responses may not isolate other variables from the mediated guidelines. Unless the existing guidelines are not followed at all, it is going to be hard to tell how much the mediated effort augmented these for the teacher to follow. Assessment of the ability to follow guidelines now that the teacher probably could not have in the past may have to rely on subjective and largely empirical reaction surveys. However, again, if the teachers could not get students to make this discrimination of legislature types in the past with guidelines that should have been used, and does get this response after following the mediated guidelines, acceptable achievement of the objective is indicated.

Testing in the Supplemental Material Approach

Testing responsibilities in the Supplemental Material Approach are limited to the evaluation of how the material can be used by the teachers within the existing instructional process to show evidence of growth in the scope of the instructional process. A secondary responsibility would be to determine if the material mediated brought forth better learner responses than did other instruction.

In this approach to instruction, the instructional responsibility is so far removed from directly affecting the learner that the responsibility in testing is quite limited. Testing should only evaluate the way the mediated material has changed the environment influencing what a teacher uses in the classroom. An increase in the scope of an instructional process is seen ultimately in how the learner responds to the use of the material.

The material, in turn, must have been used by the teacher in the classroom structure. Variables are introduced by the way the teacher uses the material and by the way the course of study is structured. Evaluation should be made of the use of the mediated material by the teacher as an *indicator* that environmental conditions conducive to the desired learner response have been changed.

For example, it is assumed that the actual legislative process (as instructional material) is unaccessible for teachers to use in the objective that specifies: "The steps involved from the introduction of a legislative bill to its final enactment as law will be so demonstrated that the learner will analyze the human factor involved in each step of the process." Here, it is clear that both the product and the process of instruction must be evaluated.

First, it is required in the objective that some form of material about the procedures of a specific legislative process be made accessible to classroom teachers to supplement an instructional process. The completeness and the mediated form of the material can be evaluated to see how teachers now use this material in their instructional process. Second, eventually the learner must display increased intellectual skills after being exposed to this mediated material in the classroom. In the way the objective has been stated, and the approach selected, it is *not* the responsibility of the designer to test whether the mediated segment alone caused the learner to analyze the human factor of the legislative process. It is assumed in design that this concept will be a part of the conventional instructional process for the learner. Supplemental material has been mediated for use in this conventional instructional process to make its display to the learner more effective and efficient. *This* responsibility of design is what must be evaluated.

The learner, for example, may not even be exposed to required material if mediated instruction had not translated its undesirable facets into a more usable form. Material was mediated to achieve the objective where it was stated: "In order for the learner to demonstrate how radioactive tracers can be used to detect bone disease, the procedures and cautions required in handling radioactive substances must be described before actual use."

The testing responsibility is simply to evaluate if the teachers are now willing to use this radioactive material they found undesirable (as dangerous to themselves or their students) in the past. In this way, to treat the Supplemental Material Approach, it is first essential to evaluate whether the material is used now in the instructional process when it hasn't been in the past. Then, it is a secondary responsibility to see whether the material for the teacher is mediated in such a way that it communicates the concept, illustrates the principle, or demonstrates a phenomenon that is a part of instruction and that, when properly used by the classroom teacher, students will learn from having been exposed to it.

Efforts to make material available to the teachers to supplement an instructional process may have been made to achieve this objective: "In order for the learner to observe the phenomena of the effects of specific gravity of liquids on solid objects, the demonstration where objects descend at varying rates in containers of different liquids must be readily available for the teacher to use in the instructional process." In this case, then, the testing responsibility would include only an evaluation of the teaching situations after exposure to the mediated segment to see if the teachers now want to use this demonstration in their instructional process.

Testing how the learner responds to the demonstration is not a direct primary responsibility of design itself. Too many things can happen between the design of such mediated material and its use in the conventional instruction that to measure the learner's response is not a primary responsibility of testing. Some teachers may use the demonstration for individual learners to extrapolate the principle themselves. Others may show the mediated demonstration and explain what is happening. Still others may ask the students to replicate the experiment after they think they have determined the principle it demonstrates. Each use is legitimate and would indicate the objective as stated has been achieved.

However, there is a responsibility to tell the teachers not only how to use the mediated material, but also how to test results in the desired kind and level of learning. Knowledge of these other test results, and the conditions both of testing and instruction, will be of value in the instructional diagnosis.

Testing in the Enriched Resources Approach

The testing responsibilities in the Enriched Resources Approach are limited to observations of how appropriate to the instructional situation the resources are. A secondary responsibility would be to see how the resources are used for the learner.

Even when designed in a systematic approach, instruction to "enrich" is difficult to test. This is chiefly because an "enriched" educational program is difficult to define objectively. Perhaps more so than in any other approach to instruction, *indicators* of the desired result must be relied on more than direct testing of a response.

Since there is some generality and ambiguity in stating objectives for this approach to instruction, caution must be exercised to guard against measuring results that were not attempted. If the objective establishes that the specific way resources are used for a learner will be accepted as evidence that the educational program has been enriched, then the responsibility in testing is to observe how these resources are indeed used for the learner. But, the responsibility in design is so far removed from directly affecting the learner. The variables of the classroom teaching structure, the course of study and the instructional process may be beyond any direct control in design. Testing of anything but the use of the resources for the learner would be highly speculative at best.

The motivation of the learner to "appreciate fine music" involves responsibilities that are deeper than the surface statement in the objective, "The learner will be exposed to enough classical music from which the rhythms and melodies of many popular tunes have been adapted that he will actively seek out additional classicial compositions to compare." It is possible to determine whether a person is motivated to appreciate fine music, as Mager has said, if "we can predict he will say favorable things about it, that he will put himself in the presence of that kind of stimulus, and that he will stay in the presence of that kind of stimulus as long as he can" (Mager, 1968).

There is an indication of motivation when we can "concentrate on increasing the incidence of 'moving toward,' or *approach* responses, and reducing the incidence of 'moving away from,' or *avoidance* responses" (Mager, 1968).

Thus, after the end of our influence over the learner in the mediated instructional segment, his motivation may have been increased if he is more inclined to approach the concept or resource than he was before he was exposed to the mediated resources. Ultimately, this apparent increased motivation should produce better learning but this effect may often be long range and must be observed over a rather extended period of time. It is important *not* to extend the testing responsibilities in design to things that were never attempted to be done.

Testing Procedures

The objectives for each approach are formulated in the larger context of a total learning sequence. Thus, it must be determined what information about results is required at all levels within the structural framework from which the mediated segment of instruction evolved.

Pretesting for Entry Behavior

If the results of testing are to be applied in the development or assessment of the instruction, the level at which the target population entered the planned instructional experience must be known. It is essential that the target population have the required entry level characteristics before exposure to the mediated instruction. Therefore, it is also essential in testing the results to identify the level of entry behavior *measured* to establish firm evidence of learner readiness or to identify the levels of entry behavior *assumed* learned previously by the target population.

The analysis of the entry level tells much about the effectiveness of the design effort. If the target population was not at the assumed entry level before exposure to instruction, then the design efforts would most likely be beyond the performance capabilities. If, on the other hand, the target population was able to perform at levels beyond the assumed entry level, the exposure could well have been redundant, even boring.

Progress Testing for Enabling Behavior

The progress of the target population toward the terminal objective can be determined by testing performance at enabling levels. In attempts to analyze the terminal response, it may often be essential to test each enabling level. In this way, it can be more easily established where the design effort may have failed to provide adequate situations for learning or for the desired environmental change to take place.

Measurement of progress toward a goal may yield as much useful information as testing at the goal level. It is, therefore, important to identify which enabling levels will require direct testing and which levels will not have to be tested because their prerequisite nature allows performance capability at other levels to be assumed from measured performance at higher levels.

Posttesting for Terminal Behavior

The specific terminal behavior must be known to determine if the instruction has achieved the specific objective for which it was designed. The terminal behavior describes the response characteristics specified in the objectives. However, in any given instructional experience, several objectives may be treated, each dependent on other performance achievement in the same or in other learning domains. Thus it is necessary to describe the specific terminal conditions that will actually be tested after exposure to instruction. It may well be, for example, that performance at one level may also document performance capabilities at other terminal levels in the same or in related learning domains. Then, testing at these other levels would not be necessary. However, it must also be recognized that if all terminal levels are not measured, failure at any given point may be difficult to analyze for corrective measures.

Test Components

The components of the actual test instrument should be structured to be in harmony with the design of instruction if the results of testing are to provide information that can be used in design.

Testing for the Nature of Response

The nature of the planned response will help determine what techniques will be used in the actual test instrument. These specific techniques will be based on the response characteristics established to show the achievement of the goal, as well as by the conditions under which the response is expected to occur. Specifications may have to be given for a medium to display stimuli to achieve either an overt response or a covert response. In a similar manner, then, the testing techniques should also reflect the nature of the anticipated response.

DIRECT TESTING FOR ACTIVE RESPONSES   Where the medium has been used to get an active response, direct testing techniques would be best. If in the objective it is stated that the learner solve a certain type of algebraic equation, then the response can be tested directly by setting the conditions under which the learner can demonstrate this mathematical intellectual skill. The overt act of working out all of the steps in the solving of the algebraic equation on a pencil-and-paper test will provide more usable information on the effectiveness of instruction than just asking the learner to recite the answer.

INDIRECT TESTING FOR PASSIVE RESPONSES   The medium may have been used in design for a more passive response. In these situations, then, the testing techniques used must be more indirect, but yet give reliable data on successful attainment of the goal or objective. Robert F. Mager, in his book, *Developing Attitudes Toward Learning*, has provided some guidelines for the development of testing (as well as design) techniques for affective learning where passive responses are more likely to occur. He maintains that "attitude" is a word used to refer to a general tendency of an individual to act in a certain way under certain conditions. Contrary to the more popularly held belief that attitudes cannot be measured, Mager maintains that attitudes are based on what someone says or what he does. It is based on visible behavior. In the measurement of an attitude then, we are making an inference from visible behavior about an internal, invisible condition (Mager, 1968).

Thus, if it desired to measure the change in an individual's attitude toward a policeman after exposure to mediated instruction, testing procedures should look for some observable or measurable behavior that will be demonstrated by the learner if his attitude has been changed. Since learning deficiencies have been clearly identified by some visible indication that a desired condition does not exist, it can therefore be assumed that there will also be some visible indication that the condition of the desired attitude change has occurred. Tests can then be designed to measure this change in attitude indirectly from some observable learner behavior.

Testing for Occurrence of Response

The times at which the response is expected to occur will also influence the structure of the test instrument. The objectives will specify not only if the nature of the response will be active or passive, but also if it is expected that the response occur immediately during or after exposure to instruction or is expected to be delayed for some extended period of time.

ISOLATED TESTING FOR IMMEDIATE RESPONSES   Isolated testing techniques can be designed where intermittent pacing has been used to elicit immediate learner responses. In this way, the effect of the mediated instruction can best be isolated from other learning variables. For example, an analog computer program is usually written to stop the progress of the instructional experience until the learner makes an immediate response to some testing function in the program itself. In some programs, the learner can then be branched to remedial, sequential or advanced instructional increments based on his response. This technique can also be used in less interactive mediation such as radio and television by providing some testing technique for the classroom teacher to measure, in isolation, learner *responses*. The technique may also provide some psychometric criteria for the observation of the *reactions* of the target population sought in design.

To assess the effectiveness of the mediated instruction itself, it is desirable, almost necessary, to use testing techniques that will measure the response immediately after exposure to the segment. For example, it may be expected that the learner will draw two-dimensional representations of various three-dimensional geometric shapes shown to him. The only reliable data on the effectiveness of the instruction (isolated from all other variables to the extent possible) would be to ask the learner to draw the desired shapes immediately after his exposure to the mediated instruction.

CUMULATIVE TESTING FOR DELAYED RESPONSES   Where continuous pacing has been used in production for, or to delay, learner responses after exposure to the instruction, cumulative testing techniques should be used.

Some responses may be designed to occur weeks, even months after the exposure to the mediated instruction. For this type of response, the testing technique will assume a totally different character. It is usually desired to measure how the learner has been prepared to respond to other stimuli with which he will be confronted during the interim between his exposure to the mediated stimuli and the time when the response is expected to occur. For example, the mediated instruction may be designed to create a disposition in the learner to respond to a policeman in different ways than before. The response can only be observed or measured when the opportunity is provided for an actual confrontation between the learner and a policeman.

However, uncounted variables in the total educational environment of the learner will have an effect on his response. The longer the time interval between the exposure to instruction and the time that the individual is expected to respond is directly proportional to the effective isolation of the contribution made by the mediated experience.

Hence, it can be seen that testing techniques would be very difficult to design for an objective that guides instruction to "expose a student now to good music so that five years from now he will be a more discriminating consumer of the fine arts." With the almost infinite number of variables and learning stimuli to which he will be exposed in the five years that follow his brief exposure to the mediated "good music sequence," it would be virtually impossible to isolate the effect which that instruction had on the ultimate response. It would be more desirable as well as more manageable to test in a cumulative fashion the tendencies of the learner to act in a certain way when confronted with other stimuli after exposure to his mediated instruction.

Testing Influences of Response Conditions

The restrictions formulated as part of the objective will introduce variables that must be considered in the structure of the test instrument. In a like manner, the academic environment in which the instruction will be used will also introduce variables to be considered in the design of tests.

NATURAL VARIABLES   Variables introduced by the natural conditions in the academic environment must be considered in the design of the test instrument. It should be recognized that aspects of the total environment in which the learner will be exposed to instruction will affect his response. Hence, the testing techniques must also reflect how these environmental variables will affect the interpretation of the results. These environmental variables include the physical conditions under which the learner was exposed to the mediated sequence (such as television or radio reception quality or the presence or absence of distractants to instruction), as well as the specific learner variables (such as an unusual emotional or tension state at the time of testing or during instruction).

STRUCTURED VARIABLES   Variables introduced by the structured conditions to the response in the statement of objective should also be considered in designing the test instrument. While it has been said that a well-written objective is, in itself, its own best test, caution should be exercised in asking others to administer tests. For example, an objective stated:

"Given large sheets of paper with ten circles, three inches in diameter, and ten three-inch squares, assorted crayons, and a smooth working surface, the student will use the crayons to fill the ten circles and ten squares within two consecutive days with no more than one linear inch per circle or square colored outside the figure outlined."

This objective, to all outward appearances, would leave little latitude for variations in the design of a specific test. Yet, in the classroom, it should not be assumed that all teachers will provide the same format for the test of this objective. One teacher, for example, may alternate squares with circles on the sheet given to the learner. Another may put all 20 figures on a single sheet. Yet others may interpret the word "large" as being notebook-size paper while colleagues may be providing wall murals for the same purpose. In comparing the results of each of these situations, any variables in the format of the test, even when designed from a quite specific objective, may affect the reliability of the information received. Therefore, in the design of a test, it may also be necessary to provide precise specifications of its format and administration.

It is not unusual for the objective to be written with a specific test in mind. The two functions are so interrelated that to separate them, even in this description of a systematic design procedure, is almost artificial. Indeed, many designers now include the formulation of the criterion test item as a component of the statement of objective itself.

Criterion of Acceptable Performance in Testing

The criteria against which the results of the test will be assessed will determine the kind of test instrument that can be used. For the statement of the degree of acceptable performance in the objective, a basic criterion for the test is known. If the learner is expected to demonstrate learning gains by how he can classify concepts in a sequential order, for example, it is necessary not only to display the concepts to be arranged, but also to establish the criteria against which the learner would be expected to perform to be acceptable as evidence of learning.

To quantify results, the criterion is often expressed as a ratio of the accepted score by the accepted number of students. For example, 65 percent of the learners may be expected to score 70 on the test to be accepted as evidence that instruction has achieved the objective to the degree that will be acceptable. Where a degree of achievement of objectives cannot be quantified, this ratio (expressed as 90/90 for example) will mean that ninety percent of the learners must achieve ninety percent of the objectives for instruction to be said to be reliable.

To measure the effectiveness of instruction, some criteria of success should also be considered in the design of a text. The criteria offered by Donald R. Miller for the California Project to Prepare Educational Planners can be used, with Mager's concept of the two-fold responsibilities of testing, to assess *results* against some *absolute* criteria with some form of *performance* tests; and to assess the *process* of design against some *relative* criteria with some form of *standardized* tests.

USE OF PERFORMANCE TESTING   Performance testing can be used where absolute criteria will determine evidence of acceptable performance in the results of instruction. According to Miller, in his "Systems Approach to Educational Management," absolute criteria facilitate the design of instruction for performance by their use in measuring "minimum levels of acceptable performance according to previously defined requirements, specifications, and objectives" (Miller, 1968).

More often than not, tests will have to be designed for the specific instructional moment. It would rarely be true that the existing published tests would provide the precise measurement structure for instruction that has been designed for the statement of a specific objective. It is not accepted practice (although it does happen) to begin with an existing test item, and then write objectives and design instruction to enable students to reply to that test item as desired. This method of "teaching to the test" should be quite clearly distinguished from designing the test to measure only what is expected that the individual learn as a result of instruction.

USE OF STANDARDIZED TESTING   Standardized testing can be used where relative criteria will determine evidence of learning. According to Miller, relative criteria measure "achievement of a performance unit in terms of levels of achievement demonstrated by other groups performing the same or related functions or tasks. Relative criteria can be structured according to efficiency, proficiency, effectiveness, costs, benefits, advances, and other factors" (Miller, 1968).

Standardized tests, such as the *Iowa Test of Basic Skills*, the *California Achievement Tests*, and others, can be used *in addition to* the performance tests formulated to measure achievement of the objective. Since it has been recommended that every objective *must* contain a statement of absolute criteria and *may* contain a statement of relative criteria, the use of performance tests would be a requirement of design, where the use of standardized tests would be an option open to design.

Scope of Testing Requirements

During the developmental phase of instructional design, the testing requirements became an integrated element of design. Formative testing during design differs somewhat in form from the kind that will be used in the actual field implementation of instruction.

FORMATIVE TESTING   One of the advantages of the validation process is that any segment of instruction can be designed, tested and revised until it works with the confidence desired. This process depends heavily on formative testing. Formative testing is done in the actual formulation of instruction and is an integral part of its design. The use of criterion tests is recommended during the entire developmental phase of design in order to locate immediately and with some precision where the weaknesses of instruction may be.

"A criterion test consists of test items or testing situations designed to demonstrate achievement of *all* objectives for a course of instruction. During the formative testing of instruction, a pretest consisting of items dealing with the appropriate objectives is given to the students before the instructional material is administered. After the students have gone through the instruction, a posttest covering the same objectives is given. The information derived from these two tests is used as a basis for revising instruction" (General Programmed Teaching, 1968).

Criterion tests measure specific *responses*. Performance tests measure general *performance*. The learner's performance is seen in the cumulative effect of what responses he makes at any given category of a learning domain. Thus, it may be possible to use performance tests to show evidence of achievement at any given step within a learning domain. Criterion tests should be used to measure responses that indicate incremental learning gains at each performance level.

SUMMATIVE TESTING   Criterion tests can be adapted to sample only those objectives needed to measure achievement in the actual field use of instruction. After instruction has been through enough cycles of formative testing to have confidence that it will do what was intended, it is field-tested with larger numbers of students in a setting closely resembling that in which the completely developed and validated instruction will be used.

Testing of this field trial of instruction may not measure achievement of every terminal objective, subobjective, and enabling objective against which instruction was designed. Rather, the performance test can be used to measure the results of instruction in actual use. This measurement can be based on a judgment of which objectives are critical to the intent of instruction, or which objectives would function as indicators of ability to respond to other objectives.

Generally, the structure of the test instrument in summative testing is more general than the criterion test used in formative testing. However, if weaknesses of instruction are evident by the persistent failure to respond as expected, the full criterion test of formative testing may have to be administered to locate and isolate the trouble spots.

Test Structure

The format of the test should be designed to give results that will be objective, reliable, and valid.

Test Format

The specific test used must be structured to get information about the instruction designed. This means that the test instruments must not only yield information on how well the mediated sequence has achieved the stated objectives, but it must be designed to provide direction for change and improvement in the design of subsequent instruction. While the statement of objectives will, to a large extent, determine the physical format of the test, the way it will be administered will also affect the format.

TAKEN TESTS   The test may be designed to be self-administered by the individual learner. Thus, its format must reflect known characteristics of the target population as well as the response characteristics for which measurement is sought. For example, a test should not be designed that depends on reading to measure learning of a nonreader's psychomotor skill. Less obvious, but perhaps more frequently violated, is the consideraation of the cultural and societal background and experiences of a learner when designing items that must be identified and classified in the test.

GIVEN TESTS   It may be expedient to allow the test to be administered by the classroom teacher to the learners either individually or collectively as a group. The test would then require quite a different format. In addition to specific instructions to administer the test, the format may also include criteria that can be applied by the classroom teacher to judge, compile, and report the responses of the target population. This test format would most frequently, for example, be provided for the classroom teacher in the teacher's guide to a television series.

MEDIATED TESTS   The format of a test would be obviously much different if it were mediated as a part of the instructional segment itself. Most computer-assisted instruction programs include the testing device to allow for branched sequences depending on the response of the learner. However, a mediated test is not uncommon to other electronic instructional devices. Countless instructional television programs in elementary mathematics have been planned to display a teacher next to a magnetboard with an incomplete equation, attempting to measure an incremental learning gain by asking: "$2A \times 4A$ = what— (pause) That's right, $8A^2$?!" However, it is rarely considered what reinforcement this style of presentation has on the learner who responded "$6A$" or on the one who fogot to multiply the A factor and responded "$8A$" during the pause allowed for the unseen response.

Hence, when mediating the test itself, the format must reflect the fact that responses are not always immediately known and adjustments must be made to acknowledge possible incorrect answers as well as to reward or reinforce correct responses. Then, too, when the test is designed to be mediated as a part of instruction itself, the resultant information must be fed back into the design effort if subsequent increments are to be built on the result of previous experience.

Testing Confidence

The confidence that can be placed in the test results will be determined by the degree of reliability, validity, and objectivity that will be accepted.

RELIABILITY   The consistency with which the test measures desired performance on various occasions establishes the reliability of the test. Reliability, as used in these design procedures, is defined as the ability of the test instrument to measure the same thing whenever it is administered. In designing tests for radio and television, for example, where the target population is most likely dispersed over a wide geographic area, it is important to rely on information gathered from varied academic situations. Hence, the importance of the instrument to consistently test the same response characteristic is essential.

VALIDITY   The accuracy with which the test measures desired performance establishes the validity of the test instrument. Validity, as used in these design procedures, can be determined simply by asking: "Does the test instrument measure *only* what was intended in the instruction leading toward the objective?"

Often designing of a valid test is not as simple as defining it.

In Project ASERT, young learners were asked to identify from a series of photographs those people, including a policeman, to whom they could turn for help if they were lost. When inconsistent results were obtained, an analysis showed that the quality of the various photographs varied so widely that what may have been measured was not the child's disposition toward a policeman but his ability to identify photographic quality.

In another Project ASERT validation attempt, actual buildings illustrating various architectural styles were shown on television. However, the test instrument asked the learner to identify these architectural styles from line drawings of the same buildings. It is doubtful if valid results were obtained since the stimuli to which the learner was asked to respond were mediated for him in different ways. Hence, it was not known whether a learner failed to identify architectural styles or failed to associate the televised image of the actual building with the line drawing in the test.

Thus, to determine the effectiveness of mediated instruction, it is essential to establish that the test will measure only the response desired rather than new and often irrelevant stimuli in the test instrument itself.

It is also a common phenomenon in testing for students to attempt to "beat the system" and to respond as they think they are expected to respond. Obviously such results would have little value to improve future instruction for this learner. If, however, even these results were used in a conscientious, systematic way, the learner will be faced with instruction he is not ready for and *may* soon realize that the instruction, not himself, was being tested.

It is at this point in design where replies are differentiated from responses. A reply can be made by the learner without any substantial base of learned competencies, simply by "parroting back" information he knows is desired. A response is a genuine indication of learned competencies.

OBJECTIVITY   The test instrument must be designed so that the same test is administered in the same way by anyone in any given situation. If the directions for administering the test are vague, or if the test itself is so ambiguous that a great deal of freedom is permitted in its administration, then the final results may be so affected by uncontrolled variables as to be useless in future design efforts.

Conditions for Testing

Mediated instruction can be guaranteed to work only when it is used under the conditions specified in design. Therefore, for confidence in the results of testing, the conditions under which it will be expected that testing be conducted should be formulated as a part of design.

There should be a high degree of control over the environmental setting and over the conditions for learning that must be present in order to reduce the variables and to isolate any reasons why the instruction did not produce the desired results.

The Population for Testing

The instruction will be validated only when used with the target population for which it was designed. In establishing the nature of the testing, it is important to know all characteristics of the individual used in the design to identify the target population.

POPULATION CHARACTERISTICS   The characteristics and needs of a specific individual identified as the target population have been the base from which instruction was designed. It is necessary as well to use this learner profile for testing. The design effort meets its objective only for the needs of the identified target population. Learning gains or environmental changes *may* be observed in individuals or for situations other than those of the target population. Operationally, however, it must be assumed that these other responses are secondary to design. Cost effectiveness and accountability can be based only on the responses of the identified target population.

POPULATION SIZE   The learner population for testing may be identified either as the total target population or as a sample.

To get the most reliable data, testing should eventually be conducted with all individuals identified as the target population. The larger the scope of influence of the mediated instruction, the more complex the task of collecting and compiling the resultant information for analysis and interpretation. However, even when the target population is relatively large, if it is geographically concentrated, it may be possible to test instruction with the total target group. Similarly, where the identified target group is relatively small but widely dispersed, more reliable information might be gained by testing the total identified population.

Often the size of the target population or its geographic dispersement may present very real logistical restraints that would prohibit testing the total target group. In these cases, it may be desired to determine a statistically representative sample of the target population which can be used. If the sample is scientifically selected, the results can be extrapolated to the response characteristics of the total target population.

While the statistical methods are beyond the scope for description in these design procedures, many publications exist to guide the designer in this effort. It is generally accepted in the business community (in test-marketing of a product or in television rating services) as well as in the academic community (in establishing national norms or the reliability of standardized tests) that a representative sample of the total population will be an accurate reflection of the responses of the total population.

It is usually accepted that the sample should be accurate to the ".05 level of confidence." This means that in only 5 times out of 100 would the response of the sample group be the same as the response of the total population merely by chance. In other words, it can usually be established that 95 times out of 100, testing a statistically representative group would produce the same results as testing the entire group.

Closed Distribution for Testing

In most cases, exposure to instruction for formative testing will be in ways other than the actual operational situation. For example, while televised instruction may be designed for broadcast, exposure for testing may use videotape within a more limited geographic area.

However, in considering the distribution mode for testing, it must be recognized that any mode other than that planned for actual field use may introduce variables that would affect the reliability of results. Pretesting of television programs has been known to be tried by playing an audiotape of the lesson to the audience or by having the television teacher present an identical lesson "live" to a classroom audience. Even less obvious, but more dominant perhaps, are attempts to pretest books with typed copies instead of the final typeset printed form. Attempts to extrapolate these results to the effect anticipated in the actual dissemination mode may not be reliable.

Medium and message are not separate and distinct entities but are so interrelated that changing one may also change the basic structure of the other. There are ways in which the design effort can be displayed only to the testing population and yet yield reliable data that can be extrapolated to the total target population.

IN-HOUSE DISTRIBUTION   A representative sample of the target population can be brought to some central location to be exposed to mediated instruction. For example, television experiences have often been pretested by bringing a representative sample class to view the program in the television studio or control room. This distribution mode has as an advantage that all performance and environmental conditions can be directly controlled to assure that the situation in which the learning or environmental changes expected are as close as possible to that planned. It is also advantageous to use in-house distribution to get the test results immediately.

In-house distribution has the disadvantage of creating an artificial environment—beyond the controlled instructional situation—often quite different from the actual learning environment. In this mode, it is almost impossible to disguise the fact that an experimental situation exists, and what degree the "Hawthorne Effect" will have on the final results may never be known.

FIELD DISTRIBUTION   The population for testing can also be exposed to instruction in their actual learning environment. Field distribution for formative testing seeks to duplicate as closely as possible the actual field conditions expected in the operational exposure of mediated instruction to the total target population. There are advantages to using field distribution. Not only are the variables of a foreign learning environment reduced to a minimum, but the way the classroom teacher manages the environment for learning can be examined.

However, this also poses an obvious disadvantage. There is relatively little direct control over the elements of the situation in which the learner is exposed to instruction. It must therefore be assumed that all conditions of entry behavior were met and tests were properly administered. Often, too, field distribution has an inherent time lag in reporting back test results.

For electronic media, such as instructional radio or television, closed field testing can be accomplished by using a recorded copy of the planned broadcast. When audio- or videotape copies of the instruction are brought to a school and played back on hardware in the classroom, the result is quite similar to that described in the in-house distribution mode. If, on the other hand, the video or audio recording is transmitted to a classroom through a central distribution system, the situation for testing would approach true in-field distribution mode.

In Nebraska's Project ASERT, for example, video recordings of the television experiences were brought to various schools equipped with videotape recorders and central antenna distribution systems. A schedule was established to play the television experiences for the target audience on a regular, sequential basis. This schedule was similar to the one planned for the operational phase and fit into the familiar pattern of classroom viewing using other television efforts.

Open Distribution for Testing

Testing of the instruction can also use the actual operational situation designed for exposure of the target population. The testing results are then compiled only for the sample of the total population exposed to instruction.

NONSCHEDULED DISTRIBUTION   The sample population for testing can be exposed to instruction by nonscheduled distribution by making the availability of instruction known only to the selected groups. However, where a nonscheduled mode such as broadcast is used, for example, no assurance can be made that other groups, with whom no communication of purpose or intent is made, will not also view or listen. This could encourage attempts to use an incomplete, and as yet untried product in some schools. The possible result of these attempts may create a negative attitude toward the instruction before it is revised and released for general consumption in its finished, tested form. However, using nonscheduled distribution does have its advantages, especially when it is desired to efficiently reach the test sample in a wide geographic area.

SCHEDULED DISTRIBUTION   The mediated experience to be tested can also be included as a part of the normal distribution schedule for other mediated instruction. This scheduled distribution mode becomes almost mandatory where the total target population has been identified as the test group. Apart from the logistical advantage of testing over a widely based target group, the use of scheduled broadcast for distribution, for example, places a product before the consumer much sooner even though its effectiveness has not been demonstrated. This may be important if funding groups require a visible and immediate result from their expenditures.

The disadvantages to the use of a scheduled distribution for testing are many. Chiefly, it places untried and nonvalidated instruction before the total population with little time to place revised material before these same learners. Usually, in this distribution mode, the first, and even second, year of learners may not benefit from a fully tested attempt to achieve the objectives.

Validation

Instruction is validated when the tested instruction gives enough consistent results for the designer to have confidence to guarantee it will do what was intended, when used under appropriate conditions for a specific target population.

Validation serves several functions. The obvious reason is to continually revise the material until it works. The designer can be satisfied only when his effort has been validated to effect the planned change in an individual or in the environment. All too often, however, attempts to "validate" mediated instruction, for example, will ask only that members of the design and production team go into an actual classroom to watch their product. Funds could be expended in other aspects of design by allowing this team to watch their product elsewhere if examination of only the product is the intent. If the purpose is to verify consistency in use of the product, the design team should be sent to watch learners respond to the mediated instruction.

Validation serves academic, administrative and logistical functions as well. A validated, mediated, instructional experience can be used with the confidence that it will work whenever used with an appropriate learner in a situation similar to the one for which it was validated. A bank of such mediated instruction could be established from which the educational system could draw, with a high degree of confidence.

Administratively, a validated instructional sequence represents a budgetary item more closely associated with a capital investment than with an operational expense. For example, relatively expensive and redundant efforts for teachers to present the same material seven periods a day, semester after semester, year after year, could be reduced. Validated instruction can keep costs from increasing with a presentational effort that has proven to be effective. This is possible by allowing a more effective presentation to be mediated and stored for retrieval. Validated mediated instruction is also as visible to an inventory as are desks and chalkboards, because it is an integral part of the educational system and not peripheral to it.

Criteria for Validation

To get the confidence required for a statement of validation, it is necessary first to conduct a face value evaluation of the mediated instruction. It is then important to subject the mediated instruction to an empirical review before conducting actual performance assessment. Then a criteria of relevancy can be applied in the analysis to determine the total validity of the mediated instruction.

Empirical Validity

Evaluation of the mediated sequence at face value for internal consistency will contribute ultimately to validation. This will determine whether the basic specifications of an operational nature have been met. Face evaluation, used to review the total effort for these basic aspects, is still a vital consideration in the design of instruction. In the past, this type of assessment has been almost the exclusive concern. Now, it becomes a functional part of a planned sequence of other important factors. The final instructional product should adhere to all display specifications and meet minimum technical standards if it is to be seen, heard, read or felt by the target population.

But validation of mediated instruction must go beyond looking at a television program, for example, to see if the recording heads were clogged during production or by listening to the fidelity of sound in an audio recording period. There must be a concern also with the possibility of the human heads being clogged in the design or of intellectual infidelity to a basic procedural scheme.

DESIGN STANDARDS   The degree to which design standards have been met can be determined by evaluating whether the objectives are consistent within a learning domain and are relevant to the instructional approach. This aspect of validation can be done by looking at the resultant instructional product. For example, in a structure designed for a cognitive goal, any affective objectives must relate directly to an affective disposition to the primary cognitive learning desired.

The intellectual performance objectives must also be sequential within the cognitive hierarchy if the learning increments are to be developed in a linear manner. It has been characteristic of many television efforts to design a program at the cognitive level of understanding and expect immediate follow-up activities to be conducted by the classroom teacher at the levels of Synthesis or Evaluation, without establishing performance capabilities in the learner for the levels within the Application and Analysis steps.

It is also not uncommon to see attempts to provide teachers with course of study guidelines designed to reinforce those mediated in other forms and then to introduce a new area of curriculum development without changing the approach to instruction. Hence, the evaluation must determine the appropriateness of the approach to instruction as well as the consistency of the sequence of instruction within a learning domain.

PRODUCTION STANDARDS   The production must adhere faithfully to the display specifications and must meet minimum technical standards. This aspect of validation can be determined by evaluation at face value. For example, if the display specifications require that the function of television is to display some object for detailed examination and no close-up is ever shown of the object, it is doubtful whether that factor of the display specifications has been met.

A display specification may identify that a subjective camera technique—for a child—be used to display an event, yet the sequence is recorded from the height and in the way an adult sees the event.

Or, if the sequence is to be displayed by broadcast television from a pre-recorded production, the videotape must be suitable to be played back according to set broadcast industry standards.

Regardless of the mode of dissemination of the mediated instruction, any electronic display must meet display specifications and technical standards in the evaluation of the total effort as a part of establishing the validity of instruction.

AESTHETIC STANDARDS   Another important factor now placed in its context of one of the elements rather than the chief element in evaluation is the appeal of the instructional segment.

Studies have demonstrated that smooth, polished professional television productions bear no direct correlation to learning. Yet, learners and those who manage their learning environment, persist in comparing (consciously or not) television in the living room and in the classroom by the same standard. Public television station managers and school media directors still prowl the halls of their operations, judging the worth of their output by how the product looks on the screen. This factor is reminiscent of the principal who prowls the halls of his school and judges the worth of his teachers by the discipline and decorum of their classes. While the evidence of good teaching is not how quiet and well-behaved the students are, neither is the evidence of good instructional television seen in how polished and well-produced the program is.

There is no inherent characteristic of using these design procedures that says that mediated instruction should not be nice to look at. The instruction designed must appeal to media directors as well as to curriculum directors. No learner is ever going to benefit from something that isn't there.

USE STANDARDS   The mediated instruction must be used under the conditions specified to achieve valid results. It was not unusual, in the first year of "Sesame Street," to hear first-grade teachers say their children really didn't get much out of the program (after it had been used in class as a "Friday Afternoon at The Movies" diversion once a week). Many kindergarten teachers, anxious to get the drop on their first-grade colleague, will expose their children to "The Electric Company" and wonder why their students aren't learning how to read. Neither program was designed for either audience. In both cases mentioned here, the programs were used to do something that was never intended in design.

It would not be surprising that test results, different from those expected in design, will be reported when the instruction is not used for what it was intended—and under the conditions for which it was intended to be used.

Absolute Validity

Evaluation for validation can also be based on the reactions of experts, about the appropriateness of the mediated sequence to the total instructional setting in which it will be used. Empirical judgments should be sought to determine the basic instructional consistency of the mediated segment. However, the reactions of teacher-planning experts cannot foretell whether a good and effective instructional sequence has been produced. They can only predict whether the final effort is consistent with known learning theory, consistent with past experiences with other mediated and conventional instruction and consistent with the goals and philosophies of the academic institution in which it is to be used.

LEARNING CONSISTENCY   The mediated instruction must be designed to do something that can actually be tested in an operational situation.

The extent to which the actual learning or environmental change can actually be measured in the school must be known. For example, in assessing all aspects of the total design effort, it may be the expert judgment of a teacher-advisory committee that the test designed may be too difficult to administer in the classroom. It may also be judged that the learning gains measured will not be universally accepted as evidence of learning in the way designed.

Often too, the judgments of various experts must be sought when environmental changes have been attempted, to see if these changes can be identified in the actual academic setting and if the effect of the mediated instruction can be isolated from other factors that may have caused such changes to take place.

INSTRUCTIONAL CONSISTENCY   The reactions of experts are also sought to establish the validity of instruction to be articulated into sequential learning patterns for the individual. For example, instructional material may have been designed to fill an identified learning deficiency in an individual's knowledge about the Spanish-American War, only to find that the social studies teacher does not provide any structure into which the learning sequence can be articulated. While this phenomenon may be discovered quite a bit earlier in the design procedures, it is not uncommon to uncover, at the time of validation, specific gaps in the sequential progression toward an ultimate instructional goal because the mediated sequence is out of phase with other stimuli more readily available in the classroom.

EDUCATIONAL CONSISTENCY   The validity of instruction can also be determined by seeking the empirical judgments on the degree to which the mediated instruction is consistent with the goals and philosophy of the academic institution that supports the effort and in which it was designed to be used.

Relative Validity

To determine whether the end product of instruction design is good—to determine whether the mediated instruction is effective—it has to be displayed to the target population under appropriate conditions to see whether the specific objectives for which the effort was designed have been reached with enough consistency to predict universal results.

The final judgment on instruction will be made by measuring, assessing, evaluating or observing the actual responses of the target population. Validity can thus be determined by predicting operational success on the basis of consistency in the findings of the testing situations. Thus validity is based on consistency of actual achievement in the content area compared against predetermined standards, and consistency of the responses that demonstrate the desired behavioral change.

CONTENT APPROPRIATENESS   A determination of content appropriateness will provide evidence on validity of the mediated sequence to display content symbols that can function as stimuli to get the desired response. For example, if, to reach instructional goals, prerequisite learning experiences were provided in design for the Direct Experience Approach, tests could be administered to the individual to determine whether the content substance provided the basic cognitive knowledge required to continue his learning by other mediated or conventional means.

Testing procedures could also be established to observe whether the learner's direct exposure to the mediated content provided the time and the opportunity for more interaction with a teacher or in group discussion activities for the extension of the knowledge gained. Thus, the content approach is valid if it can be said to consistently meet these standards of appropriateness.

PERFORMANCE ADEQUACY   A determination of the terminal response characteristics actually evidenced will provide evidence to demonstrate that instruction was consistent in providing the conditions to be effective in reaching the goal. The learner's response to the objective can be extrapolated with relative confidence to that of the total population identified for design.

Information obtained in testing a sample may have demonstrated that the objective was achieved to the degree desired. It could then be predicted that the mediated instruction would produce the same results whenever it was used as intended, under appropriate conditions. It can be held accountable in terms of the achievement of specific objectives.

INSTRUCTIONAL RELEVANCE   The responses made to all stated objectives should actually show that the goal of instruction has been reached or that progress is being made directly toward that goal before the instruction can be said to be validated. If validated instruction leads toward inconsequential goals, or toward goals that would not be supported by the community, or is not useful to the individual outside school, or is not integrated within the academic structure, it's relevancy would be highly questionable.

For more confidence in the testing, it may be advisable to establish a control group to be used to isolate the contribution of the mediated sequence to learning gains or environmental change. It may be entirely possible, for example, that in the administration of the same posttest to a control group that had not been exposed to the mediated instruction, similar results might be achieved. This would indicate, assuming instruction was based on the results of an adequate pretest, that elements other than the mediated sequence contributed to the desired response. The validity of the mediated instruction is questionable.

It may also be necessary to determine the extent of the universal acceptance of the response as evidence of the desired learning or environmental change. While instruction may be validated to produce a substantial and visible change in the learner or his environment, if the sponsor will not accept the response as evidence of learning, the fact that it has been validated will have little effect on increased or integrated use. While it may have to be decided empirically which response will show the desired individual or environmental change, the mediated sequence cannot forever stand in the protective isolation of design. At some point in time instruction must face the real and cynical world of actual use.

Dissemination

After the instructional sequence has been tested and validated, it is either released for use or returned for revisions. The results of both the testing and the validation also provide input for the research data required for the design of subsequent instruction.

Implications of Testing

In instructional design, results of testing are fed back into the procedural structure to systematize change until instruction does what was intended. In essence, the validation of instruction allows design to institutionalize change.

FRAME OF REFERENCE FOR DISSEMINATION
OF INSTRUCTION

This design function should begin from the frame of reference established by acknowledging any restraints imposed on using the results of testing to reshape instruction or to advance further design efforts.

It should be possible to use the information gathered in the design of instruction to feed input into later design elements, and to assure that adequate treatment and use is made of the existing mediated instruction.

The actual and potential distribution of the final product may impose a restraint that must be reconciled before design begins. For example, the instructional strategy would differ in the design of mediated instruction under the restrictions imposed by a desire to distribute for local consumption or to generalize the presentation for more widespread distribution. Also, basic management considerations involving rights and responsibilities would impose quite different conditions for instructional design.

Until the advent of the recent xerographic era in communications, the dissemination mode for electronically mediated instruction meant almost exclusively broadcast radio and television. However, advancements in both audio and video display systems, as well as the vast array of electronic media retrieval and storage systems demand recognition before design begins. It is quite apparent (or should be) that an instructional sequence designed to be used in the classroom on a videocassette recorder that has not only an on-off switch, but a rewind button as well, should be treated differently than would the same instruction designed for a broadcast medium.

In using these procedures, research should be regarded as the basic raw product from which instruction will be built. Without the facilities or talent to thoroughly diagnose and investigate what can be done from what has been done, one may be restrained to conduct only popularity surveys. If so, many aspects of the total design scheme will have no reliable input upon which to completely develop its function and contribute to the next interrelated step.

Restraints imposed by management contingencies of people, time or money may restrict feedback functions to only a few procedural elements of design when it should be possible to use the results of testing to close the instructional loop in *all* elements of the design procedures. For example, while it may be desired to use the results of today's learning to design tomorrow's instruction, it may not always be possible to do so. The target population may be spread across a large geographic area or instruction may have to be mediated far in advance of its actual display to the target population.

The total scope of testing makes it possible to know when to revise or remake a segment of instruction—and why. This is possible regardless of the frame of reference established by imposed restraints.

Intervals for Design

Based on the data received from the various testing functions, mediated instruction is revised or released for immediate use. George L. Hall has described the closed-loop schema concept in this way: "The process itself is the very familiar behavioral sequence that encompasses the following steps: 1) a person senses, then identifies a need and sets an objective for satisfying it; 2) decides on a likely course of action; 3) takes appropriate action; 4) monitors the apparent results; and 5) changes his strategy contingently and continues action until his objective is adequately achieved for the need to be effectively eliminated.

"The applicability of the model to instructional design is logical, resulting in the following kind of operational restatement: 1) an educator identifies a deficit in a student and helps establish a learning objective; 2) he then helps determine a likely instructional strategy; 3) he institutes appropriate, sequential action; 4) monitors the apparent learning results; and 5) modifies the instructional strategy and continues shaping student behavior until the objective is adequately achieved and demonstrated.

"Of course," Hall continues, "this is a microcosmic description of what goes on hour to hour, day after day, year in and year out in classrooms the world over. In other words, education itself is basically a closed-loop operation. But—and here is the catch—it is not invariably short-interval. Nor does it invariably enjoy the improved learning efficiencies made possible through close systemization of design" (Hall, 1969).

However, the time interval for closing the loop through the validation effort is contingent on the functions of instruction as well as on the nature of various management and operational restraints imposed. Other operational conditions related to the disposition of the mediated instruction after validation will affect both the procedures used and the confidence that can be placed in the results.

Short-Interval, Closed-Loop Development Scheme

A short-interval, closed-loop development scheme will design all succeeding efforts only after the result of the present effort are known. In this scheme, the total learning process is validated in a cumulative and sequential manner until learning or environmental change is realized. In a short-interval, closed-loop development scheme, objectives below the accepted degree require that the instruction be revised in the next increment. In this scheme, if a segment is not fully successful, another is designed for the learner's next exposure to the planned sequence of instructional experiences.

FLEXIBLE TERMINAL BEHAVIOR ON A FLEXIBLE TIME BASE
The best example of the short-interval, closed-loop development scheme was seen in the efforts of the National Association of Educational Broadcasters to restructure the educational system of American Samoa, using television to mediate a major portion of the instructional process.

In the American Samoa experience, the system's architect, Vernon Bronson, made fully operational a learning structure where tomorrow's television lesson was based on the measured learning results that were caused by today's television lesson. This learning structure is highly dependent on open channels of communication between the design agency and the schools. It also depends on the dynamics of systematic design and the capacity in the design effort to respond immediately to known learner deficiencies. In the American Samoa scheme, a flexible terminal behavior was established on a flexible time base and the learning increments were redesigned until an acceptable response was demonstrated.

FIXED TERMINAL BEHAVIOR ON A FIXED TIME BASE   Where
operational restraints or management constraints do not allow for the fully dynanic development scheme, such as that designed for American Samoa, a different approach to a short-interval, closed-loop scheme can be used for development.

In this variation, each segment of instruction that is mediated has a fixed terminal behavior established on a fixed time base. Before the sequence is displayed operationally to the total target population, it is subjected to rigorous testing and changed until it achieves the desired results. In this short-interval, closed-loop development scheme, each mediated sequence is designed well in advance in a less dynamic structure. Thus, exposure to tomorrow's lesson is based on the confidence of achievement in today's lesson.

Today's lesson, therefore, has to have been previously validated to achieve the learning gains desired. Most programs for computer-assisted instruction are structured to be validated in this way. The use of this development scheme is also seen in some of the few instructional television efforts where validation was attempted to allow more design and production lead time between testing and broadcast.

Long-Interval, Closed-Loop Development Scheme

A long-interval, closed-loop development scheme will require redesign of succeeding efforts after the initial exposure of the total target population to all of the instruction in a planned series. In a long-interval, closed-loop development scheme, the mediated instruction is generally not designed to build on the degree of demonstrated previous results but is built on fixed levels of stated entry behavior.

FIXED TERMINAL BEHAVIOR ON A FLEXIBLE TIME BASE   In this development scheme, a fixed terminal behavior is established on a flexible time base. The mediated instruction is thus validated under less dynamic conditions. These conditions may require more precise design contingencies. They place more reliance on the ability of the classroom teacher to manage the learning environment.

In most cases, mediated instruction appropriate to long-interval, closed-loop development schemes is not in a linear sequence leading toward a long-range goal, but is usually a series of self-contained units. In the long-interval, closed-loop development scheme, all instructional sequences can be designed before testing, and each treated as a separate, distinct unit. Generally, changes that are indicated as a result of testing will not directly affect the design of other instruction within the same unit.

In Nebraska's Project ASERT, the instructional television experiences were prevalidated on a sample of the target population before they were broadcast for use by the target population. The design procedures assumed that if the television experiences were designed under rigid controls, based on learning structures derived from established theory, and based also on detailed demographic data about the learner, it was not necessary to build tomorrow's lesson on the result of today's exposure to television. Therefore, in the Project ASERT efforts, a fixed terminal behavior was established on a flexible time base. The learning experiences were revised or remade as often as necessary (and as often as budget permitted) until the desired results were achieved. Using this development scheme, the designers in Project ASERT did not have the immediate press of meeting a fixed broadcast schedule.

FLEXIBLE TERMINAL BEHAVIOR ON A FIXED TIME BASE   In more than one of the Project ASERT efforts, a television experience was tested, did not achieve the objective stated, but did provide adequate stimuli to achieve a different but closely related objective. The decision was then open to the design team to determine whether the television experience should be changed to one that television experience could actually achieve. It was found that operational lapses into traditional patterns of program planning occurred when this option was made known to design personnel.

Where instruction is in a planned structure leading in a linear fashion toward a predetermined goal, there is no choice but to change the instruction to meet the stated objective actually achieved is closely related but different from the one stated, the choice is not so easy—especially when confronted with budgetary limitations and contingencies of time and facilities resources that could be directed to efforts other than to remake something that almost worked—or worked well enough.

Since early efforts in the design for validated instruction, such as those attempted in Nebraska's Project ASERT, have demonstrated that mediated instruction must often be revised or remade three or four times until it could be validated, budgetary restraints may necessitate adopting the long-interval, closed-loop scheme to effect maximum efficiencies of time and effort over any given fiscal period.

Disposition

The cyclic nature of these design procedures requires that instruction be returned to some previous point in design for revision or remake if it is not validated. Even completely tested instruction may have to be released under specific conditions of use, or with conditions that quality the confidence that can be placed in its effectiveness.

Conditions for Revision

Instruction that does not produce the desired results can be revised or remade until the results expected are achieved with the consistency desired.

TIME REQUIREMENTS FOR REVISION   The reason to test instruction is to revise or remake the segment until it does what was intended. Therefore, it must be determined how much lead time is required between the time the instruction is tested and the time it is scheduled for use. This lead time is necessary to allow for redesign or additional production efforts. It is rarely possible to afford the luxury of waiting until the entire series of mediated experiences has been validated before schedules are established to display them to the target population.

Therefore, as a part of the total design effort, it must be assumed that each mediated segment will not yield predicted test results the first time it is produced. Sufficient time must therefore be allowed to revise or remake the segment before its scheduled use.

QUANTITY REQUIREMENTS FOR REVISION   The lead time for a *revision* may be shorter, in most cases, than for a total *remake* of the mediated sequence. After the test results are diagnosed, it may be decided that only a portion of the sequence needs to be changed and that this can be accomplished by only minor revisions in design or production.

However, it may also be discovered that the entire attempt was inappropriate and the design must be changed. It could also be found that the display specifications were not faithfully followed and the entire effort must be done over to achieve the desired result.

In determining the number of segments that can be revised or remade within the time available, an important consideration is how much revision can be afforded. There is no aspect of educational endeavor that is not restrained in achieving complete fruition by lack of money to do the complete job.

Conditions for Release

After the testing procedures have been accomplished, decisions on the release of the mediated instruction must be made.

NON-VALIDATED RELEASE   Conditional approval can be given for release if, in formative testing, minor revisions were seen necessary to validate the instruction and the changes can be made without subjecting the sequence to the full testing procedures again.

Conditional approval with known restrictions can also be given. Often instruction will build on a series of increments, each with a terminal behavior specified in distinct objectives. During testing, it may be noted that the sequence has not met *all* objectives in the total structure but has provided sufficient stimuli to demonstrate a substantial movement toward the desired goal. In this case, the segment could be released *knowing* (and making it known to others) that it cannot be fully validated.

VALIDATED RELEASE   Full approval can be given for release if all design standards have been met and the desired objectives achieved.

For those mediated sequences demonstrated to be validated, it is still necessary to identify certain conditions for release. For example, no mediated instruction can be relevant to the target population for an indefinite period of time. Therefore, a condition for the release of a validated segment would be dependent on the usable life in terms of its relevancy to the learner. It may also be necessary to structure the usable life based on contract provisions with the people who have used their talents in the design or presentation of the mediated instruction.

Often professional negotiations with television teachers and producers place a limit on the usable life for the time that mediated instruction can be used. Certain copyright clearances may place a similar restriction on how long the instruction is usable. All of these contingencies, and perhaps many more, must be considered in the release of any mediated segment of instruction that is validated.

Use of Diagnostic Results

Unless the test results are used to "close the loop" in the cyclic nature of these design procedures themselves, very little is actually gained in the expenditure of the effort and resources to determine the actual response made to instruction.

Instructional Diagnosis

It may be necessary not only to test the responses for validated instruction, but to use the results to provide input for further efforts in the design, production, and use of mediated instruction.

Appropriately designed tests will verify the characteristics of the target population, and the relevancy of needs in terms of learner deficiencies. They can verity also whether the determination of the instructional intent required to fill these needs was appropriate.

For example, while initial investigations may have identified a learner deficiency in a specific content area, the instructional need indicated may have been more relevant to the academic system than to the individual learner.

It may also be found during these diagnostic procedures that the size of the actual target population is less than the potential population first identified. This might question the efficiency of using relatively costly means to mediate instruction. Hence, for future design efforts it may have to be determined not only what the size is of the *potential* target population, but also how big the anticipated *actual* target population will be.

Design has been given direction for instruction as a part of a total articulated learning sequence. Through the test results, information about the learner's performance can indicate whether the goals were set too high or too low within a learning domain. Decisions to adjust the expected response characteristics may be necessary for future design efforts. Diagnostic data can also verify the consistency in the direction taken in classifying goals. For example, data may indicate that design efforts to achieve an attitudinal response might have been more effectively directed to the attempt for a cognitive capacity for affective change.

The diagnostic information can also be used to determine the extent to which a structural discipline affected the sequence of instruction in design. For example, it is assumed in these design procedures that the most efficient approach to effective instruction is a sequence, disciplined in a step-by-step arrangement where one learning increment is based on the accepted achievement of prerequisite levels. Therefore, the results of testing can be analyzed to see if the direction of instruction was indeed sequenced in a disciplined hierarchical fashion, as well as to determine if the learner was exposed to the mediated instruction in the order intended.

Diagnostic data can verify the appropriateness of the decisions made to use a specific approach to instruction as the one most likely to reach the target population. For example, a decision may have been made to use the Supplemental Material Approach to mediate material for an existing course of study, but an evaluation of the use of this material may indicate that teachers are not following a course of study in which the material can appropriately be used. And therefore, the direction for future design efforts may be more effective if the Course of Study Guidelines Approach were used to provide a structure for the teachers to follow.

Or perhaps the decision was made to provide complete learning experiences in the Direct Experience Approach. The test data may show that other experiences are now available to the learner. Therefore, attempts to provide complete exposure to the content in a mediated form are now in conflict with other input to which the learner is exposed. From the analysis of these data, further design may well be directed to provide initial or expository learning experiences rather than continuing to try to provide complete experiences that were demonstrated to be redundant.

While the testing function is based chiefly on the structural format of the objective, it is possible not only to determine if the objective has been achieved, but also to isolate various components of the objective itself for analysis and functional feedback.

For example, it may be discovered that the stated response cannot be measured reliably in actual field conditions and should be restated in more measurable and valid terms. On the other hand, testing may reveal that the conditions of the objective were difficult to replicate in the administration of the actual test. Therefore, in order to obtain more consistently reliable results in future testing, the conditions under which the response is expected to occur must be relaxed somewhat.

In testing to measure actual learning gains, positive results are usually obtained but fall short of or far exceed the performance criteria set for the acceptable level of confidence. Where the criterion was established for 65 percent of the learners to score not lower than 75 on the test, and the test results showed consistently that 65 percent of the learners were able to score only 60 on the test, the determination would have to be made either to increase exposure to instruction to raise the scores of the target population, or to decide that the 65/60 criterion was more realistic and should be used.

Diagnostic data will also verify the appropriateness of the entry conditions identified. It would not be uncommon to discover that *assumed* entry conditions were widely divergent from *actual* entry level of the target population. Therefore, future design efforts should provide for more rigid pretesting of the entry level and a closer analysis of the conditions existing before subsequent instruction is designed.

Where some levels of enabling performance were expected in the classroom, diagnosis of results may indicate that the classroom environment prohibits adequate treatment of the conditions for these desired enabling levels. Future design efforts should provide for them as a part of the total sequence of mediated instruction.

Diagnostic data may also indicate that the media selected for the designed instruction was inappropriate to achieve the most efficient learning under the conditions that now exist.

It is the responsibility in design not only to formulate key display specifications from the output of all previous steps in the procedures, but also to assure that in the translation of the structure to the mediated form, that any specifications stated are faithfully followed. As a result of instructional diagnosis, it is possible to find out if display specifications were not exact enough to create the conditions in which learning can occur. The design specification may have been too specific and served to constrain creative expression in production.

Test data can verify the adequacy of research findings used to establish the conditions for the use of instructional media in the academic environment. For example, if initial research data showed there was adequate equipment to insure access to mediated instruction, but its actual use was sporadic, additional research would be indicated to determine the acceptance of mediated instruction in the schools in which the instruction was intended to be used. The additional research would indicate whether the design energies should be expended at all for these situations.

Ultimately, and most importantly, instructional diagnostic data can be used to tell whether it was really worth the design effort to modify the behavior of an individual or to effect change in the environment in which he learns.

In Conclusion: SO WHAT?

In the past, we have all too often planned mediated instruction for awards, not for children. We have become encapsulated in a membrane of local autonomy and apathy, appeased by continued budgets and another closet to use. We strive to fulfill our own expressive needs as well as to satisfy teacher planning committee requirements in such a way that we not offend (or even be noticed by) the administration—while 45 million children sit out there, perplexed, impatient, and bored.

Thousands of educators, teachers, and producers are exposed in workshops, conferences, and procedural manuals to philosophies of design and production different from those to which they are accustomed. They do very well at nodding their heads about the "new approach," but in their minds they carefully segregate the new as theory which, of course, will not work in any practical situation. As behavioral scientist Goodwin Watson said, "We can no longer look nostalgically at a Golden Age in the past but anticipate a Utopia in the days to come."

We can no longer afford to approach instructional technology as an extension of our own professional vanity. We can no longer afford to subscribe to the design rationale in which it is thought that the only good mediated instruction is what pleases the eye and ear. We can no longer afford to kick aside the learning demands placed on us by the educational community of today.

We can meet the challenge. It is possible to design instruction which can do a specific job with predictable results. To achieve this end, the educational community, unhappy with the product it has received in the past, must ask for a better product or be satisfied with what it gets. The media community, struggling to exist in a foreign environment, must openly acknowledge its obligation to help people learn.

After all, that's what it's all about!

C. Edward Cavert

252

Glossary

There is a great deal of inconsistency in defining terms in the field of instructional technology. The whole discipline has not as yet become so firmly entrenched in the daily operational settings of media technologies that a common jargon has evolved. Many of the terms described in this glossary may be defined in other design literature in a slightly different way. These definitions and descriptions are offered here only to describe how the terms are used in this systematic approach to instructional design. While other definitions and common usage may be acknowledged, there is an internal consistency of use within this volume.

ABSOLUTE CRITERIA. The measurement of instructional results as compared to predetermined standards. Measurement against *absolute criteria* does not compare results against other efforts, or against the abilities of other learners as may be found when using *relative criteria* against which to assess the results of instruction.

ACADEMIC ENVIRONMENT. Any formal institutional setting in which the conditions for learning can be controlled and managed. More often than not, the *academic environment* is the school—both the physical facility and the administrative structure set up to accomplish instruction. *See* EDUCATIONAL ENVIRONMENT.

ACADEMIC OBJECTIVES. The traditionally stated aims of a conventional approach to classroom or other mediated instruction. *Academic Objectives* are distinguishable from the *Performance* or *Operational* objectives required in these design procedures.

ACCOUNTABILITY. The demand for, or the ability to supply, documented evidence of instructional effectiveness in terms of learning gains or environmental change with the most efficient use of time, effort, and resources.

ACHIEVEMENT TESTS. The measurement devices used to sample learner performance at a level within a learning hierarchy. *Achievement Tests* do not necessarily have to measure achievement of *all* objectives.

ADDITIONAL INSTRUCTION. Instruction that provides experiences that build on adequate present instruction and are prerequisite to later instruction.

ADEQUATE PRESENT INSTRUCTION. The ability of existing instruction to fulfill all or part of the learner needs.

ADJUSTMENT. Conformity to set standards. For the purposes of classifying affective goals, *adjustment* describes learner performance where a hierarchy of values exists to form a standard to which the individual conforms or adjusts his daily patterns of life.

AFFECTIVE LEARNING. Development within the individual of interests, attitudes or appreciation of something; or, the formulation of some sort of value system that governs the way the individual acts in his daily life. *Affective Learning* describes the way an individual relates to information or ideas while *cognitive learning* describes the way information and ideas relate to the individual.

APPLICATION. The appropriate use of information in a concrete situation. For the purposes of classifying cognitive goals, *application* describes learner performance which involves the use of information in contexts which are novel to the learner.

APPRECIATION. Evaluation of the worth, quality or significance of something. It is also defined as a recognition of aesthetic values. For the purposes of classifying affective goals, *appreciation* describes learner performance when there is demonstrated an actual sensitivity of the worth of some concept or principle. At this stage of learning development, the learner first starts to place priorities on things he is interested in but does not use them to form a system of values.

APPROACH. A description of the proposed treatment of mediated instruction.

ASERT. *Available Supplemental Educational Resources by Television.* Project *ASERT,* funded under the provisions of Title III of the Elementary and Secondary Education Act and operated under a grant made to the Lincoln, Nebraska Public Schools from 1965 to 1969, was designed to extend and improve the use of instruction over the state's educational television network.

ASSESSMENT. The psychometric process concerned with judging the ways the teacher's classroom situation has been changed by using guidelines mediated to facilitate the structure of a course of study.

ATTEMPT. (ATTEMPTED PERFORMANCE). The learner's initial effort in doing something. For the purposes of classifying psychomotor goals, *attempt*—when associated with the performance of a motor act or manipulative skill—describes the learner's initial efforts to do something or to develop some manipulative ability. At this stage, the learner is not expected to perform an act alone, but is expected to follow either verbal or visual directions.

ATTITUDE. As defined by Robert F. Mager, an *attitude* "refers to a general tendency of an individual to act in a certain way under certain conditions" (Mager, 1967). In these design procedures, an *attitude* is more mental than emotional.

AWARENESS. Realization or perception. For the purposes of classifying affective goals *awareness* describes learner performance which involves the simple recognition of stimuli.

BEHAVIOR. The actual application of learned principles, information or skills in the learner's way of life. In these design procedures, a differentiation is made between *behavior, performance* and *response.*

CATEGORY. The description of a broad range of response characteristics within a hierarchy of a domain of learning.

CLASS OF STIMULI. Various symbols or experiences that have common traits.

COGNITIVE LEARNING. The recall or recognition of knowledge; development of the ability to use knowledge the learner already has in order to attain levels of intellectual achievement.

COMPLETE INSTRUCTION. Instruction that provides experiences that are self-contained units.

CONCEPT. An abstract idea generalized from particular instances. A *concept* is formed by putting together a series of interrelated ideas that have common traits. In these design procedures, the use of the term *concept* is used to describe the basic affective change agent.

CONFIRMATION. Feedback which informs the learner whether or not his response is appropriate and what progress he is making. In these design procedures, confirmation is also referred to as reinforcement. (*See* REINFORCEMENT.)

CONSTRAINTS. Any limitations which are inherent in the instructional setting. A *constraint* is differentiated from a *restraint* that is imposed from outside the design context.

CONVENTIONAL INSTRUCTION. Classroom situations characterized by a minimum of mediated instructional activity and a maximum of use of only a teacher, a blackboard and a textbook.

COURSE OF STUDY. The formal structure of what has to be done and what has to be used to move a learner through a given content area. Generally, in the academic community, a *course of study* is the implementation phase of a portion of the *curriculum*.

CREATE. To produce through imaginative skill. For the purpose of classifying psychomotor goals *create* describes learner performance which involves inventing new ways of doing something on the basis of the learner's mastery of a skill, and in terms of his own practical needs, or those of the situation.

CRITERION TEST. An instrument designed to measure the attainment of each objective. Each objective should have at least one *criterion test* item to document evidence of the preferred response, under the conditions specified and to the accepted degree of success specified in the objective itself.

CRITICAL RESPONSE. The response expected after exposure to a key stimulus. In these design procedures, *critical response* is used instead of *correct response*. Depending on the learner's interpretation of the stimulus and its context, a response may be correct to him, although incorrect in terms of instructional design. Generally, it isn't until the mediation stage of the design procedures that the response is referred to as the *critical response*.

CULTURAL ENVIRONMENT. The moral, intellectual and aesthetic norms of the community in which the individual must function.

CUMULATIVE TESTING. A technique of testing for responses that are intentionally delayed for a long time after exposure to instruction. Often, *cumulative testing* not only measures the ultimate response but also measures indications that the response will most likely be made at some future time.

CURRICULUM. The total influences acting on the individual in an academic environment. A *curriculum* is more narrowly described as the total arrangement of materials, events, symbols and experiences for a given content area and academic grade level(s).

DESIGN. The analysis and synthesis of specific instructional elements in a sequential scheme. In these procedures, *design* is differentiated from *planning*.

DESIGNER. One who has the total responsibilities for instructional design. The designer, also referred to as the *instructional technologist*, is required to implement or to delegate responsibilities of design, development, display, diagnosis and dissemination of the total instructional effort.

DESIRED RESPONSE. A learner response which demonstrates that the learned competencies are at the level of the learning expectations. A *desired response* is distinguishable from a *planned response* or *critical response*.

DIAGNOSIS. The analysis of instruction from the results of testing. Instructional *diagnosis*, as used in these design procedures, encompasses the tasks of *formative testing* to see what instruction has to be changed and of *summative testing* to see how consistently instruction produces the desired results.

DISCIPLINED. Tight task supervision in instructional design intended to prevent doing something that would not be used later in the design or use of instruction.

DOMAIN. A set of elements on which function is defined. In these design procedures, a *domain* is described as a hierarchy of performance capabilities in a learner, ranging from the simple to the complex; from the familiar to the unfamiliar; from the lowest level to the highest; or from the easiest to the hardest.

EDUCATIONAL ENVIRONMENT. The aggregate of all influences affecting an individual's learning. The *educational environment* includes the community, the home, the church and mass media.

EFFECTIVENESS. The management of instruction that indicates results in terms of modifying the behavior of an individual as expected.

EFFICIENCY. The management of instruction that makes the best use of both the time and money available to achieve learning in an individual.

EMOTION. A psychic and physical reaction subjectively experienced as a strong feeling and involving physiological changes that prepare the body for immediate vigorous action. In these design procedures, the *emotions* of a learner are *not* included in the descriptions of instruction toward *affective* learning. Affective learning does not involve the physiological changes associated with an emotional state, such as love, hate, fear, etc.

ENABLING CONDITIONS. Conditions essential to the mediated segment of instruction. The enabling conditions will tell how the specific approach selected should be structured to create the *terminal conditions* from the existing *entry conditions.*

ENTRY CONDITIONS. Conditions that exist in the learner or in his environment when he is introduced to instruction.

ENTRY LEVEL. The highest level within a learning domain at which the learner can demonstrate performance capability before he is exposed to instruction. The learner's *entry level* describes the baseline of known performance competency.

ESSENTIAL CONTENT. An interrelated set of symbols or experiences pertaining to a given field of study that is required to function as stimuli in the instructional experience.

ENVIRONMENT. The aggregate of all external influences on the individual. In these design procedures, the environment including the people, places, and things that directly affect an individual as a learner.

EVALUATION. 1. In design procedures, the psychometric process concerned with assessing the impact of materials on the total instructional process. 2. For the purposes of classifying cognitive goals, *evaluation* describes learner performance which involves the formation of judgements concerning the value of material for a specified purpose.

EXPECTED PERFORMANCE. The series of overt or covert *responses* that demonstrate that the learner has achieved the specific level of learning designated in the objectives for the instruction.

EXPERIENCE. (*See* INSTRUCTIONAL EXPERIENCE, *also* LEARNING EXPERIENCE.)

FORMATIVE TESTING. The process of analyzing instruction during the design phase in order to verify or modify the instruction. *Formative testing* is distinguished from *summative testing* in these design procedures.

GOAL. A general and categorical level of learned behavior in a learning domain. In these procedures, *goals* are differentiated from *objectives.* An *objective* is a specific statement of a planned learner response. A *goal* describes a learner's behavior.

HABITUAL. A behavior pattern acquired by frequent repetition or physiological dependence that is evidenced in a regularity of behavior or in an increased facility of performance. For the purposes of classifying psychomotor goals, *habitual* performance refers to behavior which the learner has practiced to the point of execution, but which he may still need to think through while he is doing.

IDEA. That which is known or supposed regarding an object or event. In these design procedures, an *idea* is a component part of an affective *concept*, where interrelated ideas with common traits are combined into a larger whole. In describing cognitive components, an *idea* is made up of bits of *information*, several *ideas* combine to form cognitive *material*.

INITIAL INSTRUCTION. Instruction that is prerequisite to a planned sequence of instruction.

INDICATORS. Visible learner responses or reactions which indicate that an internalized or covert response has been made.

INDIVIDUAL. In design procedures, a learner (not necessarily a student) who is influenced by an environment in which certain known learning expectations are imposed. The term may also be plural.

INSTRUCTION. Organized efforts to manage or control situations which produce planned change in an individual.

INSTRUCTIONAL CONDITIONS. The array of stimuli generated by an instructional experience. In these design procedures, the *instructional conditions* indicate how to select and design stimuli.

INSTRUCTIONAL ENVIRONMENT. The sum of people, places and things that comprise the situation in which the learner will be exposed to instruction.

INSTRUCTIONAL EXPERIENCE. The combination of symbols or experiences designed as stimuli to initiate the critical learner response, or series of responses. An *instructional experience* is made up of *instructional segments*, where a clearly defined response is made from an interrelated cluster of stimuli.

INSTRUCTIONAL MATERIAL. *See* MATERIAL.

INSTRUCTIONAL NEED. Any void or deficiency that results from the discrepancy between the level of instruction required to fill learner needs and the ability of existing instruction to reduce these needs.

INSTRUCTIONAL SEGMENT. A clearly defined response to a single or an interrelated cluster of stimuli. An *instructional segment* is the smallest unit of design. Several (or more) *instructional segments* make up an *instructional sequence*.

INSTRUCTIONAL SEQUENCE. A series of individual instructional segments that are combined in an orderly or logical manner. *Instructional segments* are the component parts of an *instructional sequence*. One or more *instructional sequences* combine to form an *instructional experience*.

INSTRUCTIONAL TECHNOLOGIST. One who has the total responsibility of instructional design. The instructional technologist, also referred to as the *designer*, is required to implement or to delegate responsibilities of design, development, display, diagnosis and dissemination for the total instructional effort.

INSTRUCTIONAL TASK. That which is worked with in instruction during mediation. It may encompass different stimuli or bits of content related to the same goal.

INSTRUCTIONAL TECHNOLOGY. The Commission on Instructional Technology provides two definitions. 1. "In its more familiar sense, it means the media born of the communications revolution which can be used for instructional purposes alongside the teacher, textbook and blackboard." *Instructional technology* encompasses the other items of hardware and software available to the instructional process. 2. "It is a systematic way of designing, carrying out and evaluating the total process of learning and teaching in terms of specific objectives, based on research in human learning and communication, and employing a combination of human and nonhuman resources to bring about more effective instruction." In these procedures the second definition is used.

INSTRUCTIONAL WANT. *See* WANT.

INTENT TO ENRICH. The purposeful use of media in emphasizing or extending the individual's total cultural environment.

INTENT TO ENTERTAIN. The purposeful use of media in providing the individual with diversion or escape either within or outside the formal academic environment.

INTENT TO INFORM. The purposeful use of media in presenting a body of knowledge which becomes a working part of the individual's repertoire of information.

INTENT TO INSTRUCT. The purposeful use of media in directly effecting a change in the learner performance or in altering the way in which the learner is influenced by his instructional environment.

INTEREST. A readiness to be concerned with or moved by an object or a class of objects. For the purposes of classifying affective goals, *interest* describes learner performance that demonstrates an active desire to take something into account, or to seek out things that affect the learner because he is moved by them—that is, because he likes, dislikes or has some affective-emotional concern about them.

INTERIM OBJECTIVE. As defined in the course, *Designing Effective Instruction*, "A statement written to show evidence of temporary performance which aids the student in attaining the level at which the objective is written, but which is usually dropped after the key objective is reached" (General Programmed Teaching, 1970). However, in these design procedures, the concept of an interim objective more closely approximates the descriptions of *prompting stimuli*.

ISOLATED TESTING. Tests administered to determine whether the desired response was made immediately after or during exposure to instruction.

INSTRUCTIONAL RESOURCES. The personnel, materials, equipment, facilities and repetoire of techniques available for instructional use. A distinction is made in these design procedures between *software*—the ideas generated for the use of equipment—and *hardware* the equipment devices. *Soft hardware* exists when these ideas are committed to a permanent form by the equipment devices.

JARGON. A specialized vocabulary used by those involved in the same work. For those attempting to effect learning through design, the jargon of instructional technology is a working vocabulary of phrases coined to describe new concepts or to ascribe new shades of meaning to old clichés.

LEARNED COMPETENCIES. The demonstrated ability to respond to *learning expectations. Learned competencies* establish the baseline from which learner needs are defined. *Psychomotor learned competencies* describe how closely the individuals' present manipulative abilities approach what he is expected to do. *Cognitive learned competencies* describe how closely a learner's present intellectual achievement approaches what he is expected to know. *Affective learned competencies* describe how closely the learner's present patterns of behavior approach what is expected to feel.

LEARNED EXPERIENCE. That which is retained in the learner after successful instruction. Unless otherwise specified, it is assumed that the time frame for the retention of a learned experience is long enough that the learned experience can be assumed for any future instructional design.

LEARNER NEEDS. Any void or deficiency apparent in the discrepancy between the individual's *learning expectations* and his *learned competencies.* (For the application of *learner needs* to design, see the description *of wants.*)

LEARNING. In these design procedures, the planned change in an individuals performance of what he is able to do, of what he knows or of the patterns of behavior he exhibits.

LEARNING DEFICIENCIES. The discrepancy between the *learning expectations* and the learner's ability to respond from his base of *learned compentencies. Learning deficiencies* provide the basis for recognition of the *learner needs.*

LEARNING EXPECTATION. The anticipated performance of the learner in an instructional situation. *Learning expectations* establish limits against which *learner needs* can be defined. For psychomotor learning, the individual is expected to do something in order to meet standards of skills proficiency. For cognitive learning, the individual is expected to know something in order to attain levels of intellectual achievement. For affective learning, the individual is expected to feel in a certain way in order to have accepted patterns of behavior.

LEARNING EXPERIENCES. The sum total of all the individual is exposed to that effects learning. In this context, a *learning experience* involves more than exposure to instruction. It also includes influences on the individual by all other social, cultural and academic components of his total environment.

LEARNING GAINS. The actual increase in the learned competencies of the individual resulting from instruction. *See also* QUANTIFIABLE RESULTS.

LEARNING WANTS. *See* WANTS.

LEVEL. The specific description of the response characteristics within a hierarchy of a learning domain. In these design procedures, characteristics of the learner's response are classified for instructional sequence at a definite *level* in more specifically defined *steps* within a general *category* of response characteristics.

LONG-INTERVAL CLOSED-LOOP DEVELOPMENT. A development scheme that designs future instruction on the basis of the predicted results of current instruction. In contrast to the *long-interval closed-loop development,* the *short-interval closed-loop development* scheme designs instruction based on the actual measured results of the current instruction.

MASTERY. A display of skill or technique. For the purposes of classifying psychomotor goals, *mastery* involves a degree of coordination and automatic performance without recourse to conscious mental review of the process involved.

MATERIALS. (INSTRUCTIONAL MATERIALS). Specific items or experiences provide the learner with something concrete to relate to in learning. *Material* may include as demonstrations, experiments, examples, enactments simulations and problems.

MEASUREMENT. In these design procedures, the psychometric process that tests a learner's response, performance or behavior characteristics after exposure to instruction.

MEDIATED INSTRUCTION. Instruction that is committed to some medium for display to a learner. It may use print or projected media, or the media may be electric or electronic. The media may deal with analog or digital information. A characteristic of *mediated instruction* is the ability to store information in a permanent form for later retrieval and display.

MEDIATOR. Stimulus-response units designed to aid the learner in making the critical response to a complex stimulus. *Mediators* may be internal as a part of the learner's repetoire of other learned experiences; or, they may be external. (A distinction is made in these design procedures between a *Mediator* and a *prompting stimulus*) *See* PROMPTING STIMULUS.

NEED. *See* LEARNER NEEDS; *also see* INSTRUCTIONAL NEEDS.

OBJECTIVE. A specific statement of learner responses formulated to give evidence of instructional results and to give direction in instructional planning. In these procedures, objectives are differentiated from *goals*. *Objectives* are formulated to initiate the responses that result in the performance capabilities from which the learner derives his learned behavior. *Objectives* are specific statements that describe how to get to the more general statement of the *goal*.

OBSERVATION. In these design procedures recognizing and noting the occurrence of resource utilization in order to assess any changes in the total educational process of the learner.

OPERATIONS. *(of intellectual abilities)*. Practical application of principles or processes to produce an appropriate effect. For the purposes of classifying cognitive goals, *operations* describe performance which involves the learner in working with the knowledge he has. *Operations* involve breaking apart the information in analysis and synthesizing of new information from the component parts.

OPERATIONAL OBJECTIVES. A precise statement of the learners response expected after exposure to instruction. As used in these design procedures, the term *operational objectives* is used to describe the statement, in operational terms, of the *performance objective* that has been written in pure "Magerian Form."

OVERT INDICATORS. As defined in the course, *"Designing Effective Instruction,"* an *overt indicator* is an "active response that indicates that a desired passive response has occurred." In these design procedures, *overt indicators* describe what the individual visibly does to indicate that he has made some kind of internal response, or that he would be disposed to make a covert or passive response under appropriate conditions.

PATTERNS OF BEHAVIOR. The characteristic ways a person is observed to demonstrate an interest, attitude, appreciation, value or personal adjustment. In these design procedures, this term is used to indicate the visible manifestation of *affective learning*.

PERFORMANCE. The series of overt or covert *responses* that indicate a specific level of learning.

PERFORMANCE OBJECTIVE. Objectives stated in terms of visible learner responses to a given stimulus, under controlled conditions and to a specific degree of acceptability.

PLANNED RESPONSE. The response that is expected of the learner in order to demonstrate that a specific level in the hierarchy of learning has been reached.

PLANNING. The process of putting together random known elements for instruction. In these procedures, *planning* is differentiated from *design*. *Design* is described as the analysis and synthesis of specific instructional tasks in a sequential and disciplined scheme.

PRINCIPLE. A comprehensive and fundamental law, doctrine or assumption. In these design procedures, a *principle* is arrived at by combining interrelated *concepts* that have been formed from *ideas* with common traits.

PROMPTING STIMULI. A stimulus or group of stimuli—distinct from the key stimulus—that helps the learner recognize the key stimulus and make the critical response. It indicates what the learner should actually respond to and clarifies how he will be expected to respond.

PSYCHOMETRY. The measurement, assessment, evaluation or observations of results. In these procedures, *psychometry* is used when the term, *testing*, might be interpreted by the reader as a paper-and-pencil examination designed to get correct or incorrect answers.

PSYCHOMOTOR LEARNING. The development of manipulative or motor skills in order to meet standards of skills proficiency.

PURPOSE. The state of the intentions of the design effort in mediating instruction. The statement of *purpose* is the most global description of what is being attempted in the design of mediated instruction.

QUANTIFIABLE RESULTS. The assignment of a numerical value to the results of testing so that comparisons can be made against absolute or relative criteria. Procedures described in the course, *"Designing Effective Instruction,"* quantify results in terms of a *modified gain score*. This *modified gain score* is determined by first knowing the *possible gain*. This is the difference between the pretest score and the perfect score. A pretest score of 30 and a perfect score of 100 gives a *possible gain score* of 70. Next, it is necessary to determine the *actual gain*. This is the difference between the pretest score and the posttest score. A pretest score of 30 and a posttest score of 79 gives an *actual gain score* of 49. However, to accommodate the apparent difficulty in achieving greater absolute scores with a high pretest score, Deterline recommends using a *modified gain score*. The ratio of the actual gain to the maximum possible gain. He offers this formula for calculating a *modified gain score*:

$$MODIFIED\ GAIN\ SCORE = \frac{Actual\ Gain\ Score}{Possible\ Gain\ Score}$$

Thus, where the *actual gain score* is 49, and the *possible gain score* would have been 70, the *modified gain score* is 70 percent. The weighting factor of the *modified gain score* can be seen by comparing this example to an example where on the pretest a student scored 90 out of a possible 100. Then, on the posttest, his score was 97. While his actual increase was only 7 points, his *modified gain score* was 70 percent—the same as the other student whose actual increase in score was 49 points, but who had more potential for a greater increase because he started from a lower level. (General Programmed Teaching, 1970).

REACTION. Achievement of a random nature displayed by a learner. In these procedures, *response* is differentiated from *reaction*. *Responses* imply performance of a predetermined nature. *Responses* are planned for but *reactions* are not.

READINESS. The state of being prepared mentally or physically for some experience or action. For the purposes of classifying psychomotor goals, *readiness* refers to being prepared emotionally as well as physically and mentally.

RECALL. Rememberance. For the purposes of classifying cognitive goals in these design procedures, *recall* describes learner performance which involves committing specific bits of information to memory and remembering them when asked to do so.

REINFORCEMENT. Feedback which informs the learner whether or not his responses are appropriate and what progress he is making. In these design procedures, *reinforcement* is also referred to as *confirmation*. See CONFIRMATION.

RELATIVE CRITERIA. The measurement of instructional results in comparison with other results. Measurement against *relative criteria* will compare results against other efforts to compare effectiveness or to rank a learner's progress in relation to the progress of other learners with similar characteristics. *Relative criteria* is distinguished from *absolute criteria* which measure in terms of a predetermined standard assessed against internal evidence.

RESPONSE. As defined in the course, *"Designing Effective Instruction,"* a *response* is "a unit of behavior that can be identified in terms of its relation to specific stimuli." In these design procedures, a *response* is the smallest unit of an overt or covert action demonstrated by the individual after exposure to a stimulus in instruction. (A series of *responses* make up the learner's *performance* that shows evidence of learning which is ultimately incorporated into *behavior.*)

RESTRAINTS. Any factor inhibiting instructional design which is imposed from outside the design context. A *restraint* is distinguishable from a *constraint;* a *restraint* is a limitation that is externally imposed while a *constraint* is internally imposed.

REPLY. The answer given by a student to a question on an examination. A *reply* is distinguishable from a response. *Replies* may be made by the learner without any substantial base of learned competencies, simply by parroting back information he knows is wanted. A *response* is a genuine indication of a learned experience.

SCOPE AND SEQUENCE. The nature, amount and order in which information is presented in a course of study within a given content area. The *scope and sequence* often describes ways that the course of study is implemented in a classroom setting.

SEGMENT. *See* INSTRUCTIONAL SEGMENT.

SELF-CONTAINED LEARNING EXPERIENCE. Experiences that depend solely on the design of the mediated instruction for all prerequisite and extended learning activities. A *self-contained* instructional unit may or may not depend on previously learned competencies, or other conventional or mediated instruction. Generally, it is an instructional unit that can be used in isolation from a structured sequence of experiences.

SEQUENCE. A step-by-step arrangement leading to a known end. Generally, but not always, a linear progression from lower levels of competency to higher; from simple concepts to complex; from familiar to the unfamiliar; from easiest to the hardest; etc. In these design procedures, the *sequence* describes the arrangement of response characteristics demonstrating learned competencies at certain known levels. *See also,* INSTRUCTIONAL SEQUENCE.

SHORT-INTERVAL CLOSED-LOOP DEVELOPMENT. A developmental scheme that develops future instruction on the basis of the actual measured result of current instruction. The *short-interval closed-loop development* is distinguished from the *long-interval closed-loop development* which bases future instruction on the confidence of predicted results in the present instruction.

SOCIETAL ENVIRONMENT. The interpersonal relationships necessary to advance the intellectual, moral and aesthetic norms of a culture. In these design procedures, the *societal environment* is imposed on the individual by where and how he lives. More specifically, the *societal environment* of the individual is the aggregate of people, places and things that influence him in his community.

SOFT HARDWARE. The resources and materials available for instruction. (A distinction is made in these design procedures between *software*—the ideas generated for the use of equipment and *hardware*, or equipment itself.) *Soft hardware* exists when these ideas are committed to a permanent form by the equipment devices.

STANDARDIZED TESTS. Commercially published tests which measure results in relation to the levels of achievement demonstrated by other groups of similar students. Measurement against "national norms" is most frequently associated with *standardized tests*. These norms are generally established in the design of the test by a random or selected sample, and verified through continuous feedback in field use of the tests.

STEP. A category of response characteristics with similar properties which allow for categorical classification. In these design procedures, response characteristics are classified for instructional sequencing at a specific *level* in more categorically defined *steps* within a general *category* of response characteristics.

STIMULUS. The symbol or experience to which the learner must attend in order to respond.

STIMULUS-RESPONSE CHAINS. A sequence of stimulus-response pairs in which each response acts as or produces the stimulus for the next response.

STIMULUS-RESPONSE PAIR. (UNIT). The action taken by the learner on being exposed to a symbol or experience. It is the discrete response made to a single stimuli.

STRATEGY. The organizational structure of an instructional experience. Design *strategy* includes a sequence of performance capabilities in a step-by-step arrangement leading toward the goal; an approach to instruction best suited to reach the intended audience in its academic setting; and specific objectives that are written to describe the responses that will evidence learning on the part of someone.

STRUCTURE. The component parts of an instructional experience. In these design procedures, the process of *structure* involves identifying terminal conditions stated in the objective; identifying entry conditions implied in the objective; determining what conditions will be necessary to enable the existing entry conditions to be changed to those described as the terminal conditions.

SUBOBJECTIVE. As defined in the course, "*Designing Effective Instruction*," "a specification of performance which is part of a larger terminal objective." In these design procedures, *subobjectives* are described as *objectives* at enabling levels in a learning hierarchy, or as one of a cluster of objectives formulated to show evidence of achievement at a specific level within the hierarchy.

SUMMATIVE TESTING. The process of analyzing the results of instruction by measuring, evaluating, assessing or observing actual responses of the intended target population in an actual operational setting.

TARGET POPULATION. A narrow portion of the total learner population selected by certain common social characteristics, identified by common imposed characteristics and described by common natural characteristics inherent in learners as individuals.

TAXONOMY. A classification into categories that reveals the organization and interrelation of the various parts; an orderly, sequential arrangement of classifying goals with descriptions of performance that will show evidence of learning at levels in a hierarchy.

TEACHING STRUCTURE. The pattern of events and materials used by a classroom teacher in instruction.

TERMINAL CONDITIONS. The conditions, described in the objective, that should exist after exposure to instruction.

TECHNOLOGY. (*See* INSTRUCTIONAL TECHNOLOGY.)

TERMINAL RESPONSE. Responses which demonstrate the learner's achievement of specified goals and objectives at the designated standards of skills proficiency, intellectual capability or behavioral adjustment.

TERMINAL LEVEL. The highest level within a learning domain at which the learner will be expected to demonstrate performance capability after he is exposed to instruction. The learner's *terminal level* describes the performance competency at the level on which the goal has been classified.

TEST INSTRUMENT. A device used to determine whether the expected response was made after exposure to instruction. The *test instrument* is not narrowly described to mean only a paper-pencil, true-false, multiple-choice examination usually associated with tests. Depending on the approach to instruction used, the *test instrument* could also be an objective criteria against which an observer can check the overt performance of a learner.

TESTING. The procedure used to determine the results of instruction. Testing includes both the determination of the effectiveness of the *product* and the efficiency of the *process* of instruction. In these procedures, testing is used to diagnose instruction, not to discriminate difference in students for grading purposes.

UNDERSTANDING. Acceptance of something as fact or truth. For the purposes of classifying cognitive goals, *understanding* describes learner performance which involves not only the recognition and awareness of information, but is also expected to make some use of that information, even though the learner may not fully accept the reason for doing so.

VALIDATION. The confirmation of a particular instructional design indicating a relative confidence it will do what was intended, when used under appropriate conditions, for a specific target population.

VALUE. Relative worth, utility or importance ascribed to something. For the purpose of classifying affective goals in these design procedures, *value* describes performance which involves the learner in rating what he appreciates according to some sort of priority in which he can discern varied degrees of importance or excellence.

VISIBLE RESPONSE. A measurable or observable action taken by a learner after being presented with a stimulus.

WANTS. (LEARNING WANTS). Any deficiency described as a *learner need*. *Learning Wants* are *not* the description of an affective disposition of the learner's desire for or interest in approaching some instructional moment. It is simply his awareness that he has a learning deficiency in a well-defined area of instruction that makes sense to him.

Bibliography

In addition to the direct references listed below, the author wishes to acknowledge indebtedness to Dr. George Bair, Vernon Bronson, James Fellows, Dr. Robert Gerletti, George L. Hall, Dr. Wesley C. Meierhenry, Dr. Robert E. Stepp, Lewis A. Rhodes, and countless others for a close personal association where ideas were assimilated without conscious awareness at the time to formally document those ideas as bibliographical entries.

Adler, Marilynne. "Jean Piaget, School Organization, and Instruction" in *Educational Implications of Piaget's Theory*. Edited by Irene J. Athey and Duane O. Rubadeau. Waltham, Massachusetts: Ginn-Blaisdell Company, 1970.

Athey, Irene J. and Rubadeau, Duane O. (ed.) *Educational Implications of Piaget's Theory*. Waltham, Massachusetts: Ginn-Blaisdell Company, 1970.

Ausubel, David P. "The Transition from Concrete to Abstract Cognitive Functioning: Theoretical Issues and Implications," in *Educational Implications of Piaget's Theory*. Edited by Irene J. Athey and Duane O. Rubadeau. Waltham, Massachusetts: Ginn-Blaisdell Company, 1970.

Bloom, Benjamin S. (ed.) *Taxonomy of Educational Objectives, Handbook I: Cognitive Domain*. New York: David McKay Company, Inc., 1956.

Bronson, Vernon. (Verbal statements made to a workshop conducted for the Florida State Department of Education, Tallahassee, Florida, 1968, by the National Association of Educational Broadcasters.)

Buell, Robert R. "Planning Cognitive Conflict in Inquiry Loops," in *Audiovisual Instruction*, February 1970.

Canfield, Albert A. "A Rationale for Performance Objectives," in *Audiovisual Instruction*, February 1968.

Cavert, C. Edward. "A Descriptive Analysis of the Learning Environment for the Use of Project Asert Programs in Nebraska Schools." (A report to the Lincoln, Nebraska Public Schools pursuant to a grant from the HEW/USOE under Title III, ESEA) 1968.

"Challenge: A Teacher's Utilization Handbook," Project ASERT, Lincoln, Nebraska (Lincoln, Nebraska Public Schools) 1968.

Chu, Godwin C. and Wilbur Schramm. *Learning From Television: What the Research Says*. Washington: National Association of Educational Broadcasters, 1967.

Culkin, John M. "A Schoolman's Guide to Marshall McLuhan," *Saturday Review*, March 18, 1967.

Deterline, William A. "A Curriculum is a Set of Specifications of Which of the Following: A. Stimuli, B. Responses, C. Both A and B, D. Neither A nor B." In *Educational Technology*, April, 1970.

Deterline, William A. *Instructional Technology Workshop*, Palo Alto, California: General Programmed Teaching, 1968.

Engler, David. "Instructional Technology and the Curriculum," in *Phi Delta Kappan*.

Flavell, J. H., *The Developmental Psychology of Jean Piaget*, Princeton, New Jersey: D. Van Nostrand, 1963.

Gagné, Robert M. *The Conditions of Learning*. New York: Holt, Rinehart and Winston, Inc., 1965.

Gilpin, John P. (in the forewerd to "Preparing Instructional Objectives" by Robert F. Mager.) Palo Alto, California: Fearon Publishers, 1962.

Goodlad, John I. "Providing a Dynamic Environment for Learning." in an address delivered to the 45th Annual Convention of the National Association of Educational Broadcasters, Washington, D.C., 1969.

Hall, George L. "Final Report to Project ASERT," presented to the Board of Education, Lincoln Nebraska Public Schools, November, 1969.

Hall, George L. *Television in Instruction: What is Possible*. Washington: National Association of Educational Broadcasters, 1970.

Hall, George L. In verbal comments to a workshop conducted for the Shawnee Mission Public Schools by the Great Plains National Instructional Television Library, March, 1971.

Hamreus, Dale G. *The Systems Approach to Instructional Development*. Salem, Oregon: The Teaching Research Division of the Oregon State System of Higher Education, 1968.

Harbeck, Mary B. "Instructional Objectives in the Affective Domain," in *Educational Technology*, January, 1970.

Krathwohl, David R., Bloom, Benjamin S., and Masia, Bertram B. *Taxonomy of Educational Objectives: Handbook II: Affective Domain*. New York: David McKay Company, Inc., 1964.

Lessinger, Leon G. "Accountability for American Schools," in *Educate*, March, 1970.

Mager, Robert F. *Developing Attitude Toward Learning*, Palo Alto, California: Fearon Publishers, 1968.

Mager, Robert F. *Preparing Instructional Objectives*, Palo Alto, California: Fearon Publishers, 1962.

McMurrin, Sterling M. *Innovation in Education: New Directions for the American School*. New York: Committee for Economic Development, July, 1968.

McMurrin, Sterling M. *The Schools and the Challenge of Innovation*. New York: McGraw-Hill, 1969.

Miller, Donald R. (ed.) *A Manager's Guide to Objectives*. Operation PEP: A Statewide Project to Prepare Educational Planners for California, October, 1969.

Miller, Donald R. *A Systems Approach to Educational Management*. Operation PEP: A Statewide Project to Prepare Educational Planners for California. October, 1968.

Newsom, Carrol V. "The Age of Change: A Perspective on Education," in *Educational Broadcasting Review*. Washington: National Association of Educational Broadcasters. April, 1971.

Peter, Laurence J. *The Peter Principle*. New York: William Morrow and Company, Inc. 1969.

Pulaski, Mary Ann Spencer. *Understanding Piaget: An Introduction to Children's Cognitive Development*. New York: Harper & Row, 1971.

Rhodes, Lewis A. (Producer), "A New Look at an Old Log." (16mm color, sound film) produced for the National Association of Educational Broadcasters, Washington, D.C., 1969.

Rhodes, Lewis A. *Toward a Significant Difference: Final Report of the National Project for the Improvement of Televised Instruction*. Washington, D.C.: National Association of Educational Broadcasters, 1968.

Rhodes, Lewis A. (In verbal comments made to a workshop conducted at the Shawnee Mission, Kansas Public Schools by Great Plains National Instructional Television Library, March, 1971.)

Silberman, Charles E. *Crisis in the Classroom*. New York: Random House, 1970.

Simpson, Elizabeth Jane. *Progress Report: Vocational and Technical Education Grant, Contract No. OE 5-85-104, (Taxonomy of Educational Objectives for the Psychomotor Domain).* Department of Health, Education and Welfare, USOE, 1966.

Stepp, Robert E. "Utilization of Educational Media in the Education of the Acoustically Handicapped Student," in *The Hard of Hearing Child: Clinical and Educational Management*, edited by Fred Berg and Samuel G. Fletcher. New York: Grune & Stratton, 1970.

Sylwester, Robert. "Benjamin Bloom and his Taxonomy," in *Instructor*, February, 1971.

Tickton, Sidney G. (ed.) *To Improve Learning: An Evaluation of Instructional Technology* (Volumes I and II), New York: R.R. Bowker Company, 1970.

"To Improve Learning." A Report to the President and the Congress of the United States by the Commission on Instructional Technology (Committee on Education and Labor, House of Representatives). Washington, D.C.: U.S. Government Printing Office, 1970.

Watson, Goodwin. "Resistance to Change," in *Concepts for Social Change*, edited by Goodwin Watson. Union New Jersey: Cooperative Project for Educational Development, 1969.